T0381087

The Way of

Aiki

The Way of

Aiki

a path for unity, confluence and harmony

•

Between Tradition and the Future

José Carlos Escobar Hernández, MA.

Order this book online at www.trafford.com
or email orders@trafford.com

Most Trafford titles are also available at major online book retailers.

Print information available on the last page.

ISBN: 9781425171964 (sc)
ISBN: 9781425171971 (e)

Trafford rev. 08/13/2018

www.trafford.com

North America & international
toll-free: 1 888 232 4444 (USA & Canada)
fax: 812 355 4082

Appreciations

I dedicate this book to Kurita Yutaka *Shihan,* an earnest Aiki instructor and my *Sensei,* who has devoted his life to honoring *O-Sensei* Ueshiba Morihei, the Founder of modern Aiki, after 30 years of having the privilege of being his student.

I want to express my sincere appreciation to my *Aikido* classmates, some of whom have kept a life-long interest in following and supporting Kurita *Shihan* to carry out his mission.

My gratitude to five good friends: Jason Humphrey, for his encouragement; Eduardo Hernandez, who helped me with the first English manuscript; Eric Kwiecien, for his great illustrations and the cover design; and Ricardo Rendon, my *Uke* in many pictures, as well as Carlos Tellez.

I thank my unconditionally supportive wife Rebeca and my loving children Jose Carlos and Rebeca Jr.

To my beloved parents Carlos and Socorro

CONTENTS

Foreword

Except for some published interviews Kurita Yutaka *Shihan*, one of the last living inner students (*uchideshi*) of O-Sensei Ueshiba, has never written any books or articles on his memories or the teachings he learned directly from the master. [1] This book documents only a part of his first 20 years of instruction as an international *Aikido* representative. It does not cover his most recent teachings on Aiki training which have transformed the work done in his *dojo* (practice hall). By adopting a contemporary original approach of *Aikido* as a new paradigm he is making room for new imaginative perspectives. He teaches Aiki as the basis of a new culture and his most recent core program now includes training on *ki awase*, *ki musubi*, *agatsu*, *kokyu*, *nagare*, *masakatsu*, *kokoro*, *izanau*, *renzoku waza*, *seika tanden* and *katsuhayabi* to name only the most basic contents. He has been able to transform himself to take *Aikido* a step forward in accordance with the Founder's ideal but this recent exploration is not discussed in this book.

From his perspective, the discipline and philosophical approach of *Aikido*, based on the unity of heart, body and mind, is a way to unleash the development of an intuitive intelligence that might eventually launch humanity to a higher state of consciousness. But all around the globe *Aikido* seems to be practiced now with a rather strong and almost exclusive emphasis on technique. Hence people may think of *Aikido* as a martial art consisting of techniques which are only different from those found in other arts. When Kurita *Shihan* states "*Aikido is first and technique is second*" it is clear that "*Aikido*" and "techniques" are two quite different things. Chances are somebody's practice may be "*lacking Aiki*" so the objective of this book is to review Aiki's principles and concepts by presenting it as a new paradigm.

Although each practitioner has to develop his or her own perception of Aiki, the intention is to pinpoint things that may help newcomers by discussing terms and concepts they usually misunderstand and are important to start *Aikido* correctly. Grasping the Founder's teachings is not easy so it is my sincere hope they will find a complementary guide to help them review what they learn in class. In addition, it may encourage them to try a new approach that may launch their practice into new directions. Verbal descriptions of technique have been left out given the large number of publications showing the actions found in many general *Aikido* curricula.

The information presented is based on Kurita *Shihan*'s teachings and it has been written down according to hundreds of notes taken in class and seminars, videotaped sessions, his encouragement, as well as my best understanding, and

---

[1] Japanese names are presented in this book following their usual way with the last name first.

personal interpretation. Many personal thoughts, opinions and research have been added to such notes in order to elaborate on a perspective intended to make his teachings as coherent as possible. This book has been written from a student's perspective and out of the most humble enthusiasm and love for *Aikido*, as well as a note of appreciation to Kurita Yutaka *Shihan* in his 30th anniversary.

Preface

The *Introduction* is the author's personal review of *Aikido* dissemination. Since the art is presented as a new paradigm it introduces a difference between "Aiki-do" and "Aikido" in order to establish a difference between Kurita *Shihan*'s teachings and the teachings proposed by other instructors.

Chapter 1 is a brief exploration of the Japanese mind and world vision. It provides the reader with a perspective on what *Aikido* has to offer and establishes an essential difference between *work* (Aiki) and *activity* (techniques), in order to understand Aiki-do practice in a new dimension and depth.

Chapter 2 is a brief historical review of the search carried out by the Founder and it proposes to consider him beyond his current martial artist status. It includes an analysis of the main schools known up to this date and their consistency with O-Sensei's teachings, as they are presented here and as derived from the basic Aiki-do vocabulary and concepts he promoted.

Chapter 3 describes the work Kurita Yutaka *Shihan* has carried out since he was sent abroad by the Aikikai to teach *Aikido*. It will help the reader to understand the mission of an *uchideshi* not only as it was originally assigned by the Aikikai Foundation but as it has been transformed as an attempt to follow the original vision of master Ueshiba. It offers some insight on the trends his work is taking as a formula that may eventually lead to an Aiki culture.

Chapter 4 describes the Aiki practice session and gives a meaning to what happens during practice. Based on very well-known aspects of *Aikido* practice this chapter pinpoints concepts and ideas that new practitioners usually find confusing and disconcerting. It explores *Aikido* as *misogi* (a "cleansing" practice).

Chapter 5 gathers the evolving vision and transformation of Aiki theory and the recollections imprinted on Kurita Yutaka *Shihan*'s mind that lead his very personal style. It is a sample of what he has taught in his school and an approach to the main things explored and lived in Aiki practice. Since many concepts are defined it includes a helpful vocabulary of Aiki-do terms. The reader will notice that alien concepts borrowed from other arts have not been included, whereas others have been added for the sake of clarification or because they mark the difference with other study programs and instructors.

Chapter 6 explores the multiple practical applications of Aiki which differ from its use for self-defense. It compares it to other self-improvement systems and describes its possibilities as an integral education system. It also reviews its application in the dealing with conflict and some business and leadership issues.

By approaching the teachings of Kurita Yutaka *Shihan* this book explores the ideas and perspectives he learned first-hand from the Founder. It is noteworthy that he was not only his disciple, but his personal escort and assistant, as well as his personal scribe: O-Sensei dictated to him many notes he was ordered to destroy but they remained imprinted in his memory and are now triggering his imagination, proving that *"Aiki is to nurture, develop, and help people's growth."* By the time this book is published he is re-defining Aiki practice and preparing his final legacy. I hope he will have the time to go on with his search and leave us with a solid theory for a renewed practice so that others may find his teachings inspiring in order to maintain the main purpose of Aiki practice and master Ueshiba's ideal. [2]

*"Aiki emulates a Universe which is always moving
and expanding, so we must not stop its development."*

*O negai shimasu
(Please let me start)*

---

2   Kurita Y. *Shihan* has lived in Mexico for three decades after being dispatched to Mexico City in 1980 by the Aikikai Federation in Tokyo. As a promoter of *Aikido* he first organized the Asociación Mexicana de Aikido, A.C., and now is the director of *Kurita Juku Aiki*. He is currently developing Aiki lines and training with a new solid perspective. His new thesis relates to the works of the right side of the brain, the development of an intuitive intelligence and its relationship with Aiki.

Introduction

Several decades have passed since *Aikido* arrived in the USA and grand master (*O-Sensei*) Ueshiba Morihei, *Aikido*'s Founder, passed away. Today his path is practiced in many countries and it has been taught by instructors who belong to several generations and were formed at different periods during his life-long search to develop the way of Aiki.

The fact that schools have been established at various developmental stages may be the reason why there seems to be all kinds of styles and technical variations among them. They are part of the progressive stages attained by the master throughout his career and they also reflect the sustained efforts made by leading instructors who had to work hard in order to follow him. Aikido is the product of a refined search and transformation that made "*Takemusu Aiki*" ("give life to Aiki") to be his last words and his last instruction to his disciples, as reported by Kurita Yutaka *Shihan*.

After his death many new instructors have received a second-hand instruction and chances are they may also need to review the Founder's final message. This is important because he was always changing and refining his Aiki, something somebody may well take for granted. Dramatic changes are likely to happen in a period of every ten years, and without careful consideration new adepts cannot know if their practice lacks any of the contents the master proposed by the end of his career. They might be using variations borrowed from other arts which may be rather alien to his continued and specific Aiki evolution.

Many books, magazines and films on *Aikido* correspond to such different periods too as can be seen in the emphasis renowned instructors have put on certain aspects that have influenced its present form. Some of them stress fighting forms, whereas some others put the emphasis on the concept of *ki* and others put it on weapons' practice. The speech used on tapes and books to address the general public can help us to check on this:

a) In Shioda Gozo Sensei's video from 1958 *Aikido* is seen as a series of slams and crashes, his technique emphasizes self-defense aspects and expressions like "*subduing an enemy*" are constantly used by the narrator. Another concept used here that seems to be contrary to the last Aiki of the Founder is the one conveyed by the expression "*against an enemy*" in constant reference to the practical application of techniques. The word *kata* is a third alien concept promoted in this video if it is only understood as mechanical forms which do not exist in Aiki. All this opposes to the ideals reported in this book.

b) In contrast, a 1962 video shows O-Sensei basically playing like a child and being amused by the works of his Aiki. He displays a big constant smile and he is obviously having a lot of fun as he calls out each next *Uke*. A huge change in his performance becomes apparent when comparing this video to other previously filmed demonstrations;

c) Tohei Koichi Sensei's 1962 video introduces a series of *ki* exercises that led to what is now considered to be a proprietary term of a school derived from the original teachings of the Founder and that he considered it to be different from the one he devised and conceptualized. Even the *tori fune undo* shown here varies from the one demonstrated by O-Sensei in other tapes. Techniques seem to focus more on practice partners as enemies than on the Universe and its teachings, not to mention the strong emphasis on disarming techniques found in this document;

d) In addition, some other contemporary videos (also from 1962 on) present *Aikido* basically as a martial or fighting art. They have emerged from the personal approaches of instructors in their effort to be creative and perhaps in substitution of what was considered as "obscure" words and mythological references used by O-Sensei to explain it. Many videos stress how wonderful *Aikido* techniques are but in order to go beyond its martial, fighting surface it is necessary to review all Aiki contents that may be hidden to newcomers.

Learning *Aikido* means to follow O-Sensei's heart and ideals, his way to Aiki. It also means to understand his message through correct practice in order to be able to develop an Aiki culture and not just to work at a technical or superficial level. That is the mission of his *deshi*, a Japanese term meaning "apprentice", "disciple" and "follower", and not simply a "student". [3]

O-Sensei had the *Samurai* model as his guide but he was basically interested in their way of thinking and philosophy rather than in their warfare skills, so this may be the time to check out if things have taken a different direction, since more and more instructors are likely to adopt their own personal interpretations. This is a very important issue because it may jeopardize the development of the way of Aiki and its culture, leaving it rather stagnant.

Questions arise from these concerns as to how to get *Aikido* rid of foreign elements and violent ideas, given that master Ueshiba proposed no divisions, no violence, no fighting and no competition. It is necessary to insure Aiki practice "suits the action to the word, and the word to the action", as Shakespeare would have put it. If O-Sensei foresaw his achievements would lead others and saw himself as the starting point of a path for an improved human culture –the weaponless divine warriors on this Earth he called *bujin*– it is important to see to it that these ideals are not absent in current *Aikido* practice. Incorrect interpretations might be passed on to future generations if instruction deviates from the original basic elements that should be present in practice in order to open the students' eyes towards the "hidden" aspects unveiled by the Founder.

---

[3] Linguistic remarks throughout this book are intended to contribute to the further understanding of Aiki as conceptualized and used by O-Sensei.

Kurita *Shihan*'s school does not take *Aikido* as another martial art and it does not even consider that a deeper understanding of Ueshiba's Aiki can be reached by tracing its development back to Daito-ryu since O-Sensei changed from it and adopted a brand new vision and approach. The interest in previous arts is of course legitimate and respectable but it is a path already walked by the Founder. Yet the large number of technical variations and combinations adopted by some schools leads to confusion when they engage in useless competitions to see what is the best, right, more correct or even most authentic technique or style in what is considered to be a contest-free discipline such as *Aikido*.

Aiki, the Founder's objective translated here as unity, confluence and harmony for the sake of a broader approach, is a state of being one, coincidental and in agreement with others. It must be cared for and taken a step forward if it is to be preserved and correctly launched into the future: we can not allow a formula achieved through many years of hard work and imagination to get lost. Since it goes beyond the usual paradigm, Aiki is not *martial* in a traditional sense or an *art* either, except if it is merely understood as an "ability learned by experience".

Within this context and expressed with all due respect, master Ueshiba was more than a martial artist. He said the way of Aiki is *"medicine for our sick world"* and he developed it in order to help overcome the problems, personal ghosts and weaknesses of people: fear, insecurity, selfishness, intolerance and more. Aiki is intended to help people to get rid of such weaknesses and ghosts via a physical work which does not limit itself to the practice hall or session, or to different ways of twisting an arm or throwing a person. It depends on everybody's will to make its practice help people improve their current lives and change their paradigms, their current perspective of things, and to help them to leave them behind in order to achieve another kind of personal and cultural development.

The way of Aiki is not to be used in the streets for self-defense, something practitioners may complain about. It is to help us live a great life learnt in a *dojo* (illumination hall), a space where practice is held to promote learning and understanding to educate and transform students by opening their minds and spirits. Techniques and exercises are the vehicles used between two people who work for mutual improvement and not ways to hurt each other. Self defense arts are meant for that, not *Aikido*. In the Founder's *budo* (a serious way of life inherited from martial issues) Aiki is a main element and, if it is still regarded as self-defense system, it teaches about the unity and confluence needed to keep people safe. It will eventually protect them at wider levels in their personal, family, and social lives (e.g., at home, work, and within their communities and even their country and the globe as a whole). In spite of the different *geiko* (training) forms, the way of Aiki is to be done with a partner, always in unity with others because it is not an individualistic art to be freely interpreted from any personal perspective or for the sake of a self-centered joy.

Aiki is to be used by anyone to learn about cooperation, whereas self-defense is for those concerned about enemies. We must do our best to see Aiki in a different way and to work hard in order to see what it is meant for. A general review of all the fundamental concepts originally proposed by the Founder is necessary to give them a new life. Many misunderstood concepts and misinterpretations can be avoided and training can be seen from a different perspective if the repertoire of ingenious elements O-Sensei put in his techniques is correctly observed since style differences may be the result of unnoticed misunderstandings.

It is interesting to see what happens when people from different schools get together to practice. Some *Uke* (the person starting the action, the "attacker") slap on the ground when they roll and some don't slap, some let go of *Nage*'s (the "defender's") wrist(s) when they are thrown and some keep them attached and undivided so as to maintain the attachment initially intended and conceptualized as a fundamental part of Aiki. In many schools, however, techniques are used basically to control and defeat *Uke*. Although they start trying to set some kind of union between *Uke* and *Nage*, the latter usually ends his action by means of a "good" final slam on the ground or by detaching from *Uke*.

Practitioners might not realize some of their actions may be violent from an Aiki perspective, since throwing or even pinning may be dangerous actions. This is definitely apart from the way of Aiki: terms like falling, attacking, and defending are alien to its nature. They have been used mostly because of *Aikido*'s martial resemblance and its origins but they also may have sent a wrong message.

The Founder didn't teach his students how to fall in any sense. According to Kurita Yutaka *Shihan* disciples and students started using falls and rolls *"in order to get out of the way quickly."* Instead O-Sensei taught them not to fall but to use their spirit, mind and body to grow. He was convinced the human body is like a piece of some precious and delicate glass, which has to be cared for at all costs. And part of our task is to find a way to go beyond what he accomplished too, in order to transcend medieval war practices for the benefit of our contemporary societies. Aiki must be studied in such a way as to take them a step forward if we really want to follow and extend the line he started and the goals he originally aimed at.

Such a change in history is yet to come and it makes Kurita Yutaka *Shihan* state that *"the future is big and the past is little"*:

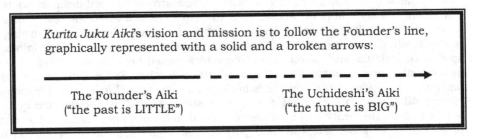

Kurita Juku Aiki's vision and mission is to follow the Founder's line, graphically represented with a solid and a broken arrows:

The Founder's Aiki   The Uchideshi's Aiki
("the past is LITTLE")   ("the future is BIG")

Students are now standing between tradition and the future

According to his ideals *dan* (black belt) ranks should be granted to those who try to understand the works of the Universe and have a good understanding of their own nature, to those who share the Founder's line and not to those who show impressive fighting skills. Kurita Yutaka *Shihan* is attempting to take Aiki into a different direction by changing its martial forms in order to make them absolutely positive, non-violent, and constructive, according to most Aiki elements and without changing their efficacy in life. He is devoting his efforts in a search for a refined Aiki practice based on his recollections of his days with master Ueshiba and his insight of how to make philosophy and technique match.

Learning O-Sensei's *bu* through Kurita Yutaka *Shihan* has never been an easy task. Thirty years of practice and three different developmental stages have been necessary to understand and fill the gaps between what he learned as the Founder's personal assistant and the levels at which he can and has been interpreted by students who have been with him at different times. Upon his arrival in Mexico City (1979) Kurita *Shihan* taught *Aikido* forms and techniques that were basically taken as part of a new amazing martial art by his first students. Ten years later he started getting into the subtleties of the art (*Kurita Juku*) and during the next decade he has switched to the creation of new ways to practice and gain a deeper insight of Aiki contents (*Kurita Juku Aiki*). He now teaches with ingenuous practical examples of the things the Founder seemingly left out on purpose after he decided to "*simplify his art for the sake of instruction*", as reported by Kurita *Shihan*. This has allowed his students to regard Aiki as a completely new paradigm suitable for everyday life together with a clear set of examples of what might now be lacking in practice.

Kurita Yutaka *Shihan* insists O-Sensei's Aiki has to be practiced correctly if adepts are to preserve it so he is determined to continue with the original line in order to launch it into the future. He compares this goal to the evolution of any other human knowledge which is always being transformed by new thinking and scientific discoveries. He is convinced that something similar has to be done with Aiki and the evolution of ideas has only been possible by those who didn't stop reviewing their current paradigms; it is a matter of cultural evolution, similar to the natural one, where living things always develop until they die. If scientists and humanists can do it, *Aikido* practitioners must also move on in the years to come.

"*The Founder understood Life is growth and to say we have learnt Aiki means we have stopped growing, so we are dead*". (Kurita Yutaka *Shihan*)

Learning from Kurita *Shihan* has been weird too because of the different perceptions regarding martial arts. But now some of his findings and recollections can be shared, knowing that learning Aiki has been a life-long task and that Aiki is something that cannot be put in words. Understood as unity, confluence and harmony, Aiki has to be lived, practiced, and felt with our five Aiki senses and not interpreted only by our intellect or biological senses: it is food for practice, and not for thought or speech. It belongs to the realms of the right side of the brain, which deals with our intuition, an element that has driven the evolution of humankind throughout history. An accurate verbal "interpretation" is not really possible because such a task is only carried out by our left side of the brain, so this book is offered for the sake of documenting Kurita *Shihan*'s first teachings.

Although writing or reading about Aiki does not really help our understanding, it can always help support what all practitioners may be able to find in due time. The following chapters only describe Aiki foundations that define *Aikido* practice and suggest an Aiki-do approach. It takes a look at concepts that will be a legacy for those who may study them in the future so as to follow and explore the Founder's original line. Many of the contemporary current practitioners of *Aikido* are not Japanese and the legacy is intended for them too since everybody can discover Aiki and benefit from it. *Aikido* is now part of Humankind but it is definitely not the deadly art some have assumed it to be and new practitioners must review and go on learning from those who preceded them. Given the right foundations, they will be able to move on taking their personal evolution forward in order to transform Aiki into an actual evolving culture.

Aikido's future

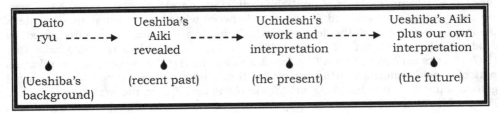

Daito ryu ----->	Ueshiba's Aiki revealed ----->	Uchideshi's work and interpretation ----->	Ueshiba's Aiki plus our own interpretation
♦	♦	♦	♦
(Ueshiba's background)	(recent past)	(the present)	(the future)

Please notice that in this book:

a)   **Aikido**, usually translated as "the way of (universal) harmony", refers to the original name given by grand master Ueshiba and the discipline promoted by the international Aikikai organization. It has Aiki as its main element but Kurita *Shihan* reminds it is a proprietary concept developed by the Founder who switched from *Aiki-budo* to *Aikido*, a name that resembles other arts' names like *Ju<u>do</u>*, *Ken<u>do</u>*, *Iai<u>do</u>*, etc., all of which have been known in America as martial arts.

b)   **Aiki**, the proprietary element developed by O-Sensei and generically translated as "union", is a term that should be linked to at least three basic indivisible concepts –unity, confluence and harmony– because a word-by-word translation jeopardizes its true broader meaning. Aiki is a three-fold term encompassing an ideal and a principle with a *do* ideogram attached to it literally meaning not only that it "emerges from experience" but that it leads you to the Grand Spirit of Aiki (union, master Ueshiba's ideal). Thus **Aiki-do** is used here to denote "the way of unity, confluence and harmony".

The following chapters explore the Founder's paradigm as a first-hand reference of the work done by Kurita Yutaka *Shihan*. There might be other serious instructors who are also exploring the Aiki-do possibilities and perspectives both in *tatami* (mats) practice as well as in real life, but this book is an attempt to honor Kurita *Shihan* and his life efforts to transform himself with the tools he learned directly from O-Sensei Ueshiba, who complained nobody was following him. His complaint is confirmed when somebody breaks an arm or wrist during practice, or when people are forced to sign a waiver to protect those who can harm them during practice. The purpose is to give Kurita *Shihan* the credit he deserves for the commitment he accepted as a disciple (*deshi*) and as a representative of the master to disseminate Aiki. A good start has been to make adepts realize that trying to understand Aiki-do leads to many questions arising from serious considerations about the constituents of practice which are to be explored during the learning process, for example:

- What was the Founder looking for and what did he eventually propose?

- Why do we have to start a movement with the left hand? Why is it wrong to work the same way with the right or left hands and feet?

- When we grab our partner or a *bokken*, why are we supposed to close our fingers in such a way as to avoid closing them as we do when making a fist?

- Why are a *bokken* (wooden sword) and a *jo* (staff) used instead of real weapons as well as in different but complementing ways?

- What is the ultimate goal the way of Aiki was originally designed for by O-Sensei?

- Where are unity, harmony and confluence to be found?

- What is *ki* made of, where is it found, and how can it be used?

- How can Aiki connect us with the Universe and what is its purpose?

- Why have programs seemingly put aside two fundamental pillars of Aiki such as *ki awase* and *ki musubi* as well as some others?

The answers to these and many other questions basically lie in our new vision and understanding of Aiki as a new paradigm.

Aiki as a paradigm

To both Japanese and Westerners Aiki is first and foremost a new *paradigm* and as such it is a way of thinking which does not necessarily conform or adjust to an already acquired set of experiences and beliefs. Paradigms are patterns which establish the limit and reach of our ideas, values and perspectives. Our behavior and thoughts are always the result of some kind of paradigm, concept, theory, perception, prejudice, tradition or framework, which in turn shapes our interpretation of the world around us.

A paradigm is created from what "others have told us" says Thomas S. Kuhn who developed and used this concept to specifically denote what we learn in school: the science he calls "normal". Such a normal knowledge, he states, is undoubtedly accepted at a given historical moment as valid, until someone comes and proves it can be understood in a completely different way. Good examples are the fact that some centuries ago people believed the Sun revolved around the Earth, until Copernicus proved the opposite, and the time when the paradigm of a "forceful education" was widespread until Comenius began to consider children as the center for Education: heliocentrism and paidocentrism became the two resulting paradigms from both changes.

Morihei Ueshiba, the Founder of the Aiki formula, discovered and created a new paradigm intended to go beyond an old tradition of combat arts. So in order to understand what he did it must be taken into account that paradigms are perspectives that ensure a certain vision and gives it a sense and an explanation making it difficult to accept new paradigms such as Aiki used to make "a friend out of a foe" simply because it opposes previous points of view. Since old paradigms served people well for a number of things in their lives they are too hard to get rid of.

Paradigms are accepted patterns nobody questions: they are preconceived ideas, and when a new way is not in accordance with a proven past experience it is difficult to accept its right dimension because it proposes that we think and do things in a very different way.

Paradigms can be detrimental to people, businesses and institutions because they hide the possibility of adopting new formulas for progress and development. Everybody has something they would like to change: a thing that needs correction in their family structure, government, education, etc. This can also be seen when business corporations struggle to find ways for an enduring success, since their efforts may be hindered by an existing paradigm that obscures their view of any new perspective. Old paradigms block new information needed as well as the ability to recognize it; they anchor us, and block any possible change.

A simple formula can be used here to demonstrate this: people are so used to the traditional paradigm "1+ 1 = 2" that they cannot recognize or accept the Aiki postulate: "1+ 1 = **1**" or "**1+ 1 = 0**". It seems easier for them to <u>divide</u> than to <u>add</u> and <u>round up</u> things because they perceive entities or components as independent from each other and not as integrated wholes. Most people separate concepts from experiences, instead of seeing them as complementing elements of an encompassing unity, as Eastern civilizations seemingly do: Westerners tend to separate and divide almost everything.

The Taoist **yin-yang** symbol is a good example of the way a paradigm is seen from a different perspective. Westerners tend to see it as a circle divided in two halves or as black and white colors when in fact they represent a unity. They complement each other while emerging from within themselves and thus constitute a whole where the black color rests on the white one and vice-versa.

According to Chinese culture, even though this symbol represents a "duality", it shows the union of a mutually complementing pair, so they can never separate and guarantee the natural order of life. When we follow the way of Aiki we learn to see things in such completely different ways.

Yin-Yang

The Founder himself gives a good example when he says that the real law of gravity makes it possible for things to be bound together harmoniously. [4] By saying this he goes beyond the general conception that the law of gravity just keeps us stuck to the ground!

Who is holding whom?

From a usual perspective, if a person grabs someone's wrist the action is taken as an attack, since he/she is probably grabbing as a clearly intended aggression. Aiki teaches that the person being held (called *Nage* in *Aikido* practice), might be the real "attacker", since he gets immediate control of his "attacker" (*Uke*) or because he might be holding a weapon (which explains the origin of this whole action).

---

[4] See John Stevens' *The Art of Peace*, a translation of the words of Morihei Ueshiba, Shambala, Boston and London, 2002, p. 47.

This can make us consider how reversed and relative a situation may be. On the other hand, which is even more important, Aiki takes the grab as a chance for *communication* and the manifestation of a positive approach to the situation and resolution of what seems to be a conflict on the surface. It is a chance to manage oneself in a positive and constructive way, an attitude that changes what usually tends to be an aggressive response into a reaction free from any negative doing and thinking. The attack is thus turned into a chance for a big smile thus making it possible to use Aiki in such a way so as *"to make friends not enemies,"* [5] something that may sound awkward in our current unfriendly societies.

Something that may seem impossible from an old perspective can be perfectly well done with a new paradigm. A long time ago nobody ever thought it was possible to heat water without domestic gas or electricity and now it is done by means of solar energy! Before the 60's grandparents were unable to imagine a man walking on the Moon and now it is such a "normal" thing: what escapes imagination today may materialize in the nearest future. People were fortunate to witness the emergence of many new paradigms in the 20th century, one of which is obviously represented by the Aiki-do, a personal developmental system that has come to change old preconceptions related to contests, encounters and even fighting and winning at any costs. Anything can always be given a different use just by changing our perspective, as can be seen in this example:

An 'umbrella' can also be... a 'sunshade'

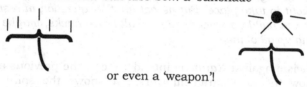

or even a 'weapon'!

It all depends on the situation: if you are sheltering from the rain, if you are trying to provide yourself with a nice, cool shade, or if you are being attacked and need to use it against someone. In any case, the use can always be harmless if you make that choice. When Aiki students practice they must ask themselves if they are learning stuff to be used as a fighting form or as a chance for their own human improvement. Other martial arts do not serve the same goal since they don't have important Aiki elements such as flexibility, communication, union and confluence: there is no such thing as a flexible kick, punch, slam or throw.

Aiki proposes to put an end to the long era of conflict human beings have lived throughout their history. History is characterized by a "clash of forces" between opposing groups, and the ideal is to begin a more prosperous and constructive millennium. This can be our "energy" era, an era full with union, confluence and harmony (Aiki) that will benefit human progress. So instead of continuing with an old paradigm where force A and force B run straight into each other and collide:

---

[5] This has always been taught by Kurita Yutaka *Shihan*. The Founder of Aiki stated: "The supreme challenge of a warrior is to turn an enemy's fearful wrath into harmless laughter" (*The Secrets of Aikido – the hidden teachings and universal truths of Aikido, as taught by its Founder, Morihei Ueshiba* by John Stevens, Shambala, Boston & London, 1997, p. 13).

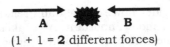

(1 + 1 = **2** different forces)

People can switch to the Aiki paradigm where Forces A and B run straight into each other in order to get together and unite by taking a different direction:

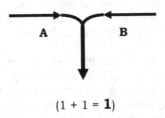

(1 + 1 = **1**)

Union makes a bigger **1,** a bigger entity and result. A short anecdote from Kurita Yutaka *Shihan* may illustrate this premise since it clearly shows the spirit of Aiki:

> *During a martial arts demo run on a TV program (ca. 1995) a Karate master was about to set a new world record: he was going to break a large amount of bricks in just a few seconds. Behind cameras, the host of this TV program, looking intently, turned to Kurita Shihan and asked him for a comment on what was about to take place. But he got another question in response: "Wouldn't it be better to build up something with all those bricks, maybe a room, instead of breaking up all of them?"* [6]

No criticism against *Karate* is intended here; the previous anecdote is just an example of how the new paradigm works: it shows the spirit of Aiki is one of construction. Aiki-do perspectives are a big change of mind; it is a personal developmental formula and its practice is intended to make us more humane and tolerant. This is in fact the original goal of general instruction all over the world: it is always conducive to change. And Aiki-do also teaches not to be afraid of change; change is mostly feared when it refers to external things but it is seen as something good and not so terrifying when transformation takes place in the individuals' self and provides them with individualized tools to face their troubles.

---

[6] This TV show was *Vibraciones cósmicas* and it was conducted by the re-known Mexican TV host Mr. Raúl Velasco. *See* the Aiki supplement at the end of this book for a complete transcription of the interview held right after this event.

The tree is beautiful because of its surroundings

[Aiki: union, confluence and harmony]

"Aiki is the Universe's order and arrangement
as a whole"

Chapter 1:

The Aiki paradigm

A GIANT CATFISH LIVING IN THE JAPANESE SEAS
IS SAID TO CAUSE EARTHQUAKES

A word on the Japanese world vision

Entering Aiki-do is exactly as starting any other Japanese art: it demands complete mastery from instructors and sincere devotion from students. And we can begin by saying that in order to understand the Aiki paradigm it is necessary to know something about its cultural origins and some aspects of the Japanese world vision. This is not the place to talk about such a topic in depth but it is necessary to start with a small reference about the nature of its concepts, with a sample of the way the world is seen in the land of master Ueshiba.

Let's start with a linguistic example. The Chinese ideogram for the word "tô" (*do*), representing everything related to a "way" or a "path", contains a stroke for "foot" at its base, and so it refers to "steps", "walking" or "moving up". In turn, this leads to the concept of "experience" as it really means in Chinese (the *tao* concept). It means

that a "way" is made by our actions and experiences, which eventually give us wisdom. The term *do* then comes from *tao*, a knowledge gained through experience, which in turn takes us to enlightenment or knowledge. We may well perceive not the whole *kanji* (ideogram) but just its particular elements, such as "the foot", and not the whole symbol if we tend to separate its elements.

Ideograms suggest that the Japanese general world vision do not appear fragmented or segmented to them. Consequently Aiki-do's work and actions (techniques) should not be learnt either as separate entities or fragments (e.g., as an attack and defenses) because they are integral parts of the same whole and they constitute a different paradigm. Kurita Yutaka *Shihan* recalls that in his last days the Founder always claimed there are no divisions in Aiki, no such things as *attack-*

defense, Uke-Nage (attacker-defender), *student-instructor,* and even no names at all since that only creates divisions.

Another example can be found in the following sketch used in Taoist medicine to provide us with an additional example of the difference between our perception of things and that from the East:

A first look at these numbers makes us perceive them as a clock-wise series. But when Chinese doctors make their interpretations of this sketch they know that number **1** is related to **4**, and that **4** relates to **2**, as **2** relates to **5**, and **5** relates to **3** in one larger integrated whole. These are not really numbers to be read clockwise: number **1** represents *happiness* and the heart, and **4** stands for *worrying* and the pancreas. So when a person is worried doctors clearly see the relationship between **1** and **4** and from that they warn patients by stating that unhappiness will have repercussions to their hearts (**1**). Consequently worrying will have a direct effect on their pancreas (**4**) too. Doctors are able to see the link between **4** and **3**, given that **3** symbolizes sadness and the lungs: a sad person's breathing is usually agitated during this condition, right?

Students should also consider the following aspects that define Japanese culture since they may find them when they learn *Aikido* with Japanese instructors:

- **aimai** (ambiguity), to which Japanese are generally tolerant for the sake of keeping up with the group.

- **amae** (dependence), which relates to the benevolence of others; children depend on their parents, younger people rely on their elders, grandparents depend on their adult children, etc.

- **bigaku** (sense of beauty), traditionally as a preference for the monochrome and with aesthetic values coming from feelings instead of what is logically considered to be aesthetic.

- **chinmoku** (silence in Japanese communication), which is a skill rather than just a form of emptiness between spoken words.

- **do** (a path), a way to be followed, a code of behavior or doctrine: "Under a master teaching without words, the adept goes through a cathartic process of emptying the mind of all passions and distinctions until it becomes a mirror of heaven and earth reflecting the multiplicity of things and goes beyond the form." [7]

---

[7] *Do* seems to be the most important aspect needed to understand *Aikido* practice. This and all of the previous terms were taken from *The Japanese Mind – understanding contemporary Japanese culture"* by Roger J. Davies and Osamu Ikeno, Tuttle Publishing, Japan, 2002.

Okuyama T.S. *Shihan* (Albuquerque Aikikai) has also pointed out that one of the most difficult things about learning *Aikido* is the lack of understanding of its philosophical aspects. He invites us to consider aspects of the Japanese culture that may help us in our "understanding of the art and its principles." [8] He touches on the subject of monotheism in the West and the totally opposite view derived from polytheism in the East. He pinpoints our so-called tendency to divide things, and to think about them in terms of independent entities and opposing pairs. As it happens in regards to the yin-yang symbol and principle, this is contrary to the Eastern way of more integrated conceptualization in terms of what he calls a "unity of harmony", a unity that leaves no room for opposites. Such a view makes everything relative because there is no need to see things as separate since "they are not really opposite and separable."

As Okuyama *Shihan* states, we tend to reduce things and thus forget to see them as interdependent, in opposition to what he calls "an Eastern integration" of concepts. Our "binary" way of thinking, as he calls it, makes us oppose things in terms of *right-left, good-bad, mind-body*, something we must be warned about since it may hinder our understanding of what *Aikido* instructors mean when they talk about *"heaviness existing within lightness"*, *"strength coming from softness"*, etc. This is another example of the way our mind-frame and our language influence the way we see and understand things alien to us like Aiki.

As an extended example we must remember that even when we have the North and South Poles there is only one Earth; there is the Sun and there are the planets, but there is only one Universe. So in order to take out from his Aiki all dividing elements, O-Sensei seemed to have used the term *kokyu* ("breath", "extension") to refer to all of his previous techniques in his last days!

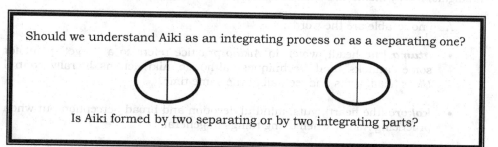

Should we understand Aiki as an integrating process or as a separating one?

Is Aiki formed by two separating or by two integrating parts?

With an additional linguistic example Kurita Yutaka *Shihan* remarks that one of the many obstacles to understanding Aiki lies in the wrong translation of *ki* simply as "energy". In his opinion, this has only contributed to the exclusion or elimination of the multiple perceptions and images Aiki-do practitioners should have in order to understand this fundamental concept in the way it was proposed by the grand master and not as it was traditionally understood in Chinese or even Japanese.

Since comparisons have been made between Aiki elements and concepts taken from our Western culture we will say at this point that this term may come

---

[8] Refer to his article: *A look at Japanese Culture* by T.S. Okuyama; this article was read on 09 /17/ 99 at <http://www.aikidoonline.com/archive/clmn_okuy.html>

close to the ancient Greek concepts of *energeia* (an active and continuous force) and *poiesis* (the creative work of transformation directed to the consecution of beauty, health and harmony of a human being), without reducing it to them:

Ki	=	***energeia***	*and*	***poiesis***
a universal force		active, continuous force		creative work of transformation

Ki may be perceived as a process, a form and an entity. For Kurita Yutaka *Shihan*, it is not only *"the force that allows life growth but the combination of both Kokoro* (heart, will) *and the 'energy-strength' plus the work done for a specific life growth goal".* [9] *Ki* is also a word that appears in many Japanese expressions related to the emotional life which specifically refer to the workings of judgment, consciousness, reason, conscience, and will.

The uselessness of trying to find the definition of *ki* in an ordinary dictionary or by asking Japanese people about it is obvious since they may not be familiar with the Aiki subject. O-Sensei conceived specific ideas for the words and terms he used in creating his paradigm, so they are part of his particular science in spite of the fact that this concept has been given varied definitions at different times in history. [10] The way of Aiki goes beyond those definitions and changes the old conceptions (paradigms) left by medieval *Samurai* warriors and thinkers.

Also noticeable are the words:

- ***atama*** (the head), which in *Aikido* practice refers to a "target" point for some "attacks" and "techniques" although Aiki actions literally control *Uke*'s head, arms and feet, all at the same time.

- ***kokoro*** (the heart], guts, mindful devotion and broad perception put when practicing Aiki or when doing things in general.

- ***hara*** (the belly], where life is born and our biological center is located.

- ***kao*** (the face], the way we face an attack and the way our actions make us look –our social face as resulting from our actions–. In fact, the Aiki movements proposed by the Founder seem to deal with touching all of these aspects that make up life. Unfortunately they cannot be described and are to be felt only through correct practice.

---

[9] Concepts like *ki* and many more are herein presented in an attempt to reproduce the words and teachings orally transmitted by the Founder to Kurita Yutaka *Shihan* so I present them to the best of my understanding. *See* the Glossary in Chapter 5 for a comprehensive list and additional details for this and other concepts. The best definition of *ki* in regards to technique seems to lie in a "body set aright" since perfection in posture leads to correct practice and in turn is the only way to understand Aiki.

[10] For more detailed information please refer to *The Spirit of Aikido* by Kisshomaru Ueshiba –the Founder's son and late Aikido Doshu–, Kodansha International, Tokyo, 1984, pp. 20-25.

Shiho-nage

It must be noticed that O-Sensei never spoke of a "killing sword" but of a sword that "kills the ills of this world", a concept interpreted in *shiho-nage* when it is seen as a technique whose practice is intended to abate evil in all four cardinal points. [11]

Master Ueshiba conceived *budo*, a life style based on martial attitude, as an art to protect our existence and not to destroy it. Consider the ideogram on the right: it represents the first part of the word *budo*.

Bu / Take

The original picture this *kanji* came from represents an advance on foot and it was then taken as a reference to military things; but the warrior may not have a challenging attitude, as this small drawing suggests. This *kanji* can also be interpreted as *"holding or stopping the spear."*

It must always be remembered that O-Sensei questioned the need to continue with the old era of clashing forces and conflict. His Aiki was indeed intended to "sheathe the sword". And although the *kanji* for *shi* in the word *bushi* represents a warrior and also means *Samurai*, it is important to make a note that such an old term has acquired a contemporary meaning currently associated with *scholar*, maybe as a result of the modern use of the term *budo*.

Kurita Yutaka *Shihan* has always taught that Aiki has in deed no such terms as *Uke* (attacker) or *Nage* (defender) because O-Sensei didn't see them as well-suited terms for the practice and instruction of his Aiki-do. They were used from earlier interpretations and at earlier stages of his career but they are definitely misleading in a culture bound towards a binary mentality such as ours. They make us divide what has to be kept united and they create divisions contrary to master Ueshiba's teachings.

In addition, given master Ueshiba never contemplated the use or practice of any kind of falling techniques or violent moves, and he never coined any term for an action which is common in other martial arts, Kurita *Shihan* asks his students *"Why*

---

[11] This is how Rinjiro Shirata understood it. Refer to: *Aikido – The way of harmony* by John Stevens, Shambala, London, 1984, pp. 61.

do you want to fall? Nobody likes falling, do they?" and he makes an analogy with an airplane to state that nobody wants it to fall either. He reports it was the Founder's students who used falling as a way to get out of the way in an efficient and quick way when O-Sensei was demonstrating his Aiki. They worked on the movement known as *ukemi,* which in spite of its rather literal meaning as "the one who receives or gets" is in fact a roll and is definitely not a passive role.

The roll was immediately interpreted as a useful activity because it helps students "polish" their bodies and spirits too. But the practice of spectacular falls for their own sake puts the practitioners' physical integrity at great risk and is absolutely opposite to the anti-selfish and anti-violent spirit of Aiki.

Breakfall is an English term coined by American practitioners and translators, but Aiki does not include falling actions of any kind or nature. A breakfall is violent and does not fit its spirit. Participants are partners, couples, and colleagues, not enemies: they have to think of themselves as equally important human beings and not as pieces of meat or garbage that can be thrown with the intention of killing or winning over them when they "attack". Such an action is definitely banned in an Aiki approach; Kurita Yutaka *Shihan* always states the body is akin to the finest piece of crystal, which may be broken just the same. He sees no need to practice any types of "falling" actions and this maybe the most important part of the true nature of Aiki, contrary to the usual goals of fighting arts.

Unfortunately, when we attend many *Aikido* demonstrations all we get is just a good "martial arts" show, full of attacks and defensive maneuvers, with the use of exotic weaponry and spectacular throws as well as Japanese garments that evoke its direct inheritance from the ancient *Samurai* warriors. This is misleading since it is rather superficial and irrelevant to Aiki, and affects the spiritual and moral content implied in the techniques being demonstrated.

From an Aiki perspective, techniques are actions considered as a *means* or *vehicles* for the integration and manifestation of one's individuality so they are always characterized by the utmost and deepest respect for life. Evidently, this cannot be learnt without a correct guidance from a good teacher, who must help students change their previous fighting paradigm and utilize the new mentality required for the development and capacity to access the human dimension embodied in the application process of what is superficially and simply seen as "techniques".

O-Sensei cautioned Kurita *Shihan* against the use of real weapons as training tools since Aiki is not military-like and its objective does not include any combat applications. Its mission is to promote what Kurita *Shihan* has called *intuitive intelligence* as well as human coexistence, not war, destruction or combat. In support of this he still recalls a personal anecdote from the day he got the idea of including *Iaido* in his study of *Aikido*. When he went to see master Ueshiba to ask for his approval to do so the grand master gave him the following straight reply: *"Kurita, why do you want to do that in my dojo?"* [12]

Kurita *Shihan*'s program, as taught in *Kurita Juku Aiki*, has never included training with any live weapons. Perhaps the opinion he got directly from the Founder

---

[12] This was a surprising comment made by Y. Kurita *Shihan* at one of our numerous and exceedingly long coffee-time chats due to the extended fact that many instructors seem to love Iaido and almost every curriculum includes "weapons" practice where the *bokken* (wooden sword) is used as a *katana* (sword).

made him realize that practice may allow the weapon's spirit to get into a man's soul, and maybe this may cast the Aiki spirit aside. The reason is simple if we notice that a sword is in fact the product of military engineering and it is definitely designed to kill.

Aiki practice doesn't need any of the highly refined killing techniques developed in Japan's medieval times.

Aikido practice with "weapons" is mainly done with a *bokken* (a wooden sword), a *jo* (a staff), and a *tanto* (a wooden knife), all of which become alive when used as an extension of the practitioner's body. They are used as tools and vehicles to learn and understand *ki* and Aiki works. It is through them that we can correct different aspects of our personalities and more important, they activate the right or intuitive side of our brains. As it will be explained in Chapter 4, the objective of this practice is to straighten out whatever might be crooked in our body, mind and spirit, since our personalities cannot be built through the use of weapons if they foster negative, destroying or violent reactions, intentions or thoughts.

This is the correct spirit of Aiki practice as a path leading to personal and social unity, confluence and harmony as it was unveiled by the Founder. Unfortunately when people hold a sword they may think of themselves as *Samurai* and they may even visualize themselves cutting enemies in half. The *bokken* and *jo* are great instruments for growth and they are also intended to be used as a means to exemplify important aspects contributing to the individual's development.

It may be difficult to realize that within the Aiki paradigm "attacks" are not directed against an enemy but against ourselves, and the use of weapons does not contribute to this either. How can it be then that through an Aiki application of "technique" we must make our best to take care of our "enemies"? Are these enemies human and imaginary, monsters such as selfishness, fear, mean intentions, etc?

The answer is not always obvious since it is ingrained in our ability to see the contents and process of an "applied technique" –e.g., to see what happens before and during an action that includes all the necessary elements to make it full of a constructive spirit and unification manifest with a whole single movement–. *Activity* and *work* are usually confused because practitioners only pay attention to the beginning and ending parts of an action, they only see an attack and its defense. This is part of a simplistic self-defense paradigm and it hides the outreach of Aiki, its profoundness and true meaning: Aiki-do is made of several unseen elements that are put to work when we practice techniques.

Aiki can help us cultivate and bring out the best of our human essence, and it does not deceive us with pretty words and intentions. Techniques are the means for a constructive manifestation of the inner self and they have tremendous favorable repercussions in our everyday and practical lives. This is what makes Aiki-do a cleansing form, a practice to help us clean our body and heart. Practice is intended to help us "clean our spirit" so we must also arrive clean to our practice, physically and spiritually free from any negative, filthy thoughts. This includes the idea of learning for the sake of competition, or to be too good to become invincible, or to be able to hurt anyone. Transcendent Aiki actually involves an "Aiki change".

Aiki Change [13]

The path for union, confluence and harmony (Aiki-do) proposes the union and coordination of people, systems and wills in order to improve an already created civilization. It might put an end to divisions among people, particularly those leading to confrontation and separation. This is a fundamental issue in an increasingly global world. The path of Aiki is already made, and anyone can now walk it by means of a correct practice which implies the use of a *good* (*harmless*), *true* (*real*) and *aesthetic* (*beautiful*) technology (Aiki work and techniques). This raises the question about the need for escalating conflict and the negative results it produces.

Do we need the clashing forces of the past?

The Founder taught that a unified body and mind means congruent techniques according to the spirit of Aiki. He also talked about the need to have all tuned to the same goal. [14] History shows man has been both the protagonist and a spectator of a long bloody fighting era of armed political and social conflicts, a "clash of forces" between fellow human beings, and an old and sad reality no one has escaped. Yet, in such a regrettable situation, the violent and conflictive "human" condition is being questioned by intellectuals who look for the failures produced in our "civilization" by the unfulfilled promises of science. A contribution gathered from Aiki principles may be here to help us change this perspective.

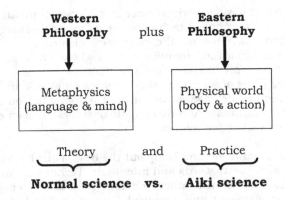

---

[13] The words "Aiki change" appear attached to the first drawing made to identify the Mexican Aikido Association, founded in 1981 by the author and a small group of enthusiasts who designated Yutaka Kurita *Shihan* as their Technical Director for life. To the author's knowledge this drawing was donated to the organization by one of *Shihan*'s first students.

[14] *See* John Steven's translation of *The Art of Peace*, by Usehiba Morihei, Shambala Classics, 2002, p. 43. This is *Kurita Juku Aiki*'s main search and goal.

When talking about the humanities Western philosophers concentrate on the Sciences of the Spirit, which seem to be useless as means to overcome the current era of conflict or have not found a clear way to be used as a technology to improve our current life. However master Ueshiba created a formula (Aiki) with a potential to remodel our human condition. Kurita Yutaka *Shihan* refers to this when he reports that the Founder said: *"We have built a civilization, and we now must learn to live in it"*. Is this is part of the meaning of *budo* as the way "to keep the sword sheathed"? Does this make Aiki a utilitarian philosophy? Can change be attained by using unity, confluence and harmony as a fundamental resource? Whatever the answer, it is embodied in the mission and vision of *Kurita Juku Aiki*, Kurita *Shihan*'s school.

Humanity has developed amid clashing and struggling forces both against nature and social institutions. It has found a way over the imposition of ideas, the conquest of nations, the creation of new borders, and the most diverse and difficult situations. Old paradigms have changed for centuries, with many exceptional cases such as the one lived by Mahatma Gandhi's "pacifist revolution". Learning the Aiki-do may enable us to find new creative ways to change old frames of mind and eventually change the continued use of destructive ways.

If Aiki performance is not correct the old paradigm's war spirit will only make us lose our chance to learn from the order of the Universe. Does this make people perceive *Aikido* as a weaker martial art? Did people start *Aikido* just because they fear being assaulted or even killed? Do we want to go on as slaves of fear? Is it really impossible to take a step further in human evolution and are we really condemned to self-destruction?

Conflict is certainly a fundamental part of life, and Aiki proposes a new approach to life and conflict. We can steer it towards our benefit if we are able to see it as an opportunity for growth and learning; that is, if we are able to adopt it as a practical constructive condition in our lives. Aiki teaches that, just as man has lived different relationships with nature, being a part of it and conquering it as much as it has been possible, there is also an enormous and encouraging chance and need to change the relationships human beings have also kept between each other.

From this perspective we can predict a series of relationships tending to positively close the historic cycle of human relationships in order to take a step towards perfecting human interaction. The Aiki paradigm states that change can only come about through daily and correct activity expressed in concrete positive actions which may promote change in our conduct and mentality.

From a psychological point of view it seems that all intentions for a change are always subdued by the superior power of the subconscious. Kurita *Shihan* sees correct Aiki practice as a means to change this. Aiki-do shows there is a direct proportional relationship between the way we move and act, and the way we think, what our mentality or paradigm is. If this is the case, we may conclude that soft, harmonic movements help model a soft, harmonic way of thinking. This may be possible only if we use the capacity our two brain hemispheres give us. So by using the intuitive (right) hemisphere of the brain Kurita *Shihan* proposes to develop an *intuitive intelligence* with its potential to develop one's self.

Aiki demonstrates that a formula contrary to the force-vs.-force one has to be used today in order to bring much better results. Instead of the usual rough and violent actions of the past we can now practice flexible vs. flexible movements, conducive to a gentler mentality. The mind is influenced by the use of our body just as honest actions result in honest characters. Refinement is acquired through a specific physical education based on careful body activities and experiences that have to be necessarily harmonious. Such an education renders a higher level and quality of psycho-motor skills that mold our mind. Vulgar movements and habits do not render such a superior order. Greeting is a good example of refinement. [15]

Peace must be practiced just as any other discipline. It can only be done through experience and not by means of lectures and discussions, which has been the preferred method for centuries. Things cannot be learnt and lived only with argumentative analysis; ideals never remain on paper or verbal exposition when people really want to follow through with them. What is the use of attending dozens of workshops and seminars of any kind if we remain in the same place or condition as those who did not attend? What is the use if we won't be able to use our newly acquired knowledge, our intellectual energy?

Our *intuition*, the main product of the right hemisphere of our brain, has been numbed by our traditional way of thinking. As a result we have an excessive dependence on logic and technology and stagnate, thinking it will automatically end our problems. In our contemporary world nobody seems to trust their senses, since up to this day empirical science has been teaching us to only trust well calibrated and tested tools and gauges, including theories, arguments and fashionable speeches more than concrete actions. Aiki teaches that no technique really works correctly without intuition.

Human experience has proved there must always be a certain "spark" of ingenuity in order to make things work well. If a leader, a thinker, or even a regular person is not able to recognize and take advantage of their own intuition, of that "gut feeling", "hunch", or knowledge that suddenly emerges out of the blue, there will be nothing else to provide him or her with an authentic feeling of security. Intuition is our capacity to understand something without any previous study or analysis but it has been discarded in academic education and might have been neglected in *Aikido* instruction.

Aiki is absolutely intuitive, and its practice makes us act right away and with no need of any previous thought.

---

[15] This is why Kurita *Shihan* refers to Aiki-do techniques as the ground for growth and refinement and not as mere punches, throws or defenses.

The two ideograms used to express the old Japanese term *bugei* (martial arts) mean "accomplished art or skills". From its early origins it proposed the control of one's self and the warrior disciplines through a paradigm based on two fundamental ideas within an honor code known as *bushido*: an effort is never enough, and a disarmed man, a seemingly "weak" one, can defeat an armed or "strong" one.

In this sense it opposes the Darwinian paradigm since the old fighting arts tested in combat always searched for a way to allow the "small fish" to protect and even defeat the "bigger" ones. Their search was also to develop intuition through mental and physical control, in order to not depend merely on instincts. Thus the Founder of the Aiki *do* was able to improve such a long-pursued ideal with a 360° twist: Aiki eliminates the differences implied in the big-small fish concept by means of a constant refinement of a person through the practice of activities that lead to the union, confluence and harmony of his/her spirit, body, and mind. Men belong to a unique species in the animal kingdom and they have a potential to grow.

Aiki provides us with a means to get rid of our enemies and of such a hideous concept. Its goal is to achieve the best in us, to heal ourselves in order to help us overcome our fears and face our crisis. From this new paradigm's ideal we may expect humankind to continue its self-discovery and to transcend in a sustainable manner. Intuition and the works of the right side of our brains have no nationalities. It does not belong to a particular country and has no creeds or political parties.

What does the Aiki paradigm offer?

Tamura Nobuyoshi *Shihan* has stated that *Aikido* is "an ascetic way that shows the direction to human accomplishment through the formation and development of: the essence (*ki*), wisdom and virtue (*toku*), and the body (*tai*)" and that "it is through this education, which includes and unites the body and the mind, that we go beyond the notions of race and boundary to form a true man." [16] This explains why it is generally stated that Aiki movements are:

a)   *harmonious* and *flexible*, like the ones found in nature. They are executed in a circular manner, from left to right and vice versa, imitating the earth's rotation and other cosmic movements;

b)   good to increase *physical stamina*. They improve glandular functioning and promote a better blood circulation, and strengthen neurological points which are important in reflexology and other systems of physiological care; and

c)   also lead to a better *overall health*. They help take care of our body and avoid even the tiniest possibility of fractures or injuries.

---

[16] Refer to *Aikido and Etiquette and Transmisión*, by Nobuyoshi Tamura , 8th. Dan, Head Instructor at the Federation Française d'Aikido et Budo, an article read on 09 / 06 / 2000 in the e-megazine found at: <http://www.aikidoonline.com./feat_0500_tmra.html>

Kokyu (extension)

Regarding the lessons inherited from *bujutsu,* or the art of fighting, Tamura *Shihan* adds: "By becoming imbued in the methods of 'life preservation', we acquire tranquility and self-confidence, and we reach peace of mind. At the same time, by the will to undertake things, perseverance and organizational skills are developed." And in an additional remark he states that "in a society that easily gives importance to technique, strength and power, rules of etiquette, a sine qua non condition to the survival of society, allows us to feel that there are superior values which are important to respect without any effort." [17]

In analyzing the main differences between Aiki and martial arts, an additional clear distinction can be made by reviewing the concepts of *efficacy* and *efficiency*. A headache can be efficaciously ended by slashing the head from the suffering person but this is not the more efficient way to stop the problem. Martial arts proven in combat represent efficacy, since they can be used to defeat and kill the enemy. Given its creative solution of conflict Aiki enables us to dissipate ill effects without having to kill anyone, its system is efficient.

It is through Aiki that we can 'look after" and even "protect" our enemies without the need to protect ourselves from them, as the old energy-wasting paradigm states. It is well-known that *Aikido* techniques are designed in such a way that you can end an attack without violence or causing any harm, one of its main precepts. There is no reason to react in a primitive way, with punches, kicks and bites. Aiki practice offers a wide spectrum of real experiences through which it is possible to obtain the harmony so widely promoted, and materialize the spirit in positive, concrete actions.

No negative conduct, technique or any other destructive intention, heart, spirit or will (*kokoro*) can be allowed in correct training if we don't want them to be part of our personality. There should be no attacks and no throws intended to destroy the opponent. This is a must in Aiki practice and the profound spiritual basis needed in our contemporary world. This promotes union, confluence, harmony and peace, the natural order of things, the same cosmic/universal order. It is based on these precepts that *Aikido* has been defined as the union between the universal and our personal *ki*.

---

[17] Ibid.

As we can see, Aiki is a way to liberate us from all confrontation by taking advantage of the works of *ki*, its central element. It shows that:

- We can neutralize the enemy in a very simple way: by changing the attack-defense concepts into relative terms, by turning our enemies into friends who won't fight against us and by creating new alliances with everybody.

- It is not necessary to compete in order to win. It is not fruitful to distract our efforts by engaging in competitions of any kind. Competition, if any, must take place within ourselves for self-improvement and not to defeat those we might consider as an obstacle or hindrance in our way.

- We can handle ill intentioned actions designed to cause us harm, we can give them a new direction where they will not hurt anyone, and we can banish them from our lives in order to develop and grow. Aiki is a *bu* way (a *bu-do*) and not a fighting art: it is not intended to destroy anything or anyone. This is Ueshiba's *ki*: a continued movement that can help clean contemporary life, an ideal to change a person's heart and a way to improve society in our contemporary world. It cannot be good to go on killing or defeating others in order to succeed; such is an old paradigm Humanity can get rid of.

The *pleasure* of no competition liberates. The practice of *Kyudo* (archery) is not a competition between archers; although they aim at the same target their practice is independent from each other. The way of Aiki goes beyond by making practitioners get together and join, communicate and share. It makes them find, multiply and apply *ki* through the correct use and care of their own beings.

Awase (unification): a very important Aiki principle

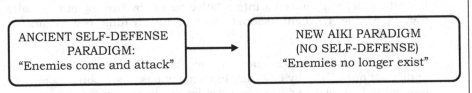

The basic Math paradigm tells us $1 + 1 = 2$, but Aiki states $1 + 1 = \mathbf{1}$ since there are no divisions, no attacks, and no differences between partners; there is union, blending and harmonious complementing.

Union means working together, in useful and complementary couples, something graphically represented as follows (notice these couples are not "pairs" but "partners"):

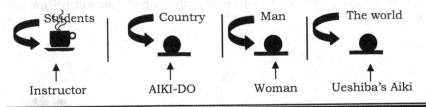

In Zen the "center" does not move and is represented like this in reference to a person:

In Aiki the union of two partners makes a bigger circle (indeed a conjoined action) and both or more participants always share a common center:

AIKI ("union") $\Rightarrow$ <u>bigger action</u>

The flower expands and flourishes by reaching for the sun

[*Kokyu*: extension and breathing]

Extending towards life, like flowers do, is necessary for us to blossom

Chapter 2

The Founder's search

TSURU
THE STORK, A SYMBOL OF GOOD LUCK

A new, energetic world

Hiroshima became a landmark in the history of men; it showed that nuclear power can be the world's greatest enemy and not just for the parties in conflict. Parallel to the armaments race, nations have seen the need to keep a power balance, acutely aware of the potentially disastrous effects they may provoke if they don't moderate their actions. As Yutaka Kurita *Shihan* teaches:

> *"Children fight, but men kill themselves when they do it; there is no need for learning how to kill since that can make you end in prison or to be executed. Think about it: children really know how to forget: after a fight, they just go back to play and have fun!"*

Administrations try to avoid international confrontations. They want to use their powers more efficiently. They know the real challenge of the new millennium should be to abandon the old clashing paradigm and to achieve more social changes in line with those produced by human rights and the fostering of fundamental values such as tolerance.

The final message from World War II is one of sensitivity and optimal use of all kinds of energies, especially nuclear. Interestingly, *Aikido* emerges as "The way to (universal) harmony", a formula logically standing as a way to evolve from old traditional fighting arts and Aikijutsu forms towards the new Aiki-do paradigm.

We have Aiki to help us make more human rights out of our human wrongs.

MASTER UESHIBA BORROWED *AIKI* DAITO-RYU TECHNIQUES AND TRANSFORMED THEM

FROM THIS    TO THIS

He switched from martial to non martial and reduced dozens of *Daito-ryu* techniques into a small bunch of dynamic contact movements, from *ikkyo* to *gokyo*, and from *irimi* to *kotegaeshi*, in order to create a different paradigm.

Ueshiba Morihei: beyond martial arts

The Aiki practice system is currently known as *Aikido* all over the world, and it is usually presented as a contemporary evolution and adaptation of preceding *budo* forms with a term loosely translated as martial arts. But it is important to be extremely careful when interpreting O-Sensei Ueshiba's *budo* as compared with ancient *bushido* since their goals differ substantially.

Contrary to what books and chronicles often describe in regards to previous martial arts *Aikido*'s history is not to be tracked too far back in time. The master certainly studied ways inherited from Japanese medieval times but he was able to develop a new paradigm he saw as a formula to improve and link all Humankind. *Aikido* practitioners think of him as the greatest contemporary martial artist who was also an outstanding visionary man. He went beyond imagination to propose a new ideal: the possibility to use physical and spirit-guided training to make a change in our minds.

To see him as a martial-fighting artist is to see only the surface of his discovery and achievements and to neglect his ideals. It may be a misleading notion for someone like him, who was able to find out a path made up of techniques meant for personal development, a fertile land for a new human being, and a profound spiritual vision of a culture capable to mirror a universal order. The Aiki-do is a means to link people with the Universe and to help them realize how to follow its laws, order and arrangement.

Ueshiba's Aiki is definitely not a new martial art. In his own words: *"It is a divine path inspired by the gods that leads to truth, goodness and beauty."* [18] All the events in his life, his life search, his findings and his eventual development can help you understand his goal. And a review of such a rich life is always worth it to see how it is that a common man can become a great one through the use of his imagination, a divine gift given to all human beings.

---

[18] Refer to *Budo*, by John Stevens, Kodansha International, New York, 1991, a book where you can find a complete version of this biography as well as concepts the Founder took as fundamental to his paradigm. .

A life in a nutshell

**Ueshiba Morihei
(Kaiso Sensei)**

Born on December 14, 1883, master Ueshiba was undoubtedly a gifted man. According to John Stevens, he was sent to a Buddhist temple to study the Confucian classics and the Buddhist scriptures at the early age of seven. And although he did not finish Middle School –according to Kurita Yutaka *Shihan*–, he was a self-illustrated man of splendid imagination, sensitivity and intuition, who won a place among other great men in universal history. According to Kurita *Shihan*'s current thesis these same qualities are achieved with the use of the brain's right hemisphere and not from accumulated data. *Kurita Juku Aiki* is a school where students can realize how Aiki-do is designed to make their right brain work.

It has been reported that the master learned traditional wrestling (*jujutsu*) and swordsmanship (*kenjutsu*) in his twenties and that he was well known for his skills and hard-working character. It is also known it was around his thirties that he met Takeda Sokaku, a Daito-ryu master, from whom he learned about *aiki* techniques and that the most definitive moment in his life occurred when his father got ill and he decided to return to his hometown, because on his way home he heard of Deguchi Onisaburo, the leader of the Omoto-kyo religion, whose influence made him change his previous fighting paradigms for good.

According to Stevens, it was after his encounter with this leader that master Ueshiba decided to search for a more spiritual life. He joined Deguchi and helped him farming his land and by so doing he also found an essential unity between *budo* and agriculture. Kurita *Shihan* reports a rather unknown aspect of *Aikido*: the Founder borrowed certain harvesting movements and incorporated them into his philosophy and techniques. And from another anecdote he recalls the curious relationship the master found between Aiki and the elaboration of a bread called *mochi* where two people take turns in order to make it: one of them mixes the ingredients and the other flips it over, a procedure curiously known as "Aiki tori" which sounds just like the grabs we use in *Aikido* practice (*katate dori, ryote dori*, etc). Master Ueshiba used this analogy to illustrate the importance of combining the work done by two partners during a grabbing (*tori*) activity.

The message cannot be more obvious and down-to-earth: we get stronger as far as we join the same efforts (1 + 1 = **1**) and gain completeness (1 + 1 = **0**). It was around this period that his practice gradually began to take on a spiritual-practical character that lead him to break away from the conventions of Takeda's Daito-ryu and opened the way to develop an original approach that breaks down the barriers between spirit, mind, and body. Although his integrating vision made him abandon ancient fighting forms from Japan's feudal past he adapted and gave a new impulse to past precepts in order to serve contemporary people (Kurita *Shihan*).

In 1922, Stevens informs, his approach became known as *Ueshiba-ryu aiki-bujutsu*, derived from the techniques learned from Takeda, whose system included an Aiki concept understood as the union of energy in battle. O-Sensei changed such a paradigm as he envisioned it as a union, confluence and harmonious work that leads to a constructive resolution of conflict, and as a path for human improvement and spiritual development. Kurita Yutaka *Shihan* points out that by shortening the number of techniques found in Daito-ryu he was able to differentiate his new non-violent Aiki paradigm. In addition, he also created *irimi-nage*, an action not found in any other *budo* or *jutsu* forms. He devoted his whole life to the study of a new Aiki, and this kept him going on, always growing, changing and evolving.

It has been reported that when he realized his way was one of unity and harmony with the Universe, he decided to change its name to *Aiki-budo* so he shifted from a fighting/technical art (a *jutsu*) to a martial life style (a *do*), a way leading to enlightenment. [19] Then his Aiki-budo became better known and attracted numerous people including Kano Jigoro, the founder of *Judo*.

According to Stevens, O-Sensei spent many busy years teaching at the Kobukan in Ushigome and in his *dojo* in Tokyo and Osaka. In 1941 there was a presentation of his Aiki-budo at the Kobukai, a governmental body that united all the martial arts under one single organization. Then he began the construction of an Aiki Shrine at Iwama in dedication to the Grand Aiki Spirit (*Aiki O-Kami*) represented in the calligraphy on the left. To Kurita *Shihan*'s knowledge, no practice hall shows the right spirit of Aiki if it does not display this *kami* representation. Without it, he teaches, the *dojo* is but a simple hall of practice and not the space provided to search and gain illumination (knowledge), understanding and insight.

The Shrine was completed in 1945, just before the war ended. *Budo* went into decline, and *Judo* aroused as a reconciliation vehicle from the Japanese as it became an Olympic sport. Then authorities granted permission to reestablish the Aikikai; the main dojo was renamed Ueshiba Dojo and then it was turned into the Aikido World Headquarters known by a shorter term of Hombu Dojo. According to Stevens, by the end of his life and during a visit to Hawaii, some time before his death on April 26, 1969, O-Sensei made the following statement:

> *"I have come (...) in order to build a 'silver bridge'. Until now, I have remained in Japan, building a 'golden bridge' to unite Japan, but henceforward, I wish to build a bridge to bring the different countries of the world together through the*

---
[19] For a detailed clarification on this subject refer to *Living the Martial Way* by Forrester E. Morgan, Maj. USAF, Barricade Books, New Jersey, 1992, p. 9-14, where you can find information on the differences between the *jutsu* arts to be used in combat and *do* practices or disciplines for spiritual improvement.

harmony and love contained in Aikido. I think Aiki (...) can unite the world in harmony..." [20]

The way to Aiki

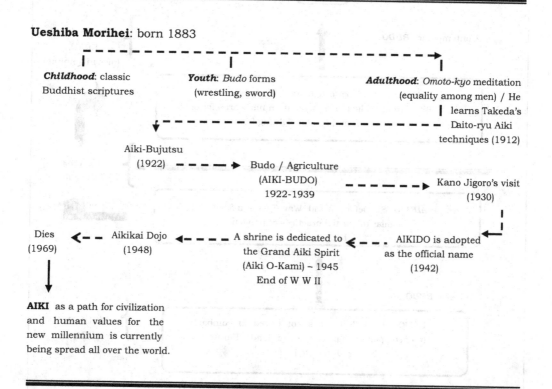

Ueshiba Morihei: born 1883

Childhood: classic Buddhist scriptures

Youth: *Budo* forms (wrestling, sword)

Adulthood: *Omoto-kyo* meditation (equality among men) / He learns Takeda's Daito-ryu Aiki techniques (1912)

Aiki-Bujutsu (1922)

Budo / Agriculture (AIKI-BUDO) 1922-1939

Kano Jigoro's visit (1930)

Dies (1969)

Aikikai Dojo (1948)

A shrine is dedicated to the Grand Aiki Spirit (Aiki O-Kami) – 1945 End of W W II

AIKIDO is adopted as the official name (1942)

AIKI as a path for civilization and human values for the new millennium is currently being spread all over the world.

The Founder's life was always permeated by spiritual and physical training. He found an expression that balances them both and makes them match through his view of Aiki as a new vision and ideal.

He changed Takeda's *aiki* concept and devoted his life to the transformation of himself. He switched from an old point of view and carried out a search which eventually leads to the emergence of *bujin*: a human being in full spirituality, an evolution from the traditional *bushi* (warrior) individual, and a step forward into contemporary *budo* (a serious way of life). This makes him the inventor and discoverer of the way of Aiki, something for which he should be better known as the *Kaiso Sensei* (discoverer master). [21]

---

[20] Refer to *Budo*, by John Stevens, pages 21-22
[21] Go to page 190 for details.

AN EVOLUTIONARY IDEAL

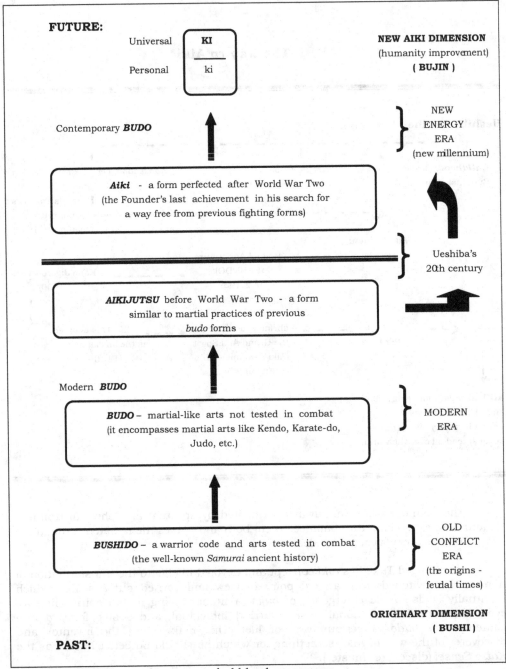

FUTURE:

Universal **KI**

Personal ki

NEW AIKI DIMENSION
(humanity improvement)
(BUJIN)

Contemporary **BUDO**

NEW ENERGY ERA
(new millennium)

Aiki - a form perfected after World War Two
(the Founder's last achievement in his search for
a way free from previous fighting forms)

Ueshiba's
20th century

AIKIJUTSU before World War Two - a form
similar to martial practices of previous
budo forms

Modern **BUDO**

MODERN ERA

BUDO – martial-like arts not tested in combat
(it encompasses martial arts like Kendo, Karate-do,
Judo, etc.)

BUSHIDO – a warrior code and arts tested in combat
(the well-known *Samurai* ancient history)

OLD CONFLICT ERA
(the origins -
feudal times)

ORIGINARY DIMENSION
(BUSHI)

PAST:

NOTE: *Aikido*: a serious way to hold back weaponry.
   Bujin: people who have been able to evolve from ancient fighting ways.

Four generations of disciples and *Aikido* dissemination

The next biographical sketch includes important events and a list of four different *uchideshi* generations. [22] Kurita Yutaka *Shihan*'s place is at the fourth and last one.

1900-1920   The Founder studies various traditional martial arts and learns Daito-ryu from Takeda Sokaku. Then he leaves him and starts his own development.

1921-1935   **1st. generation of disciples:** Tomiki Kenji (1926), Mochizuki Minoru (1930), Shioda Gozo (1932), Shirata Rinjiro (1933)

1927   Master Ueshiba teaches "Aiki techniques" (Aiki-bujutsu) since 1922.

1932-1945   **2nd. generation:** Koichi Tohei (1939), Abe Tadashi (1942)

1942   *Aikido* is adopted as a name. Some years later it will be translated as "The way of universal harmony".

1943   The Aiki Shrine is built in Iwama-Machi, Ibaraki prefecture. The grand master frequently goes there to find solace and meditate and working on the perfection of his *do* (way, code or formula).

1946-1955   **3rd. generation:** Saito Morihiro (1946), Tamura Nobuyoshi (1953), Andre Noquet (1955), Saotome Mitsugi (1955)

1948   Kaiso Sensei's son, Ueshiba Kisshomaru, is appointed as director of the Central Dojo. The foundation is set for *Aikido* to be furthered all over the world.

1956-1969   **4th. generation:** Tohei Akira (1956), Yamada Yoshimitsu (1956-7), Chiba Kazuo (1958), Sugano Seiichi (1958), Kanai Mitsunari (1959), Kurita Yutaka (1959), and Terry Dobson (1960).

Kurita Yutaka *Shihan* lives with the Founder at this time, he escorts him wherever he goes and also helps him out as his scribe. He is forced to renounce his own social and family life in order to stay at all times with his highly demanding master.

---

[22] Refer to the official Aikikai Foundation site on webmaster@aikikai.org, where you can find thorough information about the Founder's students (go to: http://www.aikikai.org/about/chrono_e.html).

Uchideshi is a term designating a very special kind of disciples (*deshi*) who used to live at the master's house (*uchi*). They had to study and take care of the master and received special instruction. This allowed students like Kurita Yutaka *Shihan* to be updated on every single detail and final evolution of the Founder's teachings. For more information on *uchideshi* check also the Aiki News Encyclopedia of Aikido (1991) at the following site: http://www.geocities.com/Colosseum/Loge/1419/Deshi.html .

Kurita *Shihan* (Uke) [23]

1958   Lee Green, producer of the US TV program *"Rendezvous with Adventure"* makes the first Aikido documentary, launching *Aikido* internationally.

1969   The master passes away and his son Kisshomaru assumes the role of its first *Doshu* ("guardian of the way").

1974   An international expansion is conducted through overseas demonstrations and the establishing of organizations outside of Japan. Instructors are sent abroad.

1979   Kurita Yutaka *Shihan* arrives in Mexico City.

1996   *Kurita Juku* starts as a project with a simple goal: following O-Sensei's line and taking it a step forward so his school takes his own name.

1999   *Doshu* Ueshiba Kisshomaru passes away. Ueshiba Moriteru, O-Sensei's grandson, is elected as the new *Aikido* guardian.

c. 1998   A *Shihan Kai* (a conference of model instructors) takes place in the USA to discuss the regulation of the future awarding of *Shihan* titles to non-Japanese, high-ranked instructors, and to keep them in check in all of the Americas. This prevents some "enthusiasts" to use this title without a real designation. Yamada *Shihan* is elected as its first president.

---

[23] This picture, the previous one, and the next five were provided by Kurita *Shihan*.

A look to schools/styles from an Aiki perspective

Different major styles and schools have been derived from the four different generations of O-Sensei's disciples: [24]

	Representative	Main characteristics and an Aiki perspective
Pre-war Schools (1921 – 1945)		
Aiki-bujutsu and first stages of Aiki-budo	**Ueshiba Morihei O-Sensei** This is how *Aikido* was first known. It was similar to the jutsu forms found in Daito-ryu Aiki-jutsu	It is considered as one of the hardest forms of *Aikido*. It is the style learnt by the first generation of master Ueshiba's students. *From an AIKI point of view this tough style was to experience a further evolution achieved by the Founder in his last years, when he was able to match his latest theories and ideology with technique as a result of his refinement of the way of Aiki (Aiki-do).*
Yoseikan	**Mochizuki Minoru** From the first *uchideshi* generation, this is a style created by an original student of Kano Jigoro, the founder of judo	This style shows Aiki budo elements combined with certain aspects of *karate*, *judo* and other arts. *From an AIKI point of view the integration of other arts gets apart from the grand master's search, becoming a separate development line.*
Yoshinkan	**Shioda Gozo** Created by a disciple from the 1930's generation, it is an independent organization started after the war	Considered as the hardest *Aikido* style, it places a great emphasis on physical efficacy and it is taught to police forces in Japan. *From an AIKI point of view this school also represents one of the different stages in the development of Aikido, which Kaiso Sensei abandoned to allow room for his next evolution stage: switching from a combative kind of practice to a more profound and more spiritual and ethical one.*

[24] Adapted from http://www.aikiweb.com (the electronic Aikido FAQ) with an additional AIKI perspective in italics. One extra row at the end was added to include some aspects of *Kurita Juku Aiki*, the most recent school started by Kurita *Shihan* in Mexico City.

Post-war Schools (1946 – 1969)		
Tradicional		
Aikikai	**Ueshiba Kisshomaru** This is the style of the Aikikai Foundation headed by O-Sensei´s son	A style taught in different manners. It has a standardized program and does not emphasize practice with weapons. *From an AIKI point of view the fact that it has been standardized might leave Aikido training focused mostly on technique. It is the most well-known Aikido style around the world and the one Yutaka Kurita* Shihan was *originally sent to teach when he was dispatched to Mexico city by Ueshiba K.* Doshu.
Iwama-ryu	**Saito Morihiro** O-Sensei's disciple from 1946. For a long time he was the grounds keeper of the Aiki Shrine.	It aims to preserve O-Sensei's teachings in the form they had and were taught during the 50´s so it is intended as a teaching system (*ryu*). It places great emphasis in weapons practice. *From an AIKI point of view this school has served as an excellent reference to contemporary generations, but if it remained unchanged it may lack the views achieved by the Founder in the following 19 years.* *The way of Aiki must never stop evolving since it still offers plenty of room for development. It cannot be a "dead" formula, it must be transformed. It cannot just be "left" in records such as books and CDs either because that may leave it stagnant.* *Societies have changed and their vision and needs are different. Aiki-do practice must be critically reviewed with no deviation from the Founder's line but on the basis of his achievements in order to give it a new life and impulse* (Takemusu).

With emphasis on "Ki"		
Shin-shin Toitsu Aikido	**Tohei Koichi** This style sees Aikido as the unification of body and mind, a concept from which this school takes its name	This style has a proprietary concept of *ki* different from the Founder's. It is one of the softest styles. *From an AIKI point of view the integration of a particular concept of Ki other than master Ueshiba's may not match the final achievements gained on O-Sensei's original search and ideal. This school started its own clear and independent development line, parallel to the Founder's.*
Sports-like		
Tomiki-ryu	**Tomiki Kenji** A student of both the Founder and Kano Jigoro	Following *judo* methods, it aims to rationalize the practice of *Aikido* as an attempt to make it easier to teach. It introduces an element of competition as a way to refine techniques. *From an AIKI point of view and according to Kurita Yutaka Shihan, this approach goes right against the Founder's spirit and goals and it is a definite step away from his ideal since Aikido is not a sport.*
Aiki-oriented		
Kurita Juku Aiki (started about 1999)	**Kurita Yutaka** An *uchideshi* who declares himself as the last one for his current attempt to take the Founder's ideals one step forward. 25	*From an AIKI point of view: It emphasizes the foundations as taught by O-Sensei in his last years and clarifies the original terminology and symbolism as well as practical values contained in "techniques" since they are regarded as vehicles for development.*

---

25 Kurita *Shihan* used to take dictation from the Founder during his last years. As he took notes for him he was very close to his Aiki concepts. Although master Ueshiba eventually asked him to destroy many of these notes, Kurita *Shihan* still recalls them and uses them in combination with his own. Kurita *Shihan* knows this *kuden*: first-hand words <u>that are to be transmitted</u>. *Kuden* refers to oral transmission and not to any "secret teachings" or "technical tricks" transmitted by the Founder.

		Kurita Juku Aiki *promotes both a different approach in the learning curricula as well as an individual and social impact of Aiki on all areas of life under the strict basis of a union, a confluence and a harmonious action.*

Given all the previous Aiki considerations regarding schools and styles one can reach the following conclusions:

1.   Styles before Second World War were harsher and tougher since they were closer to previous martial forms. Students learned and reproduced a particular style full of hand to hand combat applications and in many ways closer to Daito-ryu and other previous fighting systems.

2.   The Founder's students who have started a development line of their own have developed proprietary versions apart from fundamental concepts, something usually overseen. Their achievements have led them to multiple varieties one of which is interested on developing a competitive *Aikido* that makes it similar to other competitive sports.

3.   Some adepts would like *Aikido* to be like *Daito-ryu* so they keep track of its combat forms instead of reviewing the Founder's line. They don't seem to realize the new Aiki-do paradigm cannot be considered to belong to ancient fighting arts.

4.   Many senior instructors possess the "authentic" *Aikido* of Kaiso Sensei but their styles belong to a certain point in the master's evolution. Those who have added alien elements to their own style misrepresent the Founder's Aiki final development. It is like the story of the elephant and the seven blind men where one part is taken for the whole. The ever changing master was always perfecting and redefining his Aiki and the associated foundations present in practice (the *Aikido works*).

5.   After years of international dissemination, many *Aikido* schools and practitioners have gained diverse perspectives regarding master Ueshiba's original search and they may have made important presumptions. Kurita *Shihan* reports that by the time he was an *uchideshi* the Founder referred to every technique simply as *kokyu* (extension) and made no differences between any of the techniques included in many current teaching programs. This makes sense because there are no divisions of any sort in his Aiki.

6.   Since Kaiso Sensei traveled a lot and lived in Iwama, and because there was an organization in charge of teaching *Aikido* to the general public, much of what is taught around the world may not exactly be what he had in mind or was continuously developing. The multiple creations of schools and styles suggest that much of what is currently known as *Aikido* may be a mixture of diverse elements both proprietary and alien to Aiki.

7.   The grounds on which the way of Aiki is built in *Kurita Juku Aiki* are: perfection in practice and a practical application to a personal and social life, and to all fields of knowledge, business, and other human creations by means of an *intuitive intelligence*. A concept launched in 2001 by Kurita *Shihan* in order to give Aiki a new insight and impulse.

The original style has traveled through different venues after Second World War. One of those is the revival of the core Aiki concept that leaves the old martial paradigm behind. Using Kurita Yutaka *Shihan*'s personal search and mission as an example we can outline three stages in *Aikido* dissemination out of Japan:

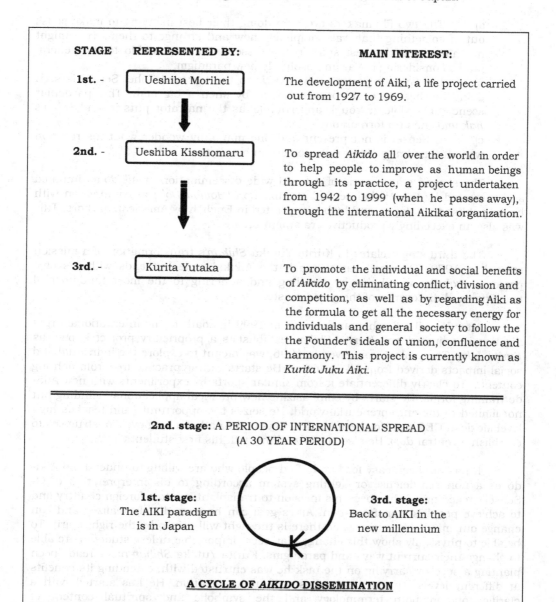

STAGE	REPRESENTED BY:	MAIN INTEREST:
1st. -	Ueshiba Morihei	The development of Aiki, a life project carried out from 1927 to 1969.
2nd. -	Ueshiba Kisshomaru	To spread *Aikido* all over the world in order to help people to improve as human beings through its practice, a project undertaken from 1942 to 1999 (when he passes away), through the international Aikikai organization.
3rd. -	Kurita Yutaka	To promote the individual and social benefits of *Aikido* by eliminating conflict, division and competition, as well as by regarding Aiki as the formula to get all the necessary energy for individuals and general society to follow the the Founder's ideals of union, confluence and harmony. This project is currently known as *Kurita Juku Aiki*.

2nd. stage: A PERIOD OF INTERNATIONAL SPREAD
(A 30 YEAR PERIOD)

1st. stage:
The AIKI paradigm
is in Japan

3rd. stage:
Back to AIKI in the
new millennium

A CYCLE OF *AIKIDO* DISSEMINATION

The first stage corresponds to the Founder's life and time. His objective was to perfect a *budo* free from negative elements such as confrontation and violence. In 1958, he is interviewed for the very first time in an American documentary (Lee Green's *Rendezvous with adventure*) where people are introduced to the master and his *budo*. He is seen as a profoundly spiritual old man, with a deep sense for life, and provides the interviewer with a small sample of the way his practice allows for a creative, violence-free handling of conflict, as well as a sample of the amazing physical skills which have made him a new legend.

Three important things have to be noticed when watching this video:

a)   The two filmmakers are seen doing their best in trying to make sense out of something that was completely new and strange to them. This might not have been the best start in the dissemination of Aikido to the general public considering it was an absolutely new paradigm;
b)   Lee Green's partner puts *Aikido* to the test and Tohei Sensei is seen doing his best to avoid been subdued by such a big man. This particular scene turns violent, 'rough and rumble' as the narrator puts it, and Tohei's *hakama* ends up torn on one side;
c)   O-Sensei is not present and one may only wonder what his reaction was after he knew about this incident in his *dojo*!

The second stage is one of a world wide dissemination of *Aikido* as initiated and promoted by the Aikikai central organization (*Hombu Dojo*) in conjunction with books published in Japan and by books printed in English by American authors. This was also an exceedingly productive era still in progress.

The third stage relates to Kurita Yutaka *Shihan's* transformation of a mission started in 1979. The goal was to teach the Aikikai style but ends with his own personal evolutionary choice by recalling and adhering to the most fundamental teachings and discoveries of the grand master.

After Ueshiba Kisshomaru's death in 1999 his oath to the international organization is adjusted and Kurita *Shihan* establishes a proprietary project known as *Kurita Juku*. The project, conceived in 1996, was meant to explore the individual and social impacts derived from Aiki practice. He starts getting practice free from fighting contents. To clearly differentiate it from similar sports he experiments with new Aikido training forms. He starts by emphasizing new practical applications including but not limited to the entrepreneurial world. He seizes the opportunity and teaches high level Mexican CEO's in Northern Mexico. This is the end of a long cycle of struggles to establish a central *dojo*. He also starts working with his first students in the USA.

It has not been easy for him to find people who are willing to understand Aikido as a non self-defense or fighting system according to his interpretation of O-Sensei's teachings. It has been his mission to transplant it into a foreign country and to achieve people's transformation. Aiki's goal can be immediately realized and can change our minds overnight when there is the right will driven by the right spirit. To be able to physically show this change may seem impossible unless students are able to change their current ways and paradigms. Kurita Yutaka *Shihan* has already been planting a seed by carrying on the task he was entrusted with, extending its benefits at different levels. His new school is still under creation. He has started with a clarification on both terminology and the symbolic and spiritual content of techniques, and with an earnest promotion of the individual and social impacts of this wonderful *do:* a solid foundation of union and confluence (*Aiki*).

Aiki transcends sports and martial arts

After Japan's defeat many grand masters had to devise ways to survive and conform to the new rules of the post war era. They had to change their ancient ways in order to adapt to our contemporary world. Such a need took their disciplines apart from the ancient martial (*bushi*) arts for war. They turned them into *budo* systems so that people could still have a martial-like life for the sake of education and human enlightenment/understanding. And as Kurita Yutaka *Shihan* sees it, the goal for the new millennium is to concentrate in recognizing our human potential and its source, as well as to determine its correct and efficient application and multiplication. This will eventually produce a positive multiplying effect of enormous social repercussions as part of an inexhaustible civilizing human impulse.

Aiki-do's primary means of expression and exploration is the human body and it is practiced in a Japanese-like environment, wearing traditional style garments. However, it is definitely not a martial/fighting art or a sport since it is not meant for competition or tournaments. Instead, as Kurita *Shihan* explains, it proposes to get knowledge and insight of one's self through the correct and almost exclusive works of the right hemisphere of our brains. This is done in an atmosphere of authentic individual and interpersonal exchange that goes beyond the one-to-one concept derived from the general sports paradigm. Individualistic training is transcended through a practice always done with a partner, and with the exclusion of *kata* (mechanical repetition of the forms involved).

Given that athletes lose their skills and weaken their capabilities until they eventually disappear, time is considered their worst enemy. But the aptitudes of those who practice *budo* always increase, refine and strengthen throughout the years. That was the case of master Ueshiba since Aiki's particular nature made him an almost mythical legend. It is really amazing to watch him as an old man who moves like a younger person, displaying a strength and technical accuracy that are definitely not muscular or athletic. Aiki helps improve your capabilities with age. Elder members who have practiced for a long period of time show the most precise execution of techniques and are usually the most powerful and efficient.

Inspired in the Founder's ideals Kurita *Shihan* suggests Aiki could also have a very unusual criteria to grant ranks: practitioners should be promoted if they improved as conscious individuals. A rank could mean they are useful to themselves and others, and less destructive-minded practitioners (*bujin*). No current sport rewards these qualities: trophies and prizes are given only and exclusively based on competitive prowess and athletes adhere to the old winning-at-any-cost paradigm that drive them to do whatever they think as necessary to win. Those who use steroids and destructive drugs show a perception trapped in a futile contest against themselves and everybody else. Unfortunately this usually results in sterile efforts to overcome their own weaknesses and destroys their careers. This gets worse as they become a negative model to others instead of what they could be and were originally pushed to be in their most glorious competitive days. This is certainly due to the pressure athletes feel and even put on them with the idea that they arc like gods who never lose because they are above everybody else.

O-Sensei's path approaches the practitioner's emotional and spiritual components in a different way: participants work and make their best for the benefit of their practice partners and their own. That is a personal achievement and not a struggle for personal brilliance. To be able to do so practitioners must put forward 100% of their best effort to make 200% or more when they add their heart and effort during practice (1 + 1 = **1**). In a progressive perspective two partners benefit by trying to achieve 1,000% quality practice. This makes them both advance in their execution and development, thus achieving *excellence*. Compared to an Olympic game Aiki can also unite all countries but it has its own way: its practice is not for individuals, it cannot be done without a partner.

Leaving an injured competitor behind or considering his harm and weakness as an advantageous factor is never the case in Aiki. The spirit and heart (*kokoro*) in Ueshiba's system opposes such idea: if an athlete has an accident, the rest must stop and render aid. They are all winners when they can continue and all make it to the finish line. We applaud competitors who make it to the goal, but it is sad to realize they are not able to have the slightest intention of helping their competitors to win. It is just impossible and even weird to do such a thing from this old paradigm. Since competitors are not supposed to help each other, they regard themselves as "the other team", "the other guys" and "the opponents", which always convey the idea that they are "the enemies to be defeated". From this point of view there doesn't really seem to be such a thing as a "good sportsmanship" present in any tournaments.

What were the ancient Greeks thinking of when they organized their Olympics? Where is the "healthy mind" in the "healthy body" found? We just know that modern sports competition makes it inconceivable to think of participants helping each other. But Aiki considers helping and caring for ourselves and others is the true victory, since it renders a win-win effect for those who help and those being helped. O-Sensei's words "*Agatsu, Masakatsu, Katsuhayabi*" (notice this word order) are usually translated as *"True victory is self-victory, victory here, right now"*. Kurita Yutaka *Shihan* rephrases them as: *"If I am well, and you are well, everything is well"* (see pages 73 and 241). Whatever the translation the Founder didn't talk of self-victory attained in isolation at all. Aiki is definitely not a sport.

SPORTS PRIZE COMPETITIVE PERFOMANCE   AIKI-DO PRIZES HUMAN IMPROVEMENT

Winning is all there is in an athletic   Helping our partner to win is a personal
contest   victory in the way of Aiki

Besides leaving out one single winner and a lot of losers, chances are the old victory paradigm found in competition and sports may turn the former into an arrogant and insecure person, not to mention a lonely and sad one, left with an unnecessary burden of pressures or "responsibilities" which can also confuse and hurt him/her. Pressure and stress may also lead to other excesses, including commercial and selfish interests by people who might do whatever it takes to gain recognition and fame for themselves. Issues related to ill understood competition are fundamental in Aiki since it goes against any form of slavery or dependence. Sincere recognition is for those who help us through difficult times, who have taught us something worthwhile and have made us feel appreciated and special. It is definitely for those who we enjoy spending time with because the people who make a difference are just the ones who care.

In spite of its superficial features, Aiki-do is not a martial art either. The formal difference between Aiki and preceding arts lies in a radical change in the traditional *budo* work and it does not correspond to the image created by commercial movies either. Some aspects not found in general *Aikido* practice are:

a)   The straight forward attacks (kicks and punches), intended to hurt, maim or kill the opponent. In other arts people turn their bodies into deadly weapons, they hold tournaments and reward their winners;

b) The grappling, throwing and holding techniques using joint manipulation moves on an opponent or "enemy". These arts also hold tournaments considered as unarmed combats;

c)   The use of real weapons such as swords, knifes, and many other tools designed to kill. In our contemporary times these are usually practiced alone or in pairs to develop skills that are no more used in real combat and assault since the *Samurai* class no longer exists. Yet these arts are tremendously admirable in themselves.

Master Ueshiba's Aiki doesn't fit any of these categories because it puts aside all confrontation, contest and competition; it eliminates tournaments and discourages students from taking part in them. O-Sensei knew how to use old things in a new era, and was able to find inspiration in the precepts inherited by the traditions inherited from his warrior ancestors. He knew they could be adapted to our contemporary life, though. Undoubtedly the *Samurai* spirit, will, and heart (*kokoro*) is still present in many aspects of Japanese culture and the big change is that whereas martial/fighting arts are used to prepare people for a good battle, Aiki prepares them for a great life.

The Founder learned from his medieval past without necessarily sharing the *Samurai* focus of using his skills on a battlefield. However, he knew the warrior class helped to create the structure of Japanese society by means of their war code (*bushido*). He realized they showed an Aiki spirit since they took good care of their own issues and promoted respect for the Emperor. They were also in search for beauty in all things around them, and thus showed sensitivity and a good sense of order and arrangement (Aiki). Coordination is crucial in *Aikido*, as well as communication among practice partners. Students practice in pairs because they follow a path to be walked with others. They are not supposed to fight among themselves and they never learn to fight against somebody else. They must learn to align with each other and to do their best to keep their performance that way. This is only possible if they follow the Aiki concept of *true respect*, the source for mutual confidence and trust between people.

Coordination and circulation are two main vehicles for growth, and everybody knows how urgent this is needed in our contemporary world!

An Aiki work applied in training guarantees there will be no losers because a training partner is never treated as an enemy. Indeed few disciplines emphasize real and authentic coordination; our paradigm stands as a deeper "self defense" paradigm seen in a much broader sense: it is a thorough, safe and civilized system that helps defend human integrity, and our spirit must grow and evolve though it.

**Nage borrows Uke's arm
and Uke lends it**

From an Aiki point of view, division and separation are found in sports and martial arts, whereas addition and multiplication define the nature of the Aiki-do. We have stated that it is efficient because it meets its objectives in the best possible way. It resolves crisis according to the noblest ends and it creatively ends conflict without any form of violence. Master Ueshiba conceived a system rooted in unity, confluence, and harmony (Aiki) and practitioners develop their individuality in a context made of interactions triggered by a series of committed "attacks and defenses" subject to a rigor meant to be non-martial, de-stressing, and re-creative. An Aiki work is characterized by *self-reflection*, *self-discovery*, *self-learning* and *self-improvement* with a positive impact among training partners. Practice makes all of these things become a vehicle for the true manifestation of our best and for the eventual emergence of our inner light. [26]

Since it teaches a new way to face our everyday life on a personal and social level, we can say Aiki-do is a *practical philosophy* which responds to the original ideal of *budo* by including sufficiently flexible and adaptable traditions that enable its

---

[26] There are two ways to make up light: one is by chemical reaction and the second is by heat. "Warming up" in Aiki, besides keeping our glands and blood flow in good shape, is also aimed to help us take our light out. Kurita Yutaka *Shihan* regards techniques as means for chemical reactions. Practice helps combine elements in order to literally produce a reaction and render a new composition in us, a new product. This is related to the meaning of *dojo*, a place for illumination or transforming understanding.

meaningful application in ordinary life. It may serve as a means to help people create new visions about themselves, their social relations, their families, and even their everyday businesses. As an example, several recent books and articles have already explored the way it may help entrepreneurs interested in creating new visions for their corporations and to find ways to achieve their mission. They suggest how *Aikido* may lead them to gain financial success by knowing themselves and transforming their current competition paradigm. Particularly, Aiki strives for the care and quality of "the human factor", an exceedingly important issue within any company.

The goal of Aiki is not to make great fighters but to form specialists in Aiki applications through a clear understanding of its philosophy, principles, values, beliefs and forms. In order to do so, techniques can be adapted and anyone can use them easily and without any risks as a means to understand things from a new perspective. From an educational point of view we could now envision the creation of an "Aiki University" too.

The way of Aiki offers practitioners a technology that allows them to holistically explore their own *being*. It is a tangible philosophy which assumes real practice of its precepts without entailing pretty words or mere intentions; it is not a philosophy of mental reflection since the union, confluence and harmony proposal must be demonstrated in the actual application of techniques. Besides, it must be lived and expressed by practitioners as they translate such precepts into actions explored between each other and not just in the practice hall but in any other aspect and context of their lives.

There is no fighting or self-defense maneuvers in Aiki training, since conflict, struggle or even a fight are resolved from an elevated perspective of quite a different sort. Practitioners follow a format of martial appearance that is real and aesthetic, but it is always free from any kind of aggressions and injuries. It follows a format supported by a constructive mental attitude and a correct body work which are the means for the student to experience and feel a true unification and reflection of the Universe. Although it has been said *Aikido* promotes a *spirit-body-mind* unification, since it certainly changes the old *body-mind-technique* paradigm of previous arts, some remarks are must be made about these three elements:

a)   The *spirit* is understood not as an invisible entity that controls human thinking and feeling but as a precise *mood, state* or *attitude* arising from a constructive will and a unifying action directly under the practitioner's control. In this sense, Aiki makes it possible to train the spirit.

b)   The *body* is not referred to in relation to our *muscles* since actions do not rely on physical strength in Aiki, and

c)   The *mind* must not be understood as *thinking* since there is no time to think during the application of a technique. According to the most recent lessons by Kurita *Shihan*, the use of our brain carries out two functions applied at two different moments during practice: the left side of our brain is used during the instructor's explanation and demonstration whereas the right side has to be in charge as soon as action starts.

According to this approach Aiki techniques make both *brain hemispheres* work together using the right, intuitive side of our brain first. This explains why practice starts with our left hand: this procedure helps practitioners to develop their intuition. And there is also the guiding application of *ki*, the element which makes practice different, unique, and non-muscular. This element breaks the barriers between spirit, body and mind, and although other elements are also activated before action, the following sentence by Kurita *Shihan* summarizes Aiki work:

"If there is Ki there is technique, and if there is technique there is Ki".

O-Sensei advised against the slightest deviation in Aiki work, since it spoils it and separates practitioners from the true path. Whereas old martial arts stress *body + mind + technique*, Aiki stresses *ki + body + mind*. Muscle work is important in all fighting arts, but Aiki action is intended to carry out a different process and to get one result of a different category. Aiki-do practitioners use *ki* first instead of their bodies or muscular strength when they work and apply technique.

Aiki training achieves the same results a ballerina or a concert musician obtains only after hours of hard work, the key to perfection. O-Sensei's Aiki has to be done in such a way that it requires full concentration on flexibility: "*Keep it simple, relax, don't use your muscles, don't block or hurt, blend, keep attached to your partner and care for him/her, never throw anybody or slam him/her on the ground, etc.,*" are some of the usual instructions given during practice. Developing these simple habits is the real challenge.

Positive circuit motion

Aiki demands the precise execution of natural, careful and caring movements. It represents some kind of a modern "gentleman's discipline" because it is a refined and educated practice of the highest nature. Its very nature helps us develop both an *emotional* and an *intuitive intelligence*, dexterity, and virtues derived from new habits. In addition, it hosts other benefits and values of extreme actual interest for our new millennium. In this new "way", "path" or paradigm, learning different techniques just to twist an arm is completely irrelevant, as well as to focus on what occurs only at the beginning (*attack*) and the end (*defense*) of a confrontation. To realize there are many different things going on even before and after an action is carried out is important for a proper performance.

All what happens before, during, and at the end of a movement, the *process* within each of its parts, is seen by Kurita Yutaka *Shihan* as the necessary *means* for the true manifestation of Aiki. The constituents of the Aiki process are the vehicle to develop a different personality and take practitioners on the right direction. A correct Aiki execution affords an extraordinary sensation of *pleasure*. What happens before and after the surface of techniques add to the refinement of students and show the direction their development is heading.

When students fail to realize this, and when they don't have good practice partners, it is common to see them getting mad when their techniques don't seem to work for them, when they find somebody who is "strong" enough as to block their intentions. It is very common to see them frustrated when they find somebody whose techniques are strange for them, when they cannot work against non-opposition, or with someone who does not fall as they expect. It is necessary to consider what happens during the application of technique:

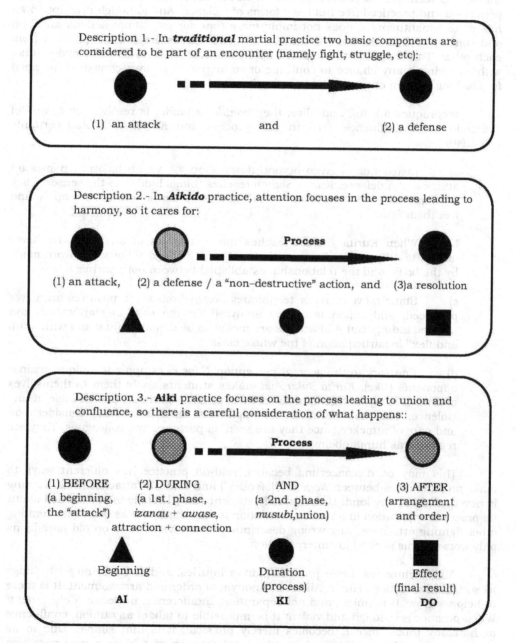

Description 1.- In **traditional** martial practice two basic components are considered to be part of an encounter (namely fight, struggle, etc):

(1) an attack   and   (2) a defense

Description 2.- In **Aikido** practice, attention focuses in the process leading to harmony, so it cares for:

Process

(1) an attack,   (2) a defense / a "non–destructive" action, and   (3) a resolution

Description 3.- **Aiki** practice focuses on the process leading to union and confluence, so there is a careful consideration of what happens::

Process

(1) BEFORE   (2) DURING   AND   (3) AFTER
(a beginning,   (a 1st. phase,   (a 2nd. phase,   (arrangement
the "attack")   *izanau* + *awase*, *musubi*,union)   and order)
                    attraction + connection

Beginning   Duration   Effect
                             (process)   (final result)
AI   **KI**   **DO**

Since Aiki is not something easily put in words, even the third description cannot show how Aiki takes into account what is previous to the action started by both *Uke* and *Nage*. It doesn't represent what remains after it either: the order and arrangement attained, the attachment used and the growth obtained, the final condition where things are perfectly squared. However, it shows that it does not contain an actual defensive phase since this is not a self-defense system. Aiki transcends technique because it is not an empty superficial event, and it has to be performed and practiced free from any forms of violence. And although description #3 has more constituents it does not imply more time for execution: actions are fluid and conclusive from the start because their constituents are not independent from each other. They require an integrated application, which automatically end conflict without giving it any chance to continue or to increase. It never considers the need for clashing with an enemy and destroying it.

Techniques are full and alive: they *breathe*. Conflict is resolved by means of the union and confluence used in this process and *Kurita Juku Aiki* certainly emphasizes this:

a)   Instruction is given beyond description #2, which basically names an attack and a defense. Kurita *Shihan* teaches things hidden to the senses. They are impossible to observe at a first glance if practitioners cannot apply and feet them first.

b)   When Kurita *Shihan* teaches the mechanics of an action he never forgets to differentiate between the *bokken* and the *jo* actions, the work made by the body, and the relationship established between both partners.

c)   Static movements or techniques begun from static postures are never practiced, and action is always analyzed for the sake of clarification and understanding. But Aiki actions are meant to be dynamic, fluid and with a full and flexible participation of the whole class.

d)   Contrary to the general perception *Nage* does apply technique against opponents (*Uke*). *Kurita Juku Aiki* makes students apply them to themselves and advises against going against their practice partners and the use of any violence. This new paradigmatic application implies extreme consideration and care of attacker since they are seen as partners and colleagues. They are regarded as human beings.

This may be disconcerting because Aiki-do practice has different ways to make no differences between *Nage* (a "defender") and *Uke* (an "attacker") and training is never a fight of any kind. Unfortunately students may become too concerned about its practical application in a real confrontation if they think of it as lacking something other fighting arts have. Any wrong description or analysis based on old paradigms only worsens this general misinterpretation.

Aiki "techniques" never produce pain or injuries, and there are no such things as soft/hard variations either. Aiki is a synonym of order and arrangement. It is there to help us grow. It is union, and not separation, indifference, neglect or detachment. When practice gets tough and violent it is impossible to talk of any union, confluence or harmony (Aiki) since it becomes merely physical; it is that simple. Due to its enormous potential, a clear and healthy interpretation of Aiki as a new paradigm results in many different perspectives of practical application in the most varied fields (see Chapter 6).

KURITA YUTAKA *SHIHAN* DEMONSTRATING THE UNION OF OUR TWO
BRAIN HEMISPHERES (ACTIONS ARE MADE OF ELEMENTS ADDED TO "TECHNIQUE")

A basic glossary of Aiki terms used by the Founder

This section presents some of the main concepts promoted by O-Sensei which all practitioners should never forget to practice and adhere to. They are part of the first-hand instruction received by Kurita Yutaka *Shihan* so it does not include terms like *zanshin*, *randori*, or "breakfall" because these terms and many others either belong to other arts or they were simply old and definitely not used by the Founder, at least when Kurita *Shihan* lived with him.

The following terms are definitely the most original ones and they are intended for those who want to follow *O-Sensei*'s ideal. They are master Ueshiba's *gengi* (fundamentals) everybody must bear in mind whenever they enter a *dojo* to start practice: they are all they need when studying his way of Aiki. [27]

---

[27] When Kurita Yutaka *Shihan* used to be O-Sensei's personal scribe and *uchideshi* he was asked by the Founder to help him write down his ideas. This was difficult for him because he did not speak the same dialect. When Kaiso Sensei dictated something and asked Kurita *Shihan* to read it back the result was usually a different message, due to the different ideograms used when he was taking notes. This made the Founder mad but it was great for Kurita *Shihan* because at that moment he received many more explanations and ideas about the given subject. This made him realize that when the Founder said something he was always meaning something else or even diffcrent. This should also alert against relying on a Japanese dictionary when trying to find the meaning of the terms used by the Founder in his Aiki theory.

Kurita *Shihan* teaches that *Aikido* is only a name, like Charles, Jason or Edward. In this sense it does not really describe what it is: its name does not describe its character, its personality, or its many qualities. In *Kurita Juku Aiki* Kurita *Shihan* states: *"Although Aikido is still the name of our practice, we do 'Takemusu Aiki'."* He states that it was by means of *Takemusu* that O-Sensei Ueshiba tied up the two extremes represented by *Bu* and *Aiki* and eventually created his new paradigm (see *Takemusu Aiki*).

A

- **AGATSU MASAKATSU KATSUHAYABI** – These words summarize the Founder's teachings and philosophy. Interpretations have stated this means that "Right victory over oneself leads to automatic light" but Kurita *Shihan* rephrases it in a very simple way: *"If I am well, and you are well, everything is well."*

  These words refer to action: if we are well and do what is correct, everything works well and our perception is transformed: Aiki prevails and wins. These words refer to the way one can manifest and make one's individuality, in connection with others and with an immediate impact around us. It changes common practice in the *Dojo* and transcends to our every-day life. Space and speed (*katsuhayabi*) practice is crucial in current *Kurita Juku Aiki*.

  When you do things right, without blocking, twisting, pulling or slamming, everybody is right and everything is fine and good. This precept transforms practice and considers the use of *katsuhayabi*. Kurita *Shihan* has always linked this victory idea with the resolutions made by people when they realize the need for a change in their lives. If people really want to change they can transform themselves immediately: if they want to be kind all they need to do is to act accordingly; they simply have to do it. Or if they intend to help somebody, they just have to do something for someone in need, thus changing automatically. It is not advisable to believe in long-term plans which are soon forgotten and never carried out. Speed, weight, and space are important elements in both Aiki training and real life.

- **AI** – Alignment.

 This *kanji* is composed of an upper part representing a lid or cover. The lower part has been considered to represent a container and it has eventually been broadly taken as "fitting" or "joining". It has two pronunciations in Japanese: **au** and **awaseru** (hence the term *awase*). Its general meanings as a verb are then: *to fit, to suit, to match* and *to agree with*. [28]

When we say that planets are aligned we mean they are located in the same position by means of the forces that keep them in their specific place so they do not "fight" against each other altering the subsequent positions we call orbits. Such forces and alignment find a resemblance in Aiki practice by using the

---

[28] The kanji used for this and other linguistic explanations was taken from: *A Guide to Remembering Japanese Characters*, by Kenneth G. Henshall, Tuttle Publishing Co., 1998

forces of attraction: practice partners are united before they start circular movements and they are kept tied that they never get apart. They never abandon their mutual connection and they do not throw each other like disposable things.

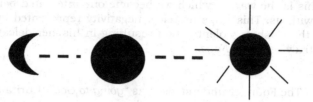

This is the "Ai" of Aiki-do

Although the Founder found **Ai** ("matching", "putting together") is akin to **Ai** ("love") it is important to remember that they are two different things: the former refers to a combination and coordination and the latter belongs to human feelings, hugs and kisses. The *kanji* for "love" is not the same as the one used by the Founder to represent his Aiki.

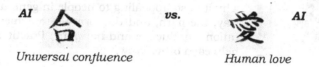

Universal confluence   *Human love*

Ai (in Aiki) refers to:

    a)   the general order of the Universe,
    b)   the union with our practice partners, which includes all natural elements, and
    c)   the alignment and union of our two brain hemispheres.

Any philosophy is useless without a concrete application so the Founder referred to three elements that help alignment to take place:

- *Izanau* (attraction)
- *Awase* (contact, relationship, union) and
- *Musubi* (undividable union kept at all times).

And union happens at many levels:

1. when we do as the Universe does,
2. when we keep in touch with our practice partners, and
3. when we work with both of our hands: we start with the left so as to activate the right side of our brain first, and then we switch to the right hand in order to give way to the left side.

By so doing we make them communicate and we develop our intuition.

The learning of *kata* (mechanical exercises) or learning in a repetitive way makes people use only their left side of the brain. The same happens when we sit down and observe our instructors. The right brain must be used as soon as we stand up to start practice. Work must let go of all conscious thoughts about technique, trying to concentrate on what we feel and sense.

This is the way by which we become one integrated being with those who practice with us. This helps us reject negativity represented by the attack of our *Uke* and the clash or violent action resulting in his/her defeat. A positive action shows a truly sensitive *Nage*.

- **AIKI** – The Founder understood it as *"going to God"* (Kurita *Shihan*).

With "order and harmony", nothing can be "crooked" and everything is put in its right place. The way of Aiki is a formula in search of such an order in our lives and communities. Aiki is full arrangement, togetherness and correspondence. That is why Kurita *Shihan* states: *"A tree is beautiful because of its surroundings."*

 The same happens with Aiki techniques when they include all necessary components. This explains why it is so appealing to people in general. Aiki-do is the way, the path, and the formula to achieve the values of union, confluence and harmony. Practitioners unite and help each other grow.

Union, confluence and harmony

Aiki is not made of techniques intended to fight and defeat an enemy. It is a way to reconcile the world. (Ueshiba Morihei)

 合氣 **AIKI**

Its way is a path to help ourselves and others by helping them reach their goals. It is a path to develop a new culture.

Aiki is a compound word standing for a single concept and it is the name Kaiso Sensei used in reference to his *budo*. (Kurita *Shihan*)

- **AIKI NO O-KAMI** – Literally: "The grand spirit of Aiki" (the spirit of union, confluence and harmony).

This is how the Founder referred to the divine entity he envisioned as responsible for the harmony of the Universe as a whole. It is the grand spirit of union and according to Kurita *Shihan* a true *dojo* must have this *kanji* as part of its *kamiza* (the place where the divinity seats).

- **AIKI NO MICHI** – A path where two become one.

This expression considers the path of "blending or uniting *ki*". Kaiso Sensei used it in reference to the point where *Uke* and *Nage* blend, where union (Aiki) between them occurs, and to the same path followed. If such a path is found in action all clashing of forces is avoided and technique becomes harmless without losing its power and sense. It must not be confused with *center*.

See Do

- **AU-NO-KOKYU** – This expression means: "Let's put your *kokyu* and my *kokyu* together," or "Let's extend your *kokyu* and mine."

- **AWASE** – A term meaning: "reaching out in order to find". It is the way the Universe joins and gets all its elements together and close to each other, crossing and overlapping as the lapels of our *keiko gi* (practice uniform).

This concept is not to be confused with "intention". *Awase* is an essential step in the approaching process between two people joining forces and finding their mutual potential. Growth is an addition and multiplication process.

See Izanau and Musubi

B

- **BUJIN** – In common *gunkan* (Japanese *kanji* dictionaries) this word means "A divine warrior" but the Founder's conception refers to it as a man completely rid of weaponry and warfare. It is a "warrior" of a different sort.

The *kanji* for *bu* is also pronounced /take/ in compound words, so it is important to remember it when referring to *Takemusu Aiki*.

C

- **CENTER**

There are diverse centers: in our body (our belly or *hara*), at the point where contact and union takes place between *Nage* and *Uke*, and the one falling vertically from our heads to our feet.

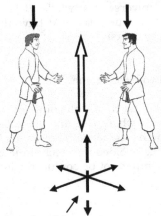

And it is here in Yoga/Zen

The center is here in Aiki

- **CHINKON KISHIN** – A salutation used by the Founder before starting his practice and right after finishing it.

It is the name of a special greeting and O-Sensei practiced it by following these steps:

a) he put both palms together, and raised them up,
b) he then brought them down to his center, and bent over twice, all the way down to the ground
c) he then rose, clapped four times, and bent over again.

He used it to calm his spirit and as a wrap up for his practice. It was his way to invite the divine to be present during training and was a farewell by the end of it. (Kurita *Shihan*)

D

- **DO** – Experience, formula (*tao*), a main road to a certain destination.

 This *kanji* originally represented a movement with an idea of chief/main. It means both a "chief means of direct movement" and "a main road" and it later acquired the connotation of "an abstract way" (to enlightenment, etc).

It is pronounced /do/ and /to/ when it stands by itself, and also /michi/ in compound expressions like: 'Aiki no michi' (the way of confluence). Aiki-do is a *budo*, a serious path with a martial appearance not meant to be applied in combat. It is a way to be walked and made together along with others willing to join us on the same journey.

"Its essence is made by its origin and its tradition, which give it a particular fragrance that makes people recognize each other." (Kurita *Shihan*)

People can recognize if they belong to the same kind or not just by the way they practice and follow Aiki. The Founder said the way is there for us to go to it because it cannot come to us. It may seem that he devised Aiki-do as some kind of cathartic process that enabled him to empty his mind of all passions and distinctions, and lead him to develop a formula that mirrors heaven and earth and is a vehicle to find our union with the Universe.

I

- **IZANAGI/IZANAMI** – Gods of harmony present in the Founder's cultural tradition and philosophy.

O-Sensei used the image of both Izanagi and Izanami to teach about the presence and intervention of these two feminine and masculine Gods as the eternal duality controlling and complementing the Universe. This image matches with all the yin-yang and *Nage-Uke* dualities which eventually are indivisible entities both in Eastern thought and *Aikido*.

- **IZANAU** – Attraction. The way gravity and magnets work.

This term refers to the first approaching and connecting action between partners; it is an "invitation" leading to confluence and union.

See Awase and Musubi

K

- **KI** – The size and scope of techniques; the force derived from the right posture and body movements all together. A concept difficult to "see" unless it is felt.

This *kanji* originally represented rice and vapors rising from cooked rice and eventually came to refer to an "invisible movement or unseen force and spirit. Practicing Aiki lets us realize the kind of unseen forces the Founder referred to as an important part of his technical subtleties. In his theory, the Universe starts from the *Big Bang* which liberated an enormous amount of energy. It eventually lost its force and gave way to something he decided to call *ki*, which is responsible for the current sustained expansion of the Universe (Kurita *Shihan*). Master Ueshiba advised his *uchideshi* to feel and use this force and to get to know it as a concrete manifestation through correct physical practice of postures, gravity, application, action, results, heart, will, etc. O-Sensei wrote this kanji in a very traditional way but associated new elements to it and thus gave it a new meaning:

Ki may involve many things: our instinct, an attitude, a heart, a mind, a spirit, a correct non-violent technical execution, flexibility, and the participation of our whole being in a united arrangement in order to allow its work to be part of our performance. *Ki* relates to correct will, intention and impulse; it is something between *Nage* and *Uke* they must feel and follow and to be used instead of muscles (physical strength), and prevents movements from being violent. *Ki* is something different from direct muscular strength since it emerges from a correct and good physical, spiritual and ethical posture. It is the direction we take in our life and the way we decide to follow it. Not being muscle or mind, it is a positive impulse and a driving concrete element. It is not a magic force coming out of our fingertips, and it is not a gimmick either: *"Ki makes things work; Aiki is then mutual function and work of two or more partners combined"* (Kurita *Shihan*).

The theory behind this fundamental concept is that:

> a)   our minds (our thinking) cannot defeat an enemy, that is part of a telekinetic or hypnotic work; and,
> b)   our bodies (our muscles) are not used aggressively to defeat or throw an enemy. Aiki requires something absolutely different to be used between practice partners, so *ki* is just *ki.*

Students are always told to "fill" their bodies with *ki*, to gather and concentrate it and to make it go where we think, want and need it to go. Many people say that is *ki* but how is it obtained? Where does it come from? It comes from the right work and compound action of *ki awase* (the approach and blending of *ki*) and *ki musubi* (the tie created by a blending *ki*).

If the right attraction or magnetism (*awase*) works together with an indivisible connection or union (*musubi)* between partners then *ki* is present and technique works as expected. If we use technique in a disconnected way from our partners, they are only thrown away and fall. But if we manage their strength and blend it with ours, by using our whole connected body, we will be using *ki,* and whenever *Uke* goes down it will be due to the effects of *ki* work and not because they are slammed on the ground.

Ki is a union of both *Nage*'s and *Uke*'s capabilities that eliminate them both and makes room for its own work. We may not know exactly what it is, but we must think about it, about its nature and the way we can manage it. When Kurita *Shihan* remarks *"If there is Ki there is technique, and if there is technique there is Ki"*, he knows they are interdependent. Otherwise only strength is present and practice becomes a struggle, a fight or confrontation. He elaborates:

> *Force is muscular, and energy puts it into action, so Ki cannot be translated as "energy", which is then a too vague and confused term since the Japanese term for "energy" may also be 'chikara', another term with a three-folded translation: calorie, light and force or energy, power and skill.*

"Only a glass full of water can spill and flow, not an empty one," Kurita *Shihan* remarks. And with this analogy he states that filling the glass up is not enough to make it spill: it is necessary to fill it up until its contents flow. The same happens with *ki* since we must be "filled up" with it to make it flow. *Ki* has also been said to be the chained relation between three elements: *mirror, sphere* and *sword* (reflection, perfection and substance).

> *"Ki is the true spiritual function and conjunction; it is the essence of things. It is life, union, harmony, and essence. Regarding space, Ki must be used when going upwards, or to the front, the left, and the right as*

well as when going down to the ground during Aikido performance. We must study and teach each one of them". Kurita *Shihan*

For the sake of instruction we can conclude that *ki* is to be understood by two inseparable things: spirit and being. And given all we have said above, we could re-define the *Aikido* of O-Sensei as:

The *way*, *discipline* and *experience* (**Do**) used to reach the necessary *conjunction* and *confluence* (**Aiki**) in a *spirit* and *will* in tune with our body (**Ki**) so that it echoes the *Ki* of the Universe.

Kurita *Shihan* states: *Ki* is the combination of both *kokoro* (heart, will), the energy/strength and the work done for the specific life growth aimed. [29]

- **KI AWASE** – The overlapping produced by *ki*.

- **KI MUSUBI** – The union created by *ki*.

- **KI NO NAGARE** – The flow of *ki*.

When used by the Founder, the term "nagare" referred to the flow of the Universe, the eternal Cosmos movement, and so it relates to past, present and future. At a technical level, it implies a flowing and continuous action.

This concept refers to the union of wills, intentions and efforts flowing together and producing an even greater flow as we find them in nature.

A river is the product of union and confluence; the common expression *ki no nagare* means "the flow of *ki*". The flow is never straight, but curvy, and it is to be used the same way during practice. In a rain-river analogy what starts as a small stream finishes as a big river which follows curved paths until it reaches the sea (an even bigger entity). This seems to be equal to the Founder's formula: 1 + 1 = **1** or 1 + 1 = **0** meaning perfection.

Kaiso Sensei learned these things from the Universe, used them in his Aiki-do and taught them accordingly. Such was his change from the traditional *budo* to his Aiki paradigm. The big lesson is that *"Nature is always correct,"* so when you have any questions just think about how natural your movements are and you will get an answer. (Kurita *Shihan*).

- **KI–SHIN–TAI** – *Ki*-Heart-Body.

These three elements have been geometrically represented as:

---

[29] Difficult concepts like *ki* are presented as an attempt to reproduce the teachings orally transmitted by the Founder to Kurita Yutaka *Shihan*. I have learned them from him even recently and I present them to the best of my understanding. *See* the Glossary in Chapter 5 for an additional list of topics.

Ki   *Shin*   *Tai*
(spirit)   (heart/intention)   (body)

All of them make *Takemusu Aiki* possible so if one is missing practice is incomplete as the following cases show:

- If technique is applied with no *ki*, practice is merely muscular or physical and it becomes only a physical activity:

Ki   *Shin*   *Tai*
(no spirit)   (heart/intention)   (body)

- If it has no *shin* (heart), practice is only physical or technical too:

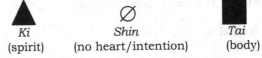

Ki   *Shin*   *Tai*
(spirit)   (no heart/intention)   (body)

- And if there is no *tai* (body) then practice is a dream, a fantasy, a mere intention independent of will and actions:

Ki   *Shin*   *Tai*
(spirit)   (heart/intention)   (no body)

These three elements are the means for the manifestation of the Universe and open the door to *Takemusu aiki*, a formula that leads to growth and development.

- **KOKORO** – Our heart. "The way I handle my God" (Morihei Ueshiba).

 This kanji evolved from a pictograph of a heart. It is also used figuratively as "feelings" or "mind". It means both heart and feelings and is pronounced /shin/ as in *Ki–shin–tai*, or /*kokoro*/. It basically means "a big mind" (Kurita Shihan).

- **KOKYU** - Extension

 Extending towards life, like flowers do, is necessary for us to bloom. Blooming is the true meaning of extending power in practice.

- **KOKYU-HO** – An extending/breathing exercise; the use of our chest and hips.

This term refers to an exercise intended to unite and control *Uke*'s energy, and to tie it to *Nage*'s. When practicing *kokyu-ho*, *Nage* must use *mawae*, the overlapping space between him/her and their practice partners. Distance also counts and must be adequate. By using *musubi*, *Nage* connects with *Uke* and keeps that union. Separation only interrupts the energy exchange between them and allows *Uke* to break the connection, and this makes them get tired.

The body and head must always be in an upright position and never bend over. *Kokyu-ho* is usually applied both in *suwate* (sitting down position) –the most usual way– or *tachi waza* (standing up). The natural way to do this is by taking one hand up while taking *Uke* down with the other hand and vice-versa. The extension "traps" and leads *Uke*. *"This togetherness elevates practice and gives it a sahō category."* (Kurita *Shihan*)

It is used to learn how to be always prepared and alert. It works like an antenna that captures the waves sent by a broadcast station (*Uke*) in order to repeat them and make them get the picture. Kurita *Shihan* reports that in his last years O-Sensei made no difference between techniques so he just called everything *kokyu* (contact and extension).

See Sahō in our second glossary (Chapter 5).

M

- **MA'AI / MAWAE** (pronounced /mabae/) – To "fill up and move".

For years it seems to have been understood as an empty space or "distance". But distance also counts in correct practice since it is used as part one of the first elements of the interaction so it is never neglected in Aiki. O-Sensei understood it as the space used to get together (*Ma* = space; *ai* = union) and not merely as a separating space between partners. It prepares and sets the right measure for all the different activities practiced.

- **MUSUBI** – Union, togetherness, linking.

This term refers to the way the universe keeps things together. It is an element dealing not just with the act of Aiki grabbing (*dori*) but with the connection needed throughout every performance and activity. After *izanau* (invitation) and *awase* (overlapping, reaching) the use of *musubi* (union) is the final Aiki touch. *Musubi* lets practitioners stay together and consolidate their mutual growth.

See Izanau and Awase

N

- **NAGARE** – Flow, current.

This word comes from the verb *nagareru* (to run, to flow, to spill). Flowing assumes a previous "filling up" and not the use of tricks or gimmicks.

S

● **SHO-CHIKU-BAI** – The pine (*sho*), bamboo (*chiku*) and plum (*bai*) used in Shinto festivities. They stand for endurance, flexibility and character.

The Founder thought of Aiki practice as a profound celebration of life. So it is inexcusable when people get hurt and put themselves in danger during practice. This made him leave the pre-war *Dayto-ryu* origins of his art behind as he learned from these three trees. They are known as "the three winter friends" because they flourish and resist even the coldest and nastiest weather.

Practicing a *budo* is a very serious task and students must develop these qualities so they don't get mad or uncomfortable in any situation, as when they attend a seminar and have to work with people they cannot communicate with. They must be tolerant of different ways and learn to blend with them.

T

● **TAKEMUSU AIKI** – This expression refers to the union or conjunction of both *bu* (*take*) and Aiki, which is in turn a way to practice according to the philosophy of O-Sensei's ideal.

To my best understanding, the Founder's expression behind this term, as it was once recalled and quoted by Kurita *Shihan* is:

1	2	3	4	5	6
" *Take*	*no*	*musubi*	*no*	*kaimi*	*Aiki*. "
(warrior)	(of)	(connection)	(of)	(instrument to see)	(unity, confluence and harmony)

These numbered words, expressed in a different word order according to English syntax results in the following statement:

"Unity, confluence and harmony (**Aiki**) as the instrument to see (**kaimi**) ∅
the warriors' (**Take**)(**no**) connection (**musubi**)."

Bu is represented by the sword (*katana*) and *Takemusu* is to learn how to draw it but even more important to learn how not to use it but to find multiple ways to put it back into the sheath (*saya*). *Takemusu* is "self control" as well as one's best potential for personal development.

Kurita *Shihan* reports that "*Takemusu Aiki*" were the Founder's last words when he was dying. He understood them as: "*Give life to Aiki, let it be victorious!*", currently rephrased as: *"Make Aiki grow, and don't let it die."* This was O-Sensei's last instruction to his *deshi*.

TAKEMUSU AIKI MEANS TO LEARN THE NECESSARY AIKI SKILLS
TO PUT VIOLENCE AWAY

The universe flows eternally in union and confluence

[Ki no nagare : "the flow of Ki"]

**Practice partners must work as equals, at the same level
and in a constant flow in order to grow**

Chapter 3
The legacy and the mission

TORA
THE TIGER, SYMBOL OF THE POWER OF FAITH

The Founder's live-in disciples (*uchideshi*) were highly motivated and in a position to learn his Aiki-do correctly. They were amazed by his efficient technique and spiritual character. That same yearning has taken Kurita Yutaka *Shihan* to search for a continuous development so this chapter is to introduce his mission perspective before going in more detail about what he learnt first-hand from the Founder. [30]

His story as an international *Aikido* instructor starts in 1979 when he is dispatched to disseminate it out of Japan and continues with a project carrying his own name: *Kurita Juku Aiki*.

Kurita Yutaka *Shihan*

Being a direct student of O-Sensei and thus having a deep knowledge and insight of Aiki, he has made and is still making a difference by following O-Sensei's line. He has been able to transform his practice and himself through Aiki.

Three decades of hard work

Since he was assigned as Hombu's Official Representative for Mexico, the most relevant features of his personality have been his earnest devotion to O-Sensei

---

[30] Chapter 5 presents a Glossary with more of the main *Aikido* aspects and concepts Kurita *Shihan* has been teaching throughout the years.

and his will to accomplish his mission. He has been out of Japan for 30 years and his task has made him not only to learn a new language but to adapt his instruction to a different culture. He has also put aside all personal and monopolizing interests in order to teach *Aikido*.

When grand master Ueshiba passed away he imposed on himself an absence of almost ten years from *Aikido*. In 1978 he was invited by two former colleagues, Yamada Y. *Shihan* and the late Kanai M. *Shihan*, to leave Japan and help disseminate *Aikido*. Throughout the first two decades he abided by the Aikikai regulations as a form of respect to the late *Doshu*, Ueshiba Kisshomaru. He waited for more than 20 years to be able to start exploring the teachings he learned first-hand from O-Sensei but being one of his most loyal followers he has eventually started *Kurita Juku Aiki*, a school devoted to follow his ideals.

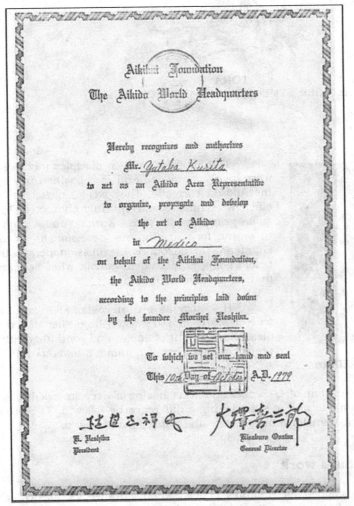

The credentials on the left were issued when he was to be officially sent to Mexico to represent the Aikikai Foundation, Japan's central Aikido organism.

He came full of expectations and a vision full of memories of the times spent with master Ueshiba, who once asked him if he would like to be sent abroad to teach the way of Aiki.

He brought with him a myriad of recollections, which are his personal heritage and treasure. He was granted with 4th *Dan* directly from the Founder, and with 6th and 7th *Dan* by Hombu Dojo.

Kurita *Shihan*'s credentials issued on October 10, 1979 by the Aikikai Foundation made him the official representative of Aikido in Mexico (signed: K. Ueshiba).

The following is a short biographic note of the life and work Kurita *Shihan* has done from the day he found Aikido to the day he was dispatched:

1940   The third of five brothers, Kurita Yutaka *Shihan* is born on April 20, in Tokyo, Japan.

c. 1956   He finds a book on *Aikido* in a bookstore. Highly interested although not fully understanding what it is all about, he looks for an address and decides to go to the *dojo* to apply for an entrance. He is forced to finish High School before being accepted as a live-in student (*Uchideshi*).

1959   A whole year passes and he finishes a period as a regular *Aikido* student. This is a memorable year because he is accepted as an *uchideshi* by the Founder, with the previous recommendation of Ueshiba Kisshomaru (*Doshu*) who is in charge of the selection process. As a live-in disciple he eventually gets his 4th *Dan* directly from O-Sensei. Then he gets a 6th *Dan* from Aikikai in order to be able to be dispatched abroad.

1965   He travels with the *Doshu* for a demonstration in New Mexico (USA) and they meet someone interested on having a guest instructor. The *Doshu* stays with the conviction that Mexico, the country, needed an instructor, a lucky misunderstanding for the *Aikido* in Mexico.

1969   O-Sensei dies and Kurita *Shihan* quits *Aikido* for 9 long years. He knows he had been fortunate to receive a 4th Dan directly from the Founder and to have served him as his scribe. The Founder dictated him lots of notes, many of which he was unfortunately ordered to destroy. However, now his memories and personal experience provide him with the material used in *Kurita Juku Aiki*, a school he starts in 1999.

1978   Kurita *Shihan* is invited back to *Aikido* by his fellow *uchideshi* friends. Yamada Yoshimitsu *Shihan* (New York Aikikai) directs him to Mexico City to a *dojo* of one of his students.

1979   He arrives in Mexico City on May 14 and he teaches classes only to instructors and advanced students at that particular place. After a few months teaching at that first *dojo*, and being highly unsatisfied in his personal expectations, he is encouraged by some of those students to leave and open a new place. After going to several locations, and facing all kinds of problems, this first group eventually dissolves, leaving him alone with the burden of a lease and no income to face it.

1980   Jose Carlos Escobar meets Kurita *Shihan* while working at the same building where he opened his first *dojo*. He is asked to help support him after he was left alone by his former group. Without realizing it he becomes his first original student since he had never practiced *Aikido* before. They are able to legally register the Mexican Aikido Association in order to go on with his mission. He cuts all relationship with almost all those first students who had followed him so far.

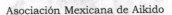

Asociación Mexicana de Aikido

This is the first official logo. It symbolizes man's union with the Universe through the practice of *Aikido*.

1981-1988   Kurita *Shihan* teaches in different places and to different people, like the Mexican President's personal guards, and works with only a small bunch of students affiliated with the Mexican Aikido Association. He also teaches some private classes that help him survive.

He reinforces the activity of the Association and goes on with renewed enthusiasm. He forms his first instructors and grants his first black belt ranks (including the author's). They are officially registered at Hombu Dojo.

1989   The *First International Seminar* is hosted, having the late Kanai Mitsunari (from Boston) as the guest *Shihan*. Seminars are instituted as a yearly event and their objective is to invite other *uchideshi* to share their approaches and ideas.

1991   The *Second International Seminar* is hosted, having Yoshimitsu Yamada (from New York IAF, East Region) as the guest *Shihan*.

1994   The *Third International Seminar* is hosted, having Shibata Ichiro as the guest *Shihan* who was again hosted for the *Fourth* (1995) and *Fifth* (1996) *International Seminars*. Okuyama *Shihan* was invited again in 1997.

Shibata *Shihan* in Mexico City

1995   *Texas Aikikai* is founded in San Antonio, Texas; it is the first school derived from Kurita *Shihan* out of Mexico, and it is promoted by Jose Carlos Escobar.

The first students abroad are Jason Humphrey, Eric Kwiecien, and Lee Escobar (Eddy Hernandez, from Laredo, Texas, appears behind).

c.1995   Kurita *Shihan* is invited to move to Monterrey city, in Northern Mexico, where he starts evolving towards new concepts of Aiki applications as part of the integral development of the self. He starts referring to the use of an "intuitive intelligence" as an essential part of Aiki practice.

A class in Monterrey, Mexico

A project known as *Kurita Juku* was to be announced at the First National *Aikido* Congress held in Mexico City. Kurita Yutaka *Shihan* decides to switch from regular *Aikido* to focus on *Takemusu Aiki*. In the background: Erick Kwiecien, Jason Humphrey, Lee Escobar, and Jose Carlos Escobar. Maria Escobar, Lee's wife, appears next to Kurita *Shihan*.

Kurita Yutaka Shihan's Family Crest
(used as *Kurita Juku*'s emblem)

1996   The First National Aikido Congress is organized by the Mexican Aikido Association. Its purpose is to announce *Kurita Juku,* a project whose objective is *"To follow the Founder's line".* Kurita *Shihan* decides to teach what he feels has been missing in *Aikido* training: both *Takemusu Aiki* and an essential Aiki approach, according to what he recalled as the most important *kuden* (the words to be transmitted) he learned from the Founder.

Other organizations are invited to participate, but they decline the invitation. Some are even opposed to this idea and take it as a rebellious action. They were not ready to understand the way of Aiki is open and free, as the Founder wished, specifically from any possible encapsulation that might hinder its development as a new paradigm.

1997   *Kurita Juku Laredo* is established as the second school representing Kurita *Shihan* in Texas. It was promoted by Eddy Hernandez with the support of Jose Carlos Escobar.

1997   The *Sixth International Seminar* is hosted, having Kazuo Chiba (IAF, West Region) as the guest *Shihan*.

Chiba and Kurita *Shihan* (Ramada Inn Hotel, Mexico City)

1997   The *Fifth and Sixth International Seminars* are hosted, having T.S. Okuyama (formerly Great Lakes Aikikai) and Mark Murashige as guest *Shihan*.

M. Murashige *Shihan* in Mexico City (1998, 1999)

1999 He decides to go deeper in his insight on Aiki and thus he starts elaborating on the original teachings he received from the Founder so as to develop his final thesis and legacy. He starts teaching Takemusu Aiki and *Kurita Juku Aiki* is started. Transformation becomes his new school asset and his motto changes to: "*Same Aiki, another view.*"

New ideas and practical applications emerge from the practice of Aiki by following a simple decision: to use past techniques in order to launch a new thesis and ways to practice. Kurita Yutaka *Shihan* points out: "*It is just like telephones, they change and modernize. If we stop Aiki development we are condemning it to die*". His ideal is to teach the Aikido of the Founder which must be taught to help in the development of people's lives.

2001 Kurita *Shihan* moves back to Mexico City.

2002 This book is conceived as an attempt to take a general look at the differences between standard instruction and the way of Aiki as an attempt to stay on the Founder's line by clarifying any possible misunderstandings or misconceptions that may affect its practice.

Kurita *Shihan*'s mission

Kurita Yutaka *Shihan* has observed that up until today most organizations have concentrated on teaching the Aikikai style. And although he was also originally dispatched from Japan to teach it he has had to renew and transform his teachings in order to honor O-Sensei by teaching his Aiki, so as to continue with the developmental line originally proposed.

It is because of this ideal, and the fact that in his opinion there might not be too many instructors devoted to the same goal, that he usually considers himself the last *uchideshi* of O-Sensei. He has pointed out that for some unknown reason many instructors seem to have neglected or refrained from doing what he is trying to accomplish. From his perspective *Aikido* and Aiki can be seen as two different development lines:

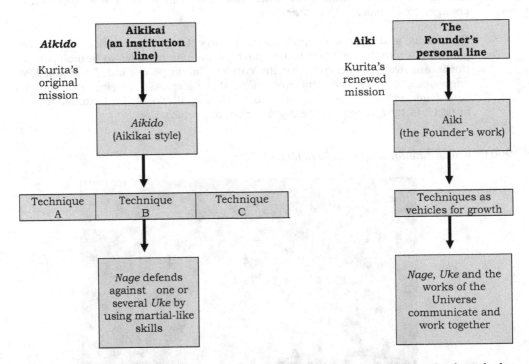

Kurita *Shihan*'s efforts are driven by the education he received and the experiences he had during his *uchideshi* days. That was a period full of sacrifices such as renouncing his personal life. He had to come along to Iwama any time the Founder ordered him to do so, and he also looked after his ancient wife. This made him miss personal family celebrations and deprived him of a common life such as having a girlfriend and eventually getting married. This was part of the life of a live-in student. Being an *uchideshi* meant renouncing everything since the grand master made no concessions. He was also taught that improvement and growth are the highest prizes in Aiki, something he was used to since effort was not traditionally prized in *budo* practice. Training was always related to everyday life, as we can see in the following remarks by the Founder:

> *"(Aiki) practice helps improve your school grades as well as your professional work; it allows you visualize problems before they arrive. You can sense the direction of the 'attack' before it gets to you and adapt immediately to the situation".*

Kurita *Shihan* now elaborates:

> *"To adapt means to know what to do in any situation and to take advantage of our own energy as well as that of the problems we are about to resolve. Without any struggle and feeling we can direct that compound energy wherever we want it. There is no use on being tense. We should be flexible and free from any pressures. We must vibrate and never clash.*

Aiki: **our vibration linked to the Universe**

> *With a good vibration we can be happy. We all have a certain vibration in us, and we must improve it every time so we can achieve an optimal development of our energy until it reaches the confines of the Universe. All of it has a vibration, which is the voice of God, his strength, his energy, and God listens to it. So Nage and Uke, as partners, must vibrate better and better each time they work; so nobody is to be tense during practice."*

He pinpoints a fundamental aspect of Aiki training when he states that one of its objectives is to perceive our own "vibration", which is done both personally and with the help of our practice partners. *"This is why we cannot talk of enemies in Aikido,"* he states. Both practitioners must vibrate together: *"Just as the energy of the Universe, in one perpetual vibration".* In his opinion techniques are complete not when they are executed with both hands and on both left and right stances but when there is "circulation". They are complete when "energy" is *received* with the left and *sent* with the right to our partner, and when the work of left and right are *clearly differentiated* and used in such a way so as to cover the axis that create a *sphere.* *"This is the only way to share the Universe's harmony circulation"*, he says. We can see this in a graphic description:

Many *Aikido* instructors make no difference in the work of the left and right hands:

↑ R / L
R / L ◄ - - - ╀ - - - ► R / L
↓ R / L

For Kurita Yutaka *Shihan* hands work different in the way of Aiki:

(space) Z axis
(left) X axis
(right) Y axis

Instructors from the first group believe hands are used in exactly the same way on both axes whereas for Kurita *Shihan* they have to be used on their own corresponding axis. Those in the first group use both right and left hands in either a horizontal or a vertical way, whereas the second way use them in such a way that they produce a circulation which makes techniques "breathe". The left hand is only used in a horizontal axis whereas the right is used on the vertical one. In addition, feet also move in a different way when standing on one foot or the other: the postures used are not the same either.

Left and right are important in Aiki. This can be noticed in the fact that *Uke* – the "attacker"– traditionally places himself on the right side of the *kamiza* [31] while *Nage* –the "defender"– stays on the left side whenever a technique is demonstrated. The reason why practice starts with *hidari hanmi* (a left stance) and uses the left hand and not the right one is because "*the left represents ourselves*" (Kurita *Shihan*). Our right hemisphere starts the fine work first whereas the right side of our body, driven by the left hemisphere and used alternatively, "*represents the help and support of others*" and is part of the shared logic of things.

Left and right also symbolize the feminine and masculine duality. They are two important elements in the Founder's representation of the Aiki universe and a tradition borrowed from Japanese mythology. According to Kurita *Shihan*, O-Sensei considered the left as "feminine" because it receives positive energy and creates life. Practice starts working on their left stance and using the left hand first. In addition, he considered the right side as "masculine" since it takes action and goes for it. This is related to the valued use of our right hemisphere during practice, a theory Kurita Yutaka *Shihan* has been using as the basis for transformation.

Analogy in action:

The feminine (−)
side receives the action; it
"defends" and "reacts".

The masculine (+)
starts the action, it "attacks".

**Together, *NAGE and UKE* create Aiki
(union, confluence and harmony)**

In his last years O-Sensei was not exploring or working on self-defense action. His masculine-feminine analogy basically shows that he saw a complementing yin-yang correspondence. He always talked of the two main Japanese deities Izanami and Izanagi and saw them as important constituents of his Aiki work. There are techniques like *katate dori kokyu Nage* where you can definitely see the different work

---

[31] In a traditional *dojo*, the *Kamiza* is the place where a small shrine or picture is placed at and is used to honor the Founder before starting a class. The *rei (salutation)* is used to ask for his permission to borrow his Aiki (it is not simply a bow or a token of adoration).

made by the left and right hands and feet in support of these statements. And since Kurita *Shihan* is currently filling the gaps on what the Founder left out for the *uchideshi* to realize, he points out:

> *"Work must not only be present on techniques, it must develop the reflection of Ki, an element everybody talks about but many don't understand or even see."*

KI [32]

According to what can be derived from practice, *ki* is life, posture, calmness, will, space, gravity, nature, biology, confluence of the left-right energy flow of our brains and bodies as well as: *"A question yet to be answered"*. This is why it is the most important element in Aiki-do. Kurita *Shihan* states: *"In Aikido we put Ki to work as a force or unseen power, which is not muscular because it is not like pulling, pushing or struggling. It is more a physical than a mental flexibility"*. He reports that according to Kaiso Sensei it is not necessary to understand *ki*; all we need is just to work with it, to use it. So in order to achieve this we need to be flexible. *Ki* may concretely be defined as *"the body set aright"* which means it is part of a correct working posture, and hence a fundamental element for correct work.

Kurita *Shihan* goes even further and adds:

> *"The body must be inside Aikido, not the other way round; this is an indispensable pre-requisite for learning the way. There are no questions in Aiki since it is mostly 'experience' (a "do"). Kaiso Sensei never allowed any questions when he was teaching, he would just demonstrate just in case someone didn't understand and all of his answers were right there."*

This system of education gave birth to the following *Aikido* maxim which has been around for years and has been used even in relation to completely different fighting arts:

> *"Don't ask; just practice and some day you will understand"*

According to Kurita *Shihan*'s most recent exploration Aiki is a way to support the works and development of the right hemisphere of our brain. This is the side in charge of intuition whereas analysis and concepts, competition, sports and martial uses is the job of the left hemisphere. Our *ki* cannot be explained, because it is not something within the left-side reach. It is an element that must be felt and sensed. Only our senses can help us gain the insight needed to see and understand it.

Ki is the most disconcerting Aiki element because it is the most multi-meaningful element in Ueshiba's system and it is not "energy". This can be easily explained once we realize that energy is a different thing for different people, as the following example related to our "natural energy" clearly shows:

---

[32] Taken from *The Essence of Aikido* by John Stevens, Kodansha International, 1993.

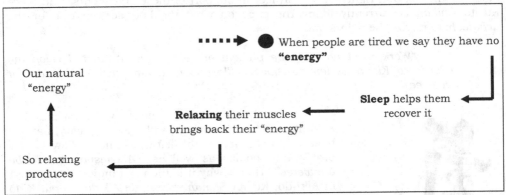

**Similarly when technique shows any kind of violence or is tense
it resembles Aiki-do but it has no *ki*.**

The self is the objective of Aiki study. And it is only from the experience gained through a correct physical activity that we can have a true perception of it. In Kurita *Shihan*'s opinion, the physical body aspect of Aiki is developed before age 35, but we can still develop its spiritual aspect after that age if we have started later. All we must do is practice accurately every day, provided we always work with *ki*. This is the basic element which makes the difference between Aiki-do and a sport or a fighting art. He remarks that if old people learn how to use *ki* they can do more and better than younger persons who only use their muscles.

***Ki* is felt and developed through *kokyu* (extension)**

The Aiki of *Kurita Juku* requires the working of *ki*, the inexhaustible concept which has simplistically been translated as "energy". Kurita *Shihan* explains:

"It is very difficult to penetrate the meaning of Ki even to the Japanese, because it is not the same as muscular 'strength' or 'force'. To work Ki makes things easier; if I don't work Ki everything becomes more difficult, so it is necessary to put it to work. It resembles a mystical strength but it is part of every single man and woman, and anyone can use it. The Founder would only ask us (the Uchideshi) to work our Ki, but when people hear this today they tend to think that Aiki-do practitioners work with some mysterious strength and Ki work is then confused with muscular work.

They are also wrong when they take the Japanese word 'ki' and relate it to the Chinese 'chi', since they are two totally different concepts. The name of Aikido comes from this Ki word, and implies we have to put it to work. It is not a mystical energy but it comes from God because it is a force given to us and is part of our own being. The Divinity does not hold anything back, everything flows from it so we should work Ki, manifest it, and let it flow as a natural part of the individual.

On the other hand, the Aiki-budo, named Aikido by the government to make it sound like Judo, Kendo, Karate do, etc., is a broader term which includes several other aspects such as "Takemusu Aiki" which represents the domain of the Aiki Budo. This last name was used by the Founder when he considered his Do represented the spontaneous 'generation' (production) of Budo, in any 'circumstance', as well as the absolute suppression of the fighting aspects it contained."

INCORRECT vs. CORRECT WORK
(FALSE vs. TRUE AIKI-DO)

In order to tell the difference we must realize that our physical senses are just different from the Aiki senses (Kurita Yutaka *Shihan*):

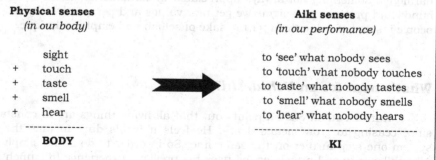

Physical senses		**Aiki senses**
(in our body)		*(in our performance)*
sight		to 'see' what nobody sees
+ touch		to 'touch' what nobody touches
+ taste		to 'taste' what nobody tastes
+ smell		to 'smell' what nobody smells
+ hear		to 'hear' what nobody hears
--------------		---------------------------------------
BODY		**KI**

Failure to use Aiki senses makes our practice incorrect and leads us nowhere:

Incorrect work/practice   ⟶   **Fake development**
(clashing forces, muscle   LEADS TO   (fantasy, untrue Aiki-do)
power, violence and tricks)

But the use of Aiki senses makes our practice correct and leads us to progress and real transformation:

Correct work/practice (union, confluence, harmony, *ki* / human essence work)	LEADS TO	*True development* (reality, true Aiki-do)

Due to the strong function of their left brains practitioners are too concerned with things alien to Aiki-do when considering correct vs. incorrect training. Things like its practical applications on the streets or its combination with other martial arts make them introduce unnecessary elements into practice as they borrow from an older paradigm instead of focusing on true Aiki stuff. Kurita *Shihan* states that everyday practice stays forever and that *effort* is the key that opens our eyes and unveils Aiki. Only sustained work can help us taste and see what others can't or to feel, see and hear what others cannot feel, see or hear. This is what we should call progress (*development*) and transformation (*metamorphosis*). The Founder's original concepts only contemplated the everyday practice of Aiki, a perspective separate from talking and speech.

It is only through active participation that we can discover its true inherent nature as it was stated in the previously quoted maxim. But many people are not able to change their current, safe martial arts paradigm and they use their practice to hurt others in class or during exhibitions. And after doing so they will still claim that happened because the person injured, their *Uke*, was "not well prepared or alert". They will even claim that *Aikido* "hurts" ignoring that good work is only possible with the voluntary participation of their training partners.

After 30 years of tireless work, Kurita Yutaka *Shihan* still wants his students to understand that Aiki-do is useful, among other things, to avoid fighting. It is important not to take it as a self-defense system, since it has absolutely nothing to do with it. Aiki-do has no violence and no confrontation but Aiki (union, confluence and harmony), something not always appreciated in exhibitions. When Aiki changes our minds and previous paradigms we get new values and perspectives by taking care of people instead of using them for the sake of selfish and empty technique.

What's next for an *Uchideshi*?

Kurita Yutaka *Shihan* points out that all living things are in constant change since ceasing to grow means death. He feels it is his duty to take the Founder's system one step further on the same line. So in order to do so he simply abides by Aiki philosophy and principles, he uses his previous experience to launch an Aiki-do exploration supported by O-Sensei's ideology. And he is adapting it to a common human identity bound by an Aiki culture. Students in *Kurita Juku Aiki* are taught Aiki is a great intercultural asset people can have in our contemporary world because it is in fact a modern tradition facing its own future.

The following chart shows the changes and evolution of Aiki through the works of Takeda Sensei, the disciples of O-Sensei, and Kurita *Shihan*. The changes proposed in the third column, which is Kurita *Shihan*'s renewed approach and understanding, are based on the Founder's original teachings shown in the second column, and reflect the dynamism and vitality he is trying to implement by still studying Aiki with a beginner's fervor. He is working only and exclusively to get to the gist of its features in order to find new forms and ways to help his students get a deeper insight and benefit from it.

Kurita Yutaka *Shihan* can do so because he is one of the few *deshi* in the world who studied full time with the master and had the opportunity to be dictated O-Sensei's theories and ideas; he was fortunate enough to grab his wrist and feel the quality and nature of his work whenever he had a chance to be his *Uke*.

Evolution of Aiki at three different historical moments [33]

Aiki was derived from Daito-ryu, but it was progressively abandoned by the grand master as he created Aikido. All the main differences and final achievements are described here (third column), but the only way to understand them is by direct experience and by tasting the difference of each kind of performance.

At any rate, the main characteristic of the technical applications of Aiki are its definitiveness and softness: there is no effort in Aiki, nor any violent clash of forces for the sake of harmony. It is well-known that when the founder of Judo saw Aikido's gentle nature he said: "This is my ideal Budo".

Daito-ryu	Aikido	Aiki
Aiki techniques inherited from ancient times	**Aiki techniques inherited from the Founder**	**Aiki techniques renewed over personal recollections**
• TAKEDA Sokaku (representative)	• UESHIBA Morihei (founder)	• KURITA Yutaka (representative)
• Its objective is to annihilate the opponent; it is a clash of forces	• Its objective is to "reconcile" with the opponent by redirecting its energy and impulse.	• Its objective is to unite with the opponent, to add and multiply each other's energies
• Participants are potential enemies and they regard practice as preparation for combat	• All schools derived from O-Sensei's teachings emphasize attacked and attacker roles (*Nage – Uke*, or other names) and many still may consider their practice as a preparation for fight or as a self-defense system	• As it was finally conceptualized by Kaiso Sensei participants are one entity, there are no divisions, no differences, and no *Nage - Uke* roles. Practice is never a combat, fight or self-defense, but a process for personal and social growth.

[33] Please note this synopsis is the author's personal interpretation.

• It is a vast system of attacks and defenses, made of blows, holds and falls	• The number of attacks and defenses is reduced to a small number	• All attacks and defenses disappear as conveyed in many styles
• The attacker is annihilated with the logical disdain towards his physical integrity and well-being	• The attacker is held or projected in order to "reconcile" his/her postures. It has been considered as "the art of peace"	• The "attacker" is taken care of as an extension of *Nage*'s own self: *Uke* is kept close and united to *Nage* at all times in permanent harmony, unity and confluence
• Movements are violent and executed in opposing and encountered directions (they clash): A —→ ←— B	• Movements are harmonious but in some styles they are executed in parallel directions that go from one side to another: A —→ ←— B	• Movements flow together in crossing and circular unifying directions overlapping as a unit: A ←—┼—→ B ↓
• It is a **reactive** art done at a physical level	• It is a **pro-active** art done at physical and moral levels	• It is a **pro-active** way done at spiritual, social and physical levels
• Action takes place between two independent beings: (A – B).	• Action consists of a combination of two or more beings: (A + B).	• Action becomes an addition or multiplication and thus an integration of beings: (A + A = **A**) or (1 + 1 = **1**).
• A and B represent two different persons mutually considered as adversaries, since one is the attacker and the other defends from him; the victim needs self-protection or self-defense	• A makes B to unite with him/her and vice versa. They are two persons assuming one of two roles: *Nage* (the one who throws) or *Uke* (the one who falls). They stop considering themselves as adversaries.	• A and B put differences aside and blend together not only as the sum but a multiplication of a vital and unique energy. Since there is neither division nor distinctions of any kind, the two participants, *Nage* and *Uke*, disappear as independent entities.

The system is made of:	The system uses:	The system uses *Aikido*'s:
• Defenses and attacks to any and all parts of the body, using all possible means (body and weapons)	• Attacks to the head, neck and stomach against which two types of defenses are applied: throws and pins. It is characterized by a series of mobilizations based on circular movements (pivots) whose objective is to nullify the attacks, something considered a reconciling means (see Chapter 4)	• **Ki** (the correct use of the body) • **Five parallel** senses • **Aiki** (union, confluence) • **Axis** of actions: X, Y, Z (depth and space) • **Izanau** (attraction) • **Awase** (contact) • **Musubi** (unification) • **Aiki no michi** (confluent, crossing "energies"), and some others fostered in *Kurita Juku Aiki* practice: **Agatsu + Masakatsu + Katsuhayabi**
• It consists of more than 100 combat techniques. When applied, these techniques are suited for combat and hence it can be used by the military or the police.	• It consists of a reduced number of harmonious techniques with multiple variables intended to improve human beings.	• It consists of a set of union, confluence and harmony techniques with multiple variations and applications in everyday life out of the Dojo and with a strong impact on our contemporary social organization with real life benefits and practical uses.

The following is an example of a technique applied according to the descriptions proposed by Kurita Yutaka *Shihan*. The arrows show the directions followed by both *Nage* and *Uke*. They are not parallel as in some *Aikido* styles but crossing, as they abide by *Aiki no michi*: the path where their "energies" meet and become one by uniting and following the same direction.

In some *Aikido* styles *Nage* confuses directions and gets away from *Uke*. He separates from his partner because there is no union (*musubi*). He loses his center and so uses violence against his arm and this produces a big slam.

In Aiki, *Nage* follows one direction and he gets close to *Uke*; and they blend because of this. They join together because *musubi* is used and kept from start to finish. They never get apart.

Practitioners must learn how different directions work and the difference they make when they are chosen. They have two possibilities: one is to move in parallel directions. This makes them follow two different and separated paths:

The other is to move in a crossing way (this is proper in Aiki), which makes them follow an *Aiki no michi*, a path where two entities become one:

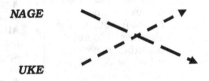

In Aiki there is no need to grab or hurt *Uke*

Nage is not grabbing *Uke*, in accordance with the Founder's precept that "*There are no slaves in Aiki*" (Kurita Yutaka *Shihan*). Aiki, as a cultural humane system, helps individuals to develop a better, honest, and integrated positive self. And in order to be much more effective within our local and world-wide communities, it opens the door of true democracy: a genuine care for people.

Aikido´s martial background usually sends the wrong message because people may only see an interaction between two "fighting" entities, *Nage-Uke*, one in control over the other. They may only see a winner and a loser instead of union. If there is no *Uke*, *Nage* cannot exist, just as it happens with a teacher, who needs students to be considered as such, or a father who needs a son, and a leader who needs followers.

Aiki-do is not meant to prepare ready-to-fight people nor athletes willing to participate in a contest. Aiki can be practiced by just about everybody without any need of strenuous exercises, as well as without any risk of getting a broken bone or any other harm against their body or their morale. Aiki is interested in much more than teaching refined ways to twist an arm or to throw a person, nor to execute the most impressive or lethal moves.

There was a time right after the Founder's death when Kurita Yutaka *Shihan's* mission outside Japan made him just abide by the objectives of Ueshiba Kisshomaru, the former *Aikido Doshu*. But things have changed and now he seems to be working back on the ideals of Kaiso Sensei in order to help promote what he thinks will be their best development: to use Aiki's force to overcome our weaknesses in all areas of our lives and culture. His position and goals are essential to promote Aiki, which is meant for freedom and individuality, in confluence and congeniality for the individual as well as among people.

There cannot be more tolerance, good will and intercultural understanding promoted by any other activity as in Aiki although it is something we still have to meditate and work upon. Kurita *Shihan* thinks he has achieved nothing yet and believes the path is beginning to be envisioned. So he takes good care in maintaining a high standard of excellence that is barely disclosing the right path. He wishes to accomplish his mission through a true uniting practice.

Aiki: an energy formula for personal and cultural development

A common way of describing *Aikido* consists in saying that it is *"The union of our personal Ki with the universal one* (the Universe's *ki*).*"* This has been the concept put on the top of the humankind development aimed by *Aikido*. But, how can we relate this to our persons and culture in general, to our family, our work place, and our society as a whole?

Let's explore this by analyzing Aiki literally as a *formula*, by putting it in mathematical terms as to see what is implied by its energy and system. Let's consider the following facts:

1. The Founder's **Aiki** is intended to express the Order of the Universe (**K**) <u>through</u> and <u>by means of</u> our human body and mind (spirit/will) (**BM**)

① $$Aiki = K\,(BM)$$

2. If this order (**K**) is correctly applied through our body (**B**), both technique (**T**) and health (**H**) flourish in a natural form.

② $$K(B) = T + H$$

3. If this order (**K**) is correctly applied to everyday life (**L**), then education (**E**), work (**W**) and personality (**P**) also flourish in a natural form, giving students a healthier and stronger self (**S1**).

③ | **K(M) = E * W * P**

4. Therefore we can express this order (**K**) in terms of body (**B**) and mind (**M**) as follows, giving us a healthier and stronger self (**S1**)

③ | **K(BM) = (T + H) * E * W * P = S1**

5. And if this order is applied to society (**S2**) in Boolean terms, the relationship between one's self (**1s**) and the self of others (**1o**) leads to naturally augmented, optimal and harmonious human relations (**1 = multiplied energy**).

④ | **K (S2) = (1s + 1o = 1)**

6. This way, humanity, just like a family, can work in unison in all fields to restore the world and find a new "human way", capable of repairing our currently devastated harmony.

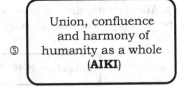

⑤ | Union, confluence
and harmony of
humanity as a whole
(**AIKI**)

Expressed as a <u>socially integrated</u> whole Aiki is the contemporary *energy* our civilization needs to drive itself safely into the future:

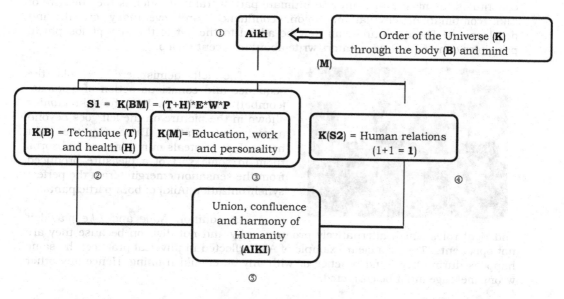

Aiki is definitely a sustainable educational paradigm, since it implies values, attitudes and visions compatible with recommendations contemporarily made by international organizations such as the United Nations for the Education, Scientific and Cultural Organization (UNESCO), and based on an eco-systemic scientific vision of the 21st century. An educational system like Aiki seems to be very helpful in the effects globalization is creating since it promotes human values adapted to the new conditions of our era and the many changes and challenges yet to be defined in new regional and global contexts. Such new contexts are being outlined via the transformations which force us to rapidly assimilate and confront the challenges currently coming from the areas of information and communications, the defense of our ecological planet systems, economic inequality, unemployment, xenophobia, intolerance, indifference and many other dilemmas.

This new line of thought is producing a change of strong values and ethical content which is taking us:

- from independence to <u>interdependence</u> among individuals
- from competition and dominance to <u>cooperation and alliance</u>
- from the individual to the <u>community</u>

Eco-education, as a contemporary educational model, is based on the fact that the planet is an ecological, integral system. This implies our natural and cultural systems are only subsystems of a larger entity, just as the heart and lungs are part of the human body. Human learning has reached a point where it integrates itself in many areas. This opens the door to a new vision between science and humanities as part of a new dynamic cultural interaction between the products of the left and right brain hemispheres, between logic and intuition.

Aiki training makes us use our left and right brains in order to work them in union and harmony: it produces a joint work of our two brain hemispheres. This allows practitioners to develop and perceive their *intuitive capacities*, and it constitutes the most important and intimate part of training. Such is the objective of Aiki: combination, circulation, union, confluence, and eventually growth and development. These features can now be added to the list of the new philosophical principles contemporary educators write about in recent books.

The left hemisphere controls the sequence and conscious action of a *kumite* (combat) with the *jo*. But the Aiki *kumi-jo* shown in the picture on the left goes beyond a real confrontation. Driven by the right hemisphere it steals our spirits and absorbs them in some sort of a pleasure produced from the sensation emerging from the perfect synchronization (Aiki) of both participants.

In addition *Nage* and *Uke* play left and right roles which alternatively produce unity and not division because they are not opponents. This is a clear example of Aiki reflected in physical practice; the same happens during free hand practice or with any other Aiki training. Hence any other wrong message must be corrected.

This brings us to the topic of cooperation and collaboration, an exceedingly common issue practitioners always discuss in class or at seminars. The interest arises whenever harmony and confluence are analyzed and conclusions always point to the fact that cooperation implies the absence of competition and the presence of a group spirit which in turn encourages positive interdependence and mutual support. This is cooperative learning in action, and this kind of learning consistently shows significant effects such as: higher self-esteem, increased confidence and enjoyment, greater achievement, more respect for the teachers, the school and the subject matters, and the use of higher-level cognitive strategies, a highly decreased prejudice, increased altruism and mutual concern.

The only hindrance to understanding the Aiki paradigm lies in the individual's potential failure to realize there are two ways of learning and knowing things. These are diametrically opposite in both their conception and perspectives between the Eastern and Western worlds. The latter promotes the study of our being through the left brain, by means of thoughts and ideas, and only partially through the body (PE classes). The former backs up a process done mainly with the right side of the brain and through the body in order to imprint it in the mind. This is what Aiki does.

In the Western world, our *being* is represented in the mind by means of an oral discourse (speech). It is an abstraction.

The *being* doesn't need any given representation in Aiki since it is perceived through the body and by means of physical activity. Moreover, Aiki accomplishes this in union and real contact with our practice partner. Aiki is a way for two, not an individual one. It promotes addition and multiplication not division.

Kurita *Shihan* states:

> *"Knowledge is acquired from top to bottom in the West (it goes from the head down to the body), whereas Aiki makes it go bottom up (from the body to the head), originating from our own body perceptions."*

This difference is central in Aiki training. It is the main reason why instructors don't write books and prefer to pass their knowledge on by oral tradition and continuous practice. According to Kurita *Shihan* the Founder thought that writing a book can be misleading because the public will read it and will tend to think they "know" the subject. Ancient masters have traditionally considered it inappropriate to write a book on the arts taught by their own instructors. The grand master himself explored *budo* from his own perspective and not from the point of view of his most influential teacher (Takeda Sokaku). And although he found out about the *Aiki* concept in ancient Daito-ryu, he eventually transformed it.

The eco-educative vision is seen by many educators as a way to make a profound change in the way education is conceived based solely on rationality: it can go from some kind of a fragmented, mechanical and linear thinking to an integrated, holistic and organic one. It is impossible not to notice the enormous coincidences with Ueshiba's physical Aiki education system:

An eco-educative vision thinks of:	Master Ueshiba's vision aims for:
• <u>networks</u>, rather than hierarchies,	• <u>networks</u> and no hierarchies,
• <u>sustainability</u>, more than exploitation	• <u>sustainability</u> through the individual's fine and intuitive self expression
• <u>sufficiency</u>, more than scarcity	• <u>sufficiency</u> (100% work multiplied by our partners in 100% respect)
• <u>processes</u>, more than structures	• free and spontaneous <u>processes</u>
• <u>relations</u>, more than objects	• <u>relations</u> among all parts or elements
• <u>totalities</u>, more than fragments	• <u>totalities</u> gained through integration, union, togetherness and collaboration
• <u>quality</u>, more than quantity	• <u>quality</u> seen as all which is correct
• <u>contextual knowledge,</u> with an orientation towards cultures, rather than an objective and independent knowledge.	• <u>contextual</u> and intercultural <u>knowledge</u>

The orientation lead by Kurita Yutaka *Shihan* is excellent food for thought. As can be clearly seen, it goes beyond the practice hall aiming to improve and benefit our experience of life.

Leaves grow on their own place, forming a unity with the plant

[*KI* : the force used by life to grow]

"When there is growth there is *Ki*, when there is *Ki* there is growth"

Chapter 4
The Aiki practice session: basics

KURITA'S *MON*

- KURITA Y. *SHIHAN* SAMURAI FAMILY SEAL -

Not a Kindergarten approach

When instructors teach *Aikido* by saying "*This is ikkyo... and this is nikyo, and now I will teach you irimi-nage, kokyu-nage, kaiten, look!*" their procedure resembles Kindergarten teachers when they say: "*This is a pen, and this is a pencil, and now I will teach you the colors, a book, an apple, look!*." A higher level of comprehension requires Aiki practitioners to see the nature, qualities and benefits derived from the positive application of all actions. They must realize their possible damaging effects when they are applied in a negative/wrong way. Any obvious and superficial contents must be left behind in order to grow in depth and understanding. Although students learn how to use a pen to write, they still have to learn how to express in writing: they still need to use their pens as vehicles for higher purposes. The same should happen as people learn the works of Aiki action and techniques.

Unfortunately this is not the case when teaching only deals with mechanical skills. This may not be such a problem for beginners but they should eventually be led to the discovery and application of *ki* and all the elements pinpointed by the Founder. Many methods are used to teach mechanical maneuvers that might take students nowhere in their vision, development or understanding of Aiki even if they devotedly practice them for years. They would easily find out they might not know how to recognize, multiply and apply their *ki*. Some instructors might tend to teach the skills needed to carry out the series of activities found in a given program but they may forget to include transcendental work. This is relevant since Aiki is not learnt in preparation for combat or competition.

In order to go beyond such an elementary level, and to reach what should be an advanced one, we must practice in a comprehensive way. We can at least try to describe contents but is necessary to go beyond words and make them a reality. But since texts are the way used by Westerners this chapter will discuss with some Aiki emphasis most of what is usually taught in Aiki-do sessions. The objective is to elaborate on fundamental teachings transmitted by Kurita Yutaka *Shihan*. A necessary word of caution is inevitable here: the ultimate definition of the real meaning of *ikkyo*, *irimi*, etc., must be directly discovered with practice as students get a better and deeper insight through their everyday constant training. It is necessary to see the Aiki-do as a holistic educational system with enormous cultural benefits derived from correct practice.

Master Ueshiba's proposal perfectly responds to the formation, adaptation and expression of the individual in our contemporary world, an awareness that has always been important to the Japanese through *misogi* (spiritual cleansing and purification), a practice usually evoked by the typical picture of a man sitting on an enormous rock and right under a waterfall. O-Sensei stated Aiki practice is *misogi*, because it is a way to clean our hearts and spirits. It goes beyond the old way done by sitting under a waterfall. Being a cleansing system, the way of Aiki looks to warrant excellence that can be reached by means of three key elements:

1.   self evaluation,
2.   self criticism, and
3.   self renovation or transformation
      (all of which involves a change of mind)

After all, an Aiki technique must be applied with a natural, sincere, and sudden smile, as many pictures of O-Sensei clearly show. When we take a look at the hundreds of pictures that have been published, we realize master Ueshiba did not show any of those ferocious, aggressive, and terrifying grins so popular in the covers of martial arts magazines. He doesn't show signs of violence, and this is the spirit and attitude he proposed as his way. What we usually do see is his great concentration so we must realize his focused and highly determined spirit instead.

This is not the usual attitude of a fighter

The place and meaning of practice

From what has been said in all our previous Chapters, it must always be stressed that:

- An Aiki class is a chance to clean our spirit through our body; it is a form of *misogi* practice and not a fighting art or a sport.
- Its objective is not to learn how to twist and break somebody's arms and bones or to slam a person on the ground, nor to learn how to win over others.
- It teaches about the order and nature of things. Kurita *Shihan* considers it as the "science of human life," as well as "the way of Universal harmony" because they are both interrelated.
- It is meant for the expression of quality: things must be done right, when they are supposed to be given purity, excellence and category (*sahō* in Japanese).
- It puts philosophy into actual practice and touches all aspects of human life.

Aiki activity is conducted in a clean *dojo*, literally considered as "the place of enlightenment or understanding" when it includes the *kanji* (ideograms) standing for *Aiki no O-Kami* ("the grand spirit of unity, confluence and harmony" next to the Founder's picture).

Then it is considered as a special place because it is the space where we learn, understand and study about our lives and their multiple aspects. Otherwise it is only an empty room, a gym, a mere practice hall, as it has been translated. It is given a special consideration because Aiki is created here, along with a relevant consciousness of what is accomplished. It is not a temple but it is the place where we grow and develop as human beings so it is worth due respect. Respect understood not only as a feeling of wonder and awe but as a sincere sense of duty to take care of our responsibilities. This is part of the master's talking about divine principles and techniques.

The *dojo* has a special place at the front called *kamiza* where practitioners usually find a picture of Kaiso Sensei. It is also considered as a place for special guests and everybody coming to class sits in front of it. When they bow they are symbolically asking for O-Sensei's permission to borrow his *budo*. Doing so is to pay our respects and offers to do whatever is due and proper to learn and benefit from practice, as well as to honor his original teachings. A couple of anecdotes recalled by Kurita *Shihan* tell us what the *dojo* meant to master Ueshiba:

a) One day somebody asked the Founder: *"Where is your Aikido?"* Then by pointing to the center of the empty hall, he said: *"There it is, make it"*. This means you enter *Aikido*, you go for it, because it doesn't come to you.

b) Once there was a man who wanted O-Sensei to show proof of the efficacy of his Aiki. He nagged at him for days trying to engage him in a confrontation in order to find out how good it was. Tired of this, the master Ueshiba invited him to the dojo, asked him to put on his *gi* (practice garment) and promised him he will try his best Aiki with him. When they met, O-Sensei asked him to enter the mats, then he did the same, they bowed at each other showing they were ready but immediately after bowing the grand master said:

> *"This (bow) is what I call perfect practice: there was no harm done between the two of us and no bad feelings can derive from it, now if you excuse me..."*

O-Sensei stood up and left the man sitting there, by himself, in the center of the empty room. That was the spirit of Aiki the grand master always had in mind.

Being a spiritual man, Kaiso Sensei was able to see his work as connected with the *kami*. And what he meant by sacred practice seems to have consisted of doing whatever it was necessary to make each and every Aiki-do class a good chance for *misogi*, a chance to get rid of any dirt we might have in our hearts, in order to find and make consistent relations with our partners. This extends our practice to our family and our professional lives, and also connects ourselves with our own essence. Not doing so is disrespectful to the *dojo* and the instructor.

As an example, *katate dori*, the basic grab consisting of holding our partner's wrist, is not an attack but a chance to get close, to communicate and to learn about our relationship. Grabbing too hard and injuring a partner makes the action violent and represents the kind of conflictive relationships where one partner suffocates or stops the person he is supposed to be relating to. There is obviously no cooperation. On the other hand a weak grab is negligent within the established relationship since only one partner works and gives his/her best whereas the other person just waits. Yet *Nage* has to be in control to make the necessary moves in order to adjust and compensate any missing aspect. This is what a "sincere attack" requires without having to be violent on either side. Regarding grabs they have to be done keeping the index finger open and with the whole palm in full contact with our partner's wrist and not as a fist or claw. Grabs are firm not violent.

Our actions (techniques) are vehicles for the true manifestation of our hearts. They are ways to be used to start a deeper understanding of our relationships with others. They are also practiced to learn about how such relationships work so next time we have a problem we won't blame innocent people or to complain of lack of understanding if we are guilty. And the worst case is to react with violence. Aiki-do is a way to discover the kind of relationships we have and maintain as part of our lives and the lives of others. When we make harmonious relationships in class we are really practicing and following the way of Aiki and it can be extended to many other relationships. In fact this will be the result of an exceedingly serious practice.

Harmony: the spirit and goal of practice

Kurita Yutaka *Shihan* teaches that training, to the eyes of the Founder, should be like a special celebration (*sho-chiku-bai*). This may be the reason why we see him smiling in many pictures. We must enjoy our activity and work and not suffer them. The symbols of a celebration give it a meaning and the occasion puts every one in tune with everybody else. Not surprisingly musicians do something similar, they understand harmony well. Our *dojo* can be easily compared to a concert hall, where harmony is expressed:

Concert hall	*Dojo* (illumination place)
• It is a special place reserved for the musicians to make music	• It is a special place reserved for practitioners to make Aiki
• Musicians get together to play, to perform and to express themselves through their art	• Practitioners get together to play, to perform and to express themselves through Aiki
• They play something written by somebody else (Chopin, Lennon-Mc Cartney, etc) and they can modify and play with it as they wish. They may modify it and sometimes even leave small recognizable pieces from the original	• They play something created by somebody else (master Ueshiba), but they cannot modify it as they wish. Leaving small recognizable pieces from the original jeopardizes the original Aiki and makes it loose its nature.
• There is no music until they play correctly	• There is no Aiki until they practice correctly
• If they don't play harmoniously they will sound terrible: no harmony means no music and no communication	• If they don't practice harmoniously they will look and feel terrible: disharmony means no unity, no communication and violence
• Harmony is found in the right combination of notes, rhythm (timing) and arrangement	• Harmony is found in the right combination of spirit, attitudes, work, and will, as well as in its timing and arrangement (order, *Cosmos*, Aiki)
• Musicians need to show disposition to perform well and show their feelings	• Practitioners need to show respect which means doing as they are expected, with kindness and cooperation, and a disposition to perform well in order to show and explore themselves

• Each instrument contributes with a different voice to the same musical piece; authors have found ways to combine those differences very well	• Each person contributes with a different role to reach the same goal; O-Sensei found the best way to combine and benefit from such a combination
• If these elements are not found there is no harmony	• If there is no harmony, unity nor confluence, there is simply no Aiki. Only correct practice can lead to a correspondence between action and philosophy

Enlightenment and cleansing

It is necessary to note that "enlightenment" and "illumination" are two words clearly pointing out a "making of light". When related to a human being, it can be taken as a metaphor but it is something quite real. We have an inner light and Aiki-do practice is meant to make us shine (Kurita Yutaka *Shihan*). We know from Physics that one way to make light is by heating or warming things up: practice starts with a "warm up", and its goal is also to enlighten and push our personalities ahead. The

warming up part in Aiki-do does not consist of simple calisthenics or stretching: a traditional session includes an exercise called *Tori fune undo* (a rowing-like exercise) intended to advance our spirit. It also symbolizes union and togetherness among participants. The most traditional warm up rowing exercise makes everybody work in unison. When everybody chants "*Eeeihhh hooo!, Eeeihh sahh!*" they resemble rowers on a boat who row together and sail in some infinite sea, all knowing they head to the same destination and all wanting to help the rest to reach their goal and to benefit from their mutual support and effort. The Founder learnt this Aiki action from the fishermen at his hometown.

When our body is warmed up it sends out light, a personal light that can help us see our own nature too.

Besides, there is also the issue about cleansing and polishing our bodies through Aiki-do practice which relates to the fact that a lot of rolling is used as a conclusion of the dynamics applied in actions. In this regards Kurita *Shihan* uses a simple analogy to explain the purpose of rolling (*ukemi*): by means of constant rolling a river rock pushed by the water becomes eventually polished, getting rid of all its previous irregularities. As water moves the rock rolls and its sharp corners disappear, leaving it round and soft. The same is said to happen when we roll and execute a technique by following circular patterns: we are refined by this process. Yet some schools prefer judo-like or other kinds of squared rolls which include straight action.

This explains why there are no break falls in Aiki-do practice. Falling or being slammed on the ground opposes the flowing process rolling produces and it jeopardizes the physical integrity of participants. Instead, a good deal of time may be devoted to rolling since it is a movement intended to enable students to polish themselves as they learn how to do it correctly. This is seen as cleansing and refinement from training, although it has also been considered as some kind of a personal "insurance": it protects practitioners from getting hurt after a bad fall. Practitioners are like river stones in Aiki, and as they learn how to "take the ground" and "roll" they gain flexibility and soften themselves. They improve by getting rid of all the irregularities found in their personalities.

The Aiki roll is an elegant, soft and safe movement, which must be done with a perfectly rounded body. Kurita *Shihan* recalls the Founder used to tell when someone's technique was wrong just by the sound their bodies as they rolled. This is a good analogy to use for refinement, and etiquette. It is rather obvious now that practicing the way of Aiki helps individuals with the irregularities in their tempers, characters and lives in general. This is the kind of work and education we can call Aiki-do and its main difference from fighting arts.

MISOGI

A CLEAN BODY   +   A CLEAN GI   +   A CLEAN TECHNIQUE
All these elements add up for a correct Aiki-do practice
(*Misogi* involves a physical, mental and practical cleansing)

An Aiki session

Although Aiki-do cannot be learned from books and a good instructor's guide is always mandatory, the following sections take a look to the practice session. They present an exploration of some of the main parts of a regular class and the main teachings/concepts students must always bear in mind. There are no step-by-step illustrations of the numerous Aiki technique details since presenting them through pictures is *"as tasteless and odorless as the food pictures in a menu"* (Kurita *Shihan*). Even words are useless when it comes to describe and explain the internal and spiritual contents of the most refined Aiki.

Our premise is to avoid sending people the wrong impression that Aiki can be learnt through pictures or animated cartoons. The ones included here are meant as a mere reference, and only when they have been absolutely necessary. Practicing the hidden-to-the-eye principles explored here are much more important than any picture sequences used to illustrate them.

This picture is misleading because it is not a fighting action; however, Aiki-do dynamics are exceedingly powerful

The garments

The uniform used for practice is called *keiko gi.* It consists of pants, a jacket and a belt. Black belt students and women wear a split, skirted-like trouser called *hakama.* This garment has one pleat in the back and five more in the front representing five highly valued virtues taken from the ancient *Samurai: justice, honor, truth, bravery,* and *loyalty.* (Kurita Yutaka *Shihan*)

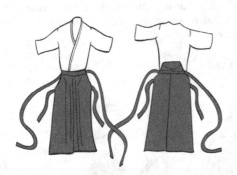

It is a Samurai-like garment which means it demands the practitioner to abide by a code of honesty and human dignity.

The black belt indicates the person who wears it has started the path or way (*do*), his own personal search for union, confluence and harmony (Aiki). It is never intended to show a mere *status* position placing those who wear it above others. That would be a token of arrogance in opposition to the true Aiki spirit.

More than a garment

Sitting (seiza): returning to ourselves

Every movement has precise and objective purposes and meanings in Aiki-do practice. The class starts as practitioners enter the *dojo*. A sitting posture (*seiza*) is assumed before jumping into the practice area, the mats (*tatami*), in order to show the student's willingness to participate. It is a way of asking for permission and when they are late they have to wait for the instructor's indication to step in. Then they choose a place to sit and assume *seiza*, mentally preparing their frame of mind to help them set the emotional tone needed in the training about to start.

Seiza, according to Kurita *Shihan,* is a return-to-one's-self activity that helps us to perceive our being, to clearly contemplate who we are, where we are, and what we want to accomplish with our practice. It is a meditation posture and it keeps our concentration smoothly running and alert.

It constitutes a first battle against our own selves. Nobody is able to stand it for more than 3 to 4 minutes when they lack the flexibility needed and their legs usually go numb quickly. Enduring this posture strengthens will and resolution, and helps us harness our energy. Japanese people believe that a child capable of sitting quiet in *seiza* shows much more energy than a child who is always jumping around. Concentration (bringing to the center) is crucial in Aiki and practitioners must realize there are several centers to pay attention to (refer to the glossary of basic terms in Chapter 5).

As they get used to this posture students are gradually able to stand it. They also learn it is definitely not a passive posture at all because it requires a lot of hard work from strong yet flexible legs. As practitioners progress they eventually find a certain degree of comfort in *seiza*, and feel just as if they were sitting on a soft air-cushion. Since it constitutes a personal struggle against our own will and determination, this posture teaches that we have the potential to grow and to carry out an enterprise. It proves we are capable of doing what everybody else does and it is a way to be victorious over one's self.

This posture is assumed when instructors teach, and when it hurts it is too hard to pay attention. Besides, students must be ready to stand up when resuming practice or when they are called by their instructor to demonstrate. Kurita *Shihan* points out how we must use both brain hemispheres in the sitting (static) and standing (dynamic) postures during class: the left, analytic side works while the instructor is demonstrating and explaining. But it has to be replaced by the work of the right intuitive hemisphere as soon as we stand up and start practice. At this moment no more thinking is to be done because it must give room to Aiki through the works of *ki awase* (joining through a *ki* action) and *ki musubi* (keeping attached and united by means of that same *ki* action).

Seiza is also Aiki-do's *shugyo* (transformation process). Kurita *Shihan* explains: "*It is a process similar to the hatching of a chicken, an action by which it opens its way to life.*" It is a transcendental process involved in a seemingly relaxing posture. *Shugyo* is considered a method for evolution and personal development, a method for the transformation of our life and conscience. Besides providing the preparatory mind frame or mentality for correct training, since it represents each one of the participants' wills and dispositions, *Seiza* had a specific and practical use in medieval times. It was a habit carried over by the ancient *Samurai* who remained in this posture whenever they were in the presence of a lord (*Shogun*). This was particularly true when they belonged to the enemy's army and came to deliver a message. Such a rule ensured they wouldn't be able to reach him, since a standing posture is obviously more dangerous: a lord could be unexpectedly attacked by a traitor if he was standing up before him.

The beginning of a session

But that meaning has nothing to do with *seiza* in current *Aikido* practice. When instructors sit closer to their students they sit as their equal. If they sit closer to the *kamiza*, where master Ueshiba's portrait is placed, they sit as O-Sensei's representatives. For obvious reasons only *uchideshi* can sit closer to it. If they sit close to their class they do so as a token of brotherhood and companionship, indicating they are also a part of the class. Additionally, *Seiza* is an expression of equality, a way to show there are no hierarchies, no differences, and no divisions. Everybody is at the same level.

Bowing (rei): asking for permission

The instructor sits close to his students as an elder brother

Besides being a way of giving O-Sensei the recognition he deserves, our bow is a sincere and humble promise to learn and do our best. It is Aiki's concept of respect as taught by Kurita *Shihan* because it is a way to ask master Ueshiba to give us his permission to try his Aiki. Practice must be correct and consistent with his teachings at all times.

The term for bowing is *rei* in Japanese and every session always begins and ends with a "thank you" bow as an act of respect and gratitude. It is given and received by people who are all at the same level since no body is superior in Aiki. Even the word *Sensei* means "one who came first" so instructors are like elder brothers and sisters, individuals who have many more responsibilities according to their broader experience.

Practice can be taken and practiced as a special ceremony too. As we have previously described, *chinkon kishin* is the name of the special salutation practiced by Kaiso Sensei at the beginning and end of his practice and it was "*to invite his God to come and be present during practice, so he had to finish with a similar movement as a farewell to the divine.*" (Kurita Yutaka *Shihan*)

We don't go to the *dojo* just to exercise our muscles, because Aiki-do is not a sport practiced in a gym. Its objective is to literally squeeze or wring out all dirt in our hearts, minds and bodies. The body and the practice uniform (*gi*) must always be clean and be a source of dignity. Training with dirty people who have not washed and ironed their uniforms, or who have long and dirty nails is uncomfortable and disgusting. The same happens when our partners don't show a clean, non-violent mentality during practice. Kurita *Shihan* says: "*Working with a violent person is like working with a rabid dog*" and there must be no hard feelings during an Aiki practice or any showing off behavior as a result of it.

The external appearance and cleanness of people reflect their internal spirits, minds and hearts. This is demonstrated in practice when we look for a clean and healthy execution of technique which are Aiki's means for a healthy expression and manifestation of our best as persons. A violent technique, one that causes pain of any sort or forces it and makes it unnatural and difficult denotes selfishness. Technique must then be *real* (not fake), *aesthetic* (beautiful) and *good* (constructive), which means *not bad* or intended to injure *Uke*. The persons receiving the action of *Nage* are used in combination with them in order to make Aiki possible, since it is by lending their body their *Nage* learn. *Nage*, the ones who are in control of Aiki, cannot act selfishly and hurt their own spirits, minds, and personalities by hurting others. If they act selfishly they never grow.

As can be seen, a session begins by working on attitudes, by changing them, and by being alert and ready, extending this attention towards the experience about to be lived. *Kokyu* (extension) is an element used in every single action or technique to develop *ki*. And the state of alertness it produces becomes the fundamental element of union between the different dimensions employed in the correct execution of techniques: it "channels" the energy of our *being* by means of it. *Kokyu* is an important part of Aiki breathing.

Spirit: attitudes in and out of the Dojo

Some people have interpreted attending a class as a chance to "steal" knowledge from their instructors. But Aiki has no thieves, except when practitioners really steal somebody else's energy during practice by not making their best effort and by just standing there with no interest to learn, to open their minds and to collaborate. Practice needs what has been called "a committed attack", which Kurita Yutaka *Shihan* understands as correct, flexible and united work. There is no such thing as soft and hard styles, but only violent (incorrect) or non-violent (correct) and flexible (Aiki) ways of doing things.

Arrogance must never be displayed since everybody must help each other to achieve the common goal of union and confluence Aiki practice is meant for. From the *kohai* (junior student), to the *sempai* (senior students), the *shidoin* (teaching assistants) and the *sensei* (instructors), everybody is there for each other.

When there is no humbleness even *seiza* puts practitioners at risk of falling to the ground, since an arrogant posture makes them bend backwards in such an angle that they may fall back: instructors and students must all be well balanced. The first token of humbleness is shown when they bow to each other, showing nobody is above anybody else in any sense.

After the initial bowing to the *kamiza*, instructors turn toward students and mutually bow to each other and say "*O negai shimasu*". This expression means "please"; used by students it means "*Please demonstrate*" and used by the instructor it means "*Please do as shown*". A mutual word is given to do each other's best. Practice will imprint in their minds all of the values they learn, such as non-violence, respect, compassion and mutual trust. Once they give their word they must keep it. Bowing to their instructor and classmates is a way to ask for permission to benefit from their mutual energy, will and work, since Aiki lets them share and multiply them by acting together so it is not a competition.

The responsibility of an instructor (*sensei*) is enormous: any lack of care, quality and category in practice leads Aiki to its extinction since any understandard practitioner may eventually become a poor instructor.

Advancing our personalities with "Tori fune undo"

Tori fune undo has been and still is an exercise practiced in "traditional" *dojo*. In Kurita *Shihan*'s school it has symbolized a rowing movement used to advance through an eternal Sea, as a train going towards the top of a mountain. O-Sensei saw it as representing a spiritual and imaginary journey throughout the Universe, although the unaware practitioner tends to see it as a mere warm up exercise. Some practitioners call this exercise *misogi* without realizing that the whole practice session is a cleansing opportunity and not only this initial exercise. As it helps advance our personality, it prepares our entrance to the path to Aiki. It is not supposed to be substituted by any other warm-up exercises borrowed from Yoga or other disciplines.

In *Kurita Juku* this exercise used to be made having in mind that it makes participants unite their efforts by "rowing" together in unison (Aiki), keeping the rhythm while moving forward, and using one and the same voice. It helps to concentrate the energy and equilibrium students must keep throughout the whole training session. Its execution denotes enthusiasm, ascendancy in life, advancement of our personality, and also group unity.

Aiki is always present and whenever the session begins it gives us a chance to discard and let go of any negativity. To learn how to fight is easy, but to learn how not to do it is not only harder but even more important: if it was easier our world would now be living in peace. Throughout history humanity has searched for this dream. To learn how to fight or just how to do a technique in order to annihilate an enemy goes against the true goals and practice of Aiki-do. Kurita *Shihan* has always stated: "*If everybody practiced the way of Aiki no one would need to practice it at all, since everybody would be living in harmony and peace, in true civilization.*"

After the rowing action is finished, students then start a simple warm up consisting of:

a)   A series of circular movements which start with a small concentrating and energetic shaking action made with the hands held together, with the left hand under the right one. This peculiar exercise is meant to gain concentration of the whole body.

b)   A series of movements done with the hands still held together starting to the left and switching to right following the Earth's rotation first. It is interesting to notice that just as our planet goes from left to right, movements in Aiki-do start with the left hand and in a left stance, allowing our right brain hemisphere to activate intuition first in order to use it as the foundation for practice. Careful attention is paid to keeping centered during the whole session.

c)   A series of movements where flexibility is used by bending over the sides as well as back and front. Attention here is paid to the effect of stretching in a similar way as that of a metal spring that returns to its original position. It is meant as a stretching and not a straining exercise.

d)   A series of movements where practitioners massage their bodies from knees to neck, and then their arms and wrists, to end with the feet, toes and soles of the feet for the sake of general health and as part of a gentle massage that works on our glands and blood circulation.

All of these exercises are designed to be part of action (techniques) so it is not necessary to combine them with any of the warm-up forms found in yoga or in sports since they serve a different purpose. Given that Aiki is not a sport, we don't really warm up as athletes do before they start practicing. Stretching exercises must be done with a "spring" effect which is looked for in order to be able to produce a "sling shot" or "bouncing" effect that will help us to go beyond mere muscular work; in fact, such an effect is used in the execution of techniques.

Warming up, making light: glandular massage and blood circulation

The series of warm-up exercises described in (d) above make a big difference between *Aikido* and other arts. They are not the usual sit-ups, push-ups, jumping and stretching exercises one could expect as the usual training preparation. They are done in *seiza* as shown below and consist of a series of light and rhythmical tapping over our arms, neck base, shoulders, thighs, and lower back. It includes some work to develop flexible wrists and ankles by rotating them both clockwise and counter-clockwise. This strengthens our joints and keeps us healthy.

This kind of warm-up is not found in other arts because their activity is different in class and they don't have to stimulate our glands but our muscles. The Aiki-do particular warm-up is basically a set of reflexology exercises that stimulate nervous points in our feet. As we grab our partners other points are stimulated with our grab (*dori,* in Japanese). By means of their grab our practice partners (*Uke*) also act positively on certain points found in their own palms at the same time they stimulate nerve points on our wrists.

As with any other Aiki action, some grabs are also done in circular ways. Aiki-do promotes a healthier body and it never compromises its safety to any risk of injury. Master Ueshiba's perfect practice meant zero injuries, which is possible only with a high level of technical execution. A good performance reduces the risk of injury. Movements are precise and harmonious because the way of Aiki fosters our well-being.

A unifying posture (hanmi)

A pyramid is the more stable geometrical posture and it is supposed to "capture" energy. The truth is that when we stand up in front of our practice partners, a triangular stance (*sankaku*) is used to reduce the area that can be touched or run over by an attack. By assuming this posture, our frontal body area is somehow "minimized" (*han* is half, and *mi* is body), something the Founder called *hito-e-mi* (which can be understood as a "minimal body front"). This posture is natural and has nothing to do with a challenging or defensive stance.

Hanmi affords absolute firmness and balance. Aiki-do practice has no kicks that may weaken it so it is also used to concentrate and steer our personal center (see the glossary in Chapter 5). Along with the fact that it helps us keep our weight balanced and holds our vertical (*north-south*) axis, *sankaku* is a triangular posture that results when feet and hands are placed just as when a person is holding a sword. Thus it is indeed a means to capture the Universe's energy from the ground because it works like the roots of a tree. It is used only with right stance since the left stance uses *hito-e*, which is not a triangle.

Hanmi is our working posture, and it can be practiced having the right (*migi*) or left (*hidari*) foot to the front. This leads to what is known as *ai hanmi*, when both practitioners have the same foot to the front (right or left), or *gyaku hanmi*, when they have a different foot to the front. These postures also promote the use of both right and left brain sides in sequential turns.

Hito-e and *sankaku* **allow us to "take" energy from the Earth and the Universe. It roots our body and helps us grow so kicks are never used in Aiki. (Kurita *Shihan*)**

FOOT WORK (*ASHI SABAKI*) IS IMPORTANT IN *AIKI*

WE MAY USE

OMOTE SANKAKU   OR   **URA SANKAKU**

THIS STANCE LEAVES
US IN FRONT OF UKE

THIS ONE IS USED TO KEEP OUT
OF THE LINE OF ATTACK

Used only in reference to right-hand stances, *ura sankaku* is much safer and helps avoid confrontation. It is a natural stance from which a lot of varied movements are done, right upon two distinct basic directions (*omote*, front, and *ura*, back) and two mobilizations (*irimi*, entering, and *tenkan*, pivoting or opening). An Aiki posture affords the weight or quality necessary for an adequate technical execution so as to help us capture the flow of the Universe. Practiced individually or in combinations, and through the right use of *ma'ai* (overlapping) and *kokyu* (extension), only the right postures help us work with confluent actions.

Grabs and strikes: our chance to grow

There are diverse grabs (*dori*) and strikes (*uchi*) in *Aikido* practice and they are used by our *Uke* (practice partner) in order to create a chance for us to grow. They help us realize the works of the Universe since they make us experience centripetal and centrifugal forces in the over-lapping and continuous turn-taking actions.

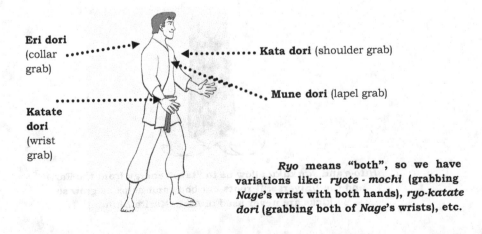

Eri dori (collar grab)

Kata dori (shoulder grab)

Mune dori (lapel grab)

Katate dori (wrist grab)

Ryo means "both", so we have variations like: *ryote - mochi* (grabbing *Nage*'s wrist with both hands), *ryo-katate dori* (grabbing both of *Nage*'s wrists), etc.

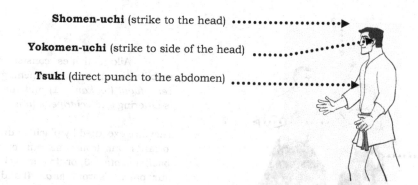

Shomen-uchi (strike to the head) ••••••••••••••••••▶

Yokomen-uchi (strike to side of the head) ••••••••••••

Tsuki (direct punch to the abdomen) •••••••••••••••••

These grabs and strikes are part of all *Aikido* programs. They were inherited from previous combat arts, from a paradigm consisting of attacks and defenses between two enemies. Aiki considers them as detonators or vehicles for the cause-effect interaction between two or more partners. By means of the application of such vehicles ("techniques") they have a chance to express a constructive and positive mind set and the right attitudes intended to improve their lives.

FROM AN OLD MILITARY POINT OF VIEW, THESE STRIKES ARE INTENDED:

1. As an attack to the head of an army (the leader): SHO-MEN UCHI
2. To separate the head from the body (the army): YOKO-MEN UCHI
3. As an attack to the nucleus of the army (its center): TSUKI

(Kurita Yutaka *Shihan*)

Both grabs and strikes are part of the process of learning Aiki. According to Kurita *Shihan* we must ask ourselves why or what is the purpose in practicing them. Let's take *katate dori* as an example: we might say it constitutes the first stage in the communication we establish with our practice partner. If we grab (*dori*) with too much strength without a real connection our practice may turn into a fight and blocks our chance for development. The Aiki grab is always done by closing our fist starting with the little finger up to the index middle and the thumb, except for the index finger as it is done when holding a *bokken* (wooden sword). The same may happen in our everyday lives: subdue your friends, workmates or relatives, and you will lose their respect and consideration.

Action: the Universe's dynamic movements

After an action starts, the next thing we do is to place ourselves in a unifying and strong position, in a safe area from which we are able to absorb our partner's action and to redirect it towards a non-existent target and nullifying it. Aiki movements imitate those of the Universe, they are harmonious and they never antagonize.

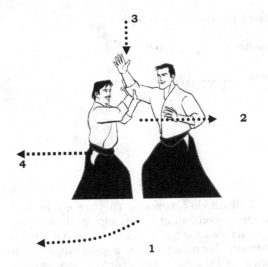

Aiki activities consist of two mobilizations: one is opening and *centrifugal* (*tenkan* – **1**) and the other is entering and *centripetal* (*irimi* – **2**).

They are executed by placing ourselves towards our front and our partner's back (*omote* – **3**) or to our back and our partner's front (*ura* – **4**) and they cover diverse circular trajectories or paths and thus follow the Universe's order (*Ai*) by using its core force(*ki*). Their purpose is to eliminate any possibility of clashing or running over practice partners.

These actions create a dynamic that literally suck up our partner's action and enables *Nage* to nullify *Uke's* weight in order to be able to lead, hold and take them to the ground (never to throw them). Such movements are commonly described to act as forces similar to those of a hurricane or a tornado, and are always both centripetal and centrifugal in nature, in left-right and right-left combinations.

FROM AN OLD MILITARY POINT OF VIEW THESE MOBILIZATIONS ARE INTENDED:

1. To change your perspective in order to surprise an army (TENKAN)
2. To surprise an army by entering against its perspective (IRIMI)
3. To work on the front view point of an army (OMOTE)
4. To work on the rear, hidden or blind point of an army (URA)

(Kurita Yutaka *Shihan*)

Again, these mobilizations are part of Aiki's learning process and they are the continuation of the grabs previously mentioned. So we must find out and understand their particular purposes.

Uke's rolling (and sometimes jumping) is a common practice but it must always be done in an active way. *Uke's* role is never passive in Aiki, he doesn't play the role of "the defeated one" so his/her work must be as active, continuous, and correct as the one done by *Nage*.

Irimi, tenkan, omote and ura: four different actions

There is an important footwork (*ashi sabaki*) that must be described in order to make our practice more precise. The correct application of these movements lets us place our body in the right spot and direction. Their goal is to teach *Nage* how to adapt (*ai*) to a situation and to learn about the direction their life is heading to.

● When *Uke* steps in, *Nage* has two choices: to accommodate his body right at the front (*omote*) or to make an entrance (*irimi*) –note the numbered sequence– The foot work is done with *tomo-e* (crossing feet, **CF**).

O M O T E

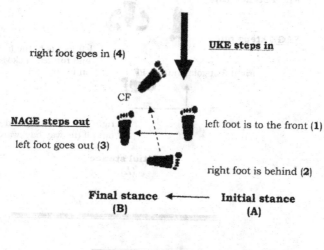

I R I M I

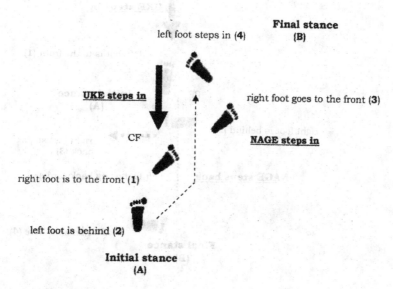

When *Uke* steps in, *Nage* has two additional choices: to pivot behind *Uke* (*tenkan*) or to take his direction (*ura*) –the sequence is numbered–. Here the foot work is with *go-ho* (parallel feet, **PF**).

TENKAN

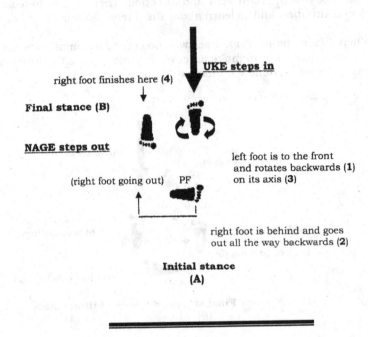

UKE steps in

right foot finishes here (**4**)

Final stance (B)

NAGE steps out

left foot is to the front and rotates backwards (**1**) on its axis (**3**)

(right foot going out)   **PF**

right foot is behind and goes out all the way backwards (**2**)

Initial stance (A)

URA

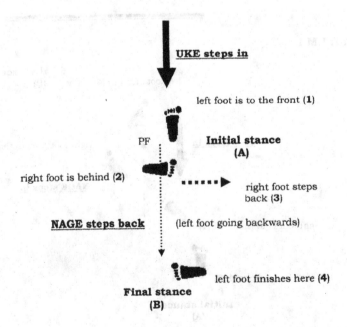

UKE steps in

left foot is to the front (**1**)

PF   **Initial stance (A)**

right foot is behind (**2**)

right foot steps back (**3**)

NAGE steps back   (left foot going backwards)

left foot finishes here (**4**)

Final stance (B)

In addition to the different mobilizations and the use of space when they are performed in *ai hanmi* (same side posture) or in *gyaku hanmi* (opposite sides), there is one more difference taught by Kurita *Shihan*: left and right movements are not used in the same way and they produce a different effect because the latter is descending and *contracting*, whereas the former is ascending and *expanding*.

MOBILIZATIONS TO THE LEFT AND RIGHT ARE NOT THE SAME:

A CONTRACTION MOVEMENT TO THE LEFT PUSHES IN	AN EXPANSION MOVEMENT TO THE RIGHT PULLS OUT
(IT'S LIKE PUSHING A SCREW IN OR LIKE THE HELIX OF A BOAT)	*(IT'S LIKE PULLING A SCREW OUT OR LIKE THE HELIX OF A CHOPPER)*

 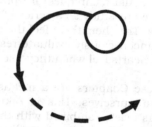

A CONCENTRATION ACTION (FROM RIGHT TO LEFT) STARTS FROM AWAY	A DECONCENTRATION ACTION (FROM LEFT TO RIGHT) ENDS AWAY

Kurita *Shihan* complains many of these things are not taught anymore, or just barely, but they are part of the most serious and deepest nature studied by the Founder. These contracting and expanding mobilizations make for a complete sphere and total Aiki-do as they use two complementing actions similar to the works of both brain hemispheres. They are also present in the works of the *jo* (a staff), which is intended for the left side of the body (to activate the right side), and the *bokken* (a wooden sword), intended for the right side of the body (to activate the work of the left side). Both are used to practice concentrating and expanding actions in order to cover every angle.

Holding or pinning is part of common practice

Static and dynamic forces working together

Aiki-do practice has two complementing *waza* (lines of action): *katame* (locking and 'pinning') and *nage* ('throwing') to promote the work of both static and dynamic forces. In regards to *katame waza* (the 'pining' lines of action) there are five basic "chapters," as O-Sensei called them: *ikkyo, nikyo, sankyo, yonkyo,* and *gokyo* (chapters 1, 2, 3, 4 and 5). He envisioned our partners' bodies as the "books" from which we learn. So it is not good to "tear" their pages off, to hurt them. Aiki-do cannot be practiced in a fighting martial way because that jeopardizes the physical and moral integrity of all practice partners.

These chapters do not constitute a self-defense program: they are means for self-exploration. From this perspective techniques are not applied against one's partner but mainly "against one's self" (Kurita Yutaka *Shihan*). This is amazing and might seem absurd or even shocking when the true nature of Aiki practice is not understood. Aiki techniques are proactive, not reactive. In addition, these chapters are to guide our study as a series of sections that make room for students to express themselves. They help them feel the quality and category of their performance, so that they can unconsciously evaluate results and realize what their spirits work like and what their hearts feel when they use them.

These Chapters are a means to an end which is never to destroy or defeat anyone but ourselves. This is Aiki victory (*Takemusu*). Since Aiki doesn't see its chapters as twists combined with throwing movements, the holding moves described here are to be done taking a continuous care of ourselves and our partners: the more comfortable *Uke* is, the more Aiki the technique is. This is a real challenge if we consider this is to be done in a context of real attack-defense sequences. Martial arts don't make fighters look after their challengers and themselves!

A big difference in *Kurita Juku Aiki* is that practice has also changed. Instead of practicing the usual "*katate dori – ikkyo*" Kurita *Shihan* makes his students practice "*katate dori– shomen-uchi – ikkyo*". Or, instead of the usual "*shomen–uchi – ikkyo*" he makes them practice "*shomen–uchi – katate dori – ikkyo*", as well as many other combinations. From his point of view these variations are helping him fill what he considers to be gaps master Ueshiba left on purpose for the sake of simplification. However they are presented here as they have been traditionally taught, together with the grabs and strikes they are a series of five complementing centripetal and centrifugal forces. They are explained here following the usual way –with only two components– in order to avoid confusion among readers who might find *Kurita Juku Aiki* concepts disconcerting.

- *Ikkyo* – "Chapter One" gives us a chance to learn about reaching out. Self-control is practiced by taking and holding *Uke*'s arm as he/she comes, say, with *shomen-uchi* (a strike to the head), *katate-dori* (a grab to the wrist) or *tsuki* (direct punch) while having control of their whole body and moving the arms in a circular way while they are led by the body. When we play *Nage*'s role we never go beyond our own level (our center is aligned with that of our partner).

Ikkyo is meant to discover the work of *ki* and it is the most important *katame waza* to be learnt.

START:

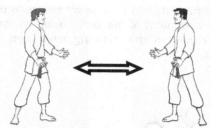

When action starts, both *Uke* and *Nage*'s centers (hips) are at the same "level", but when action starts and finishes *Uke* is taken at a lower level.

IKKYO (finish)

- **Nikyo** – "Chapter Two" is designed to control and help us to know ourselves by taking and holding our partner's wrist and body but now from a physically higher position or level. The challenge here is to make it effectively without hurting *Uke* at all, allowing for flexible responses on *Uke*'s part and without abusing him/her by inflicting pain on his/her wrists, which is always easier. *Ki* works in a different direction and allows for *Uke* to be flexible and relaxed. *Uke*'s center (at the hips) is always at a lower level than *Nage*'s.

NIKYO (middle)

- **Sankyo** – When working as *Nage* we are positioned at a lower level in this "Chapter Three". The idea is to explore what happens by using *ki* upwards in a situation where we control ourselves by holding *Uke* with a rotary movement of his/her hands, wrists, head and body as we lift his/her elbows in an ascending action here that directs and controls at all times.

START:

Uke's center (hips) is above *Nage's*

SANKYO (finish)

- **Yonkyo** – "Chapter Four" is indeed a great chance to exercise a crossing *ki* in order to control ourselves by taking *Uke* with both of our hands upon his/her wrist together with a following downward rotation of our whole body together with *Uke*'s.

START:

Uke's center (hips) is taken right below Nage's center level

YONKYO (almost finished)

- **Gokyo** – "Chapter Five" is the last of the most common and simplest series of Aiki actions. It gives us a chance to explore our *ki* and ourselves by trapping *Uke's* wrist and body by making a big circle that goes up, out and down right in front of him/her. It is similar to *ikkyo* but it is done with our hands crossing in front of *Uke*.

START:

Uke's center (hips) is above *Nage's* in a different stance.

GOKYO (almost finished)

All of these five actions complete an approaching process that puts both *Nage* and *Uke* in communication. They require the active participation of both partners, which can be lacking when *Uke* turn themselves into just passive recipients of *Nage*'s work. The work required from *Uke* should be explored in a separate book.

Variations from behind (ushiro)

There is one more situation, called *ushiro* (coming from the back), in addition to the numerous combinations and angles of frontal Aiki practice. As an analogy it translates as unexpected situations since action is started by *Uke* standing and coming from behind. This means people learn to react even when they cannot see the problem since correct application helps overcome any difficulties.

NAGE BRINGS *UKE* TO HIS FRONT SO HE CAN ALWAYS FACE HIM

The resolution must always be harmonic, no matter how terrible, difficult and out-of-sight the situation might seem. So Aiki-do works with four *ushiro* attacks":

USHIRO KUBISHIME   **USHIRO RYO-KATATE DORI**

USHIRO ERI DORI   **USHIRO RYO-KATA DORI**

Dynamic ways that emulate the breathing Universe

The second line of training contents, the "throws" or dynamic actions, was taught by the Founder as a way to emulate the continuously moving forces of the Universe. They are called *nage waza* and they make use of both centripetal and centrifugal forces, an interaction that makes technique breathe and gain true life. Hence these actions cannot be considered throws or slams.

This second set of movements consists of a series of actions that can be used against any of the different previously mentioned "attacks". But indeed they are part of the universal breathing since the forces used in them reflect the Universe's inhaling-exhaling processes. It must be emphasized that *nage waza* are not throwing techniques because they are not meant to slam our partners or to treat them like bags of trash that can just be just disposed of without any consideration. When these dynamic movements are applied, *Uke*'s balance is taken from him/her so they can be taken to the ground in a controlled manner and not because *Nage* throws them.

All of the activities developed by master Ueshiba show the work of the Universe. Centripetal and centrifugal forces overlap and cannot be clearly differentiated because what is centripetal for *Nage* is centrifugal for *Uke,* and vice versa. They are equivalent to our inhaling and exhaling actions and they are always present working together during practice.

-      ***Kokyu-ho*.-** This breathing action helps practitioners to learn how to join and direct *Uke*'s energy. It is the foundation from which *Nage* learns how their mutual energies may be overlapped (*ki awase*) and it helps to work in such a way that does not only make them add, but also multiply their energy.

SUWATE (SITTING) KOKYU-HO

By means of *kokyu-ho*, *Nage* attracts and connects with *Uke* in a centripetal (*inhaling*) force and leads him/her to the right or left in a centrifugal (*exhaling*) force. As a continuation of this movement *Nage* leans towards *Uke* always holding and tying their mutual energy by means of *musubi* (the union-keeping factor).

Without ever detaching or getting apart, they go back and resume their initial position, fluently proceeding to the other side without stopping. This is repeated three more times and they switch roles. Holding and manipulating somebody else's energy involves one's own personal control and it must be done effortlessly. Unfortunately some schools might miss this point and they may cut their union after each and every action causing a detachment and a waste of energy. In regards to the rest of the actions described herein, such a performance only causes a definitive interruption of *ki no nagare* (the flow of *ki*).

- **Kokyu-nage**.- This is an "extending" action done by describing a large *tenkan* circle in order to produce attraction in a centripetal (*inhaling*) force. *Nage* receives *Uke*, changes the relative position, and leads, inviting *Uke* to follow the original direction. When applied, *Nage* attracts *Uke*, and leads in a non-stop movement, allowing him/her to do as they initially aimed. This action usually finishes with an extension by *Nage* in a centrifugal (*exhaling*) force that puts *Uke* down.

There is no conflict or confrontation in Aiki: *awase* is dynamic and *musubi* works to keep a physical and a spiritual contact between *Nage* and *Uke* until they start each subsequent new action and after "squaring" all things up.

- **Irimi-nage**.- This is an "entering" action emulating a sea tide. When applied, *Nage* attracts *Uke*, leading into his/her personal space, as an invitation to enter in a centripetal (*inhaling*) force, and then *Nage* puts *Uke* "back into the sea" in a centrifugal (*exhaling*) force, whilst protecting them. *Nage* protects *Uke* just as the Sea protects fish, so it is never a violent or projection or slamming action.

AWASE is dynamic too, and MUSUBI works as a uniting tidal wave

- **Shiho-nage**.- This is an "entering-and-turning" action by which *Nage* attracts *Uke*'s energy in a centrifugal (*exhaling*) force by means of his/her arm's length, whilst entering or pivoting in order to make a final, non-violent and non-hurting "cut" that makes *Nage* join with *Uke* in a centripetal (*inhaling*) force.

In the usual AIKIDO style NAGE grabs UKE

But when an Aiki action is applied, it allows *Nage* to take care of *Uke* in a completely different way, allowing *musubi* to be present all the way from start to end. In fact, there is no need to grab *Uke*'s hand!

The AIKI style is different: *NAGE* does not grab *UKE*

- ***Kote-gaeshi*.-** This is a "pivoting" action that finishes with a movement equal to the one made when a faucet is turned; it allows energy to "run" just like water.

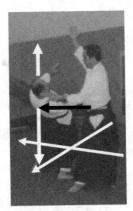

CENTRIFUGAL / CENTRIPETAL

When *kote-gaeshi* is applied the Aiki way, *Nage* attracts *Uke*, leads onto his center and to the side, and eventually makes *Uke* describe a big circle that takes him/her to the ground and not necessarily into the air. *Awase* starts from the pivot, and *musubi* is kept all the way to the end and even after. *Kote-gaeshi* must be performed free from any violence, but many *Aikido* styles do this in such a way that *Uke* goes to the air and slams. Although quite impressive, it should be checked if the action is being merely used in a way that *Uke* is treated as a disposable thing by *Nage* and without the slightest consideration of *Uke* at all!

(*Chapter 3 offered a brief analysis of the differences between Daito-ryu, Aikido and Aiki, as taught by Kurita Yutaka Shihan*)

- **Kaiten-nage**,- This is an "entering and leading" action differentiated from the previous one by a mobilization that allows *Nage* to step under *Uke*'s arm or to step outside with a *Tenkan* (the circular, outside movement) so that *Uke* is lead towards his/her own center in a centripetal (*inhaling*) action and is then led into a natural centrifugal (*exhaling*) roll.

It also emulates a tidal wave as *irimi*, but the relative positions of both partners change. When applied, *Nage* attracts *Uke*, leads all the way down to the ground, and by a twist of the arm *Uke* is brought in and out to finish with an exiting move. Both *irimi* and *tenkan* are used and *Uke*'s head should always be kept facing towards the exiting movement so he/she can never face *Nage* and counter his/her action. *Awase* and *musubi* are found here in a different angle application.

- **Tenchi-nage**.- This is an "attracting/entering", centripetal/centrifugal (*inhaling/exhaling*) action. As its name indicates, it unites us to Heaven (*ten*) and Earth (*chi*) taking advantage of a vertical axis that uses, as in some of the previous actions, the centripetal and centrifugal forces of the Universe. *Nage* attracts *Uke*, leads into his/her own personal space, and then connects with both heaven and earth, attracting *Uke* and leading him/her to exit as he enters.

**AWASE and MUSUBI combined in a TEN-CHI
(heaven-earth) action**

Some additional lines of action schools include in their *Aikido* programs are:

- **Aiki-nage**.- This is a "non-clashing" action where confrontation is completely avoided since it prevents both *Nage* and *Uke* from running into each other.

Although this action is designed to avoid any conflict, it implies an enormous risk of injury: the absence of *awase* and *musubi* elements implies *Uke* remains undetached from *Nage* and depends 100% on his experience to safely get out of the way. Since this is usually done by means of a fall or an excellent clean roll this is a quite different example of a non-fighting, Aiki action that manifests the centrifugal forces of free objects in the Universe.

- **Koshi-nage**.- This spectacular move is very popular. It resembles a traditional martial art throw since it allows *Nage* to slam Uke. It may be dangerous or lethal if wrongly applied, and *Nage* can get a bad injury on his/her back if anything goes wrong. There are certain variations that help students practice it in such a way that they don't need to engage in a violent slamming throw.

- **Sumi-otoshi**. – This is another simple and efficient action to take *Uke* down. It is usually applied by stepping diagonally forward to *Uke*'s side. The idea is to lift his/her legs in order to make them go to the ground. Again, it is not necessary to throw them away as a piece of trash. *Nage* may control *Uke* by extending power and by entering but always taking care of them. If it is done wrongly this action is not being practiced in a non-violent Aiki way.

- **Juji-garami**. – In this action an entrance is made after holding *Ukes*' arms and locking them onto each other. *Nage* is able to bring them to the ground just by stepping in. In *Kurita Juku Aiki* there are not really such things as falling or slamming, since there is always a way to take *Uke* down and put him/her on the ground without ever detaching.

UKE trusts and depends completely on NAGE

Noteworthy: all of these actions (*waza*) are not to be taken as separate or independent from each other. They are elements that can be combined and so add contents in order to avoid an empty practice. In *Kurita Juku Aiki* training they are integrated in order to be used in a true Aiki way. The fundamental approach is this: *ki* must be used in all of them and *kokyu-nage* was designed to sense and develop it. Once understood, it becomes an integral and indivisible part of all other actions (*irimi-nage, shiho-nage*, etc).

Schools that may have traditionally taught all of these techniques in a separate way, as if they were independent of each other, might have been practicing them incompletely. As Kurita *Shihan* states: "*When they are only beautiful or impressive, the activity performed is like an empty but gorgeous box used for a present: they appear nice to the sight but they contain nothing.*"

Fundamental concepts taught by Kurita Yutaka Shihan

The following concepts are additionally implied premises contained in the practice of the "chapters" and "dynamic" line of actions described.

✓   **Level** - It is an important aspect related to *weight* and *heaviness*. The heavier the posture, the more we are rooted to the ground and thus the greater quality of our technique. Things with quality are mostly heavy and sturdy. For example, take a look at: cars (compare a Cadillac with a VW), books (hard vs. paper back covers), furniture (real wood vs. plywood), etc. Even O-Sensei's calligraphy changed through the years becoming thicker and thicker. Hence we can say that cheap things are usually thin and light both in a literal or figurative way.

In spite of this, the objective of Aiki controlling movements is not just to see how they work on *Uke* in order to harm them, but to see how *Nage* can be able to find in all of them a way to develop his/her self, to find imaginative ways to end conflict, and to be correct. They are reminders of a fair play and a positive spirit (heart), something "heavier" and more serious than fighting and competition. Furthermore, they must always have the following *izanau*, *awase* and *musubi* elements to insure they are in a state of real Aiki which makes partners join in order to find, add and multiply their energies.

✓   ***Izanau, awase and musubi*** – These elements are also related to category. *Quality* must always be a part of our practice. Otherwise it will be simple, incomplete, incorrect and worthless, not to say violent and aggressive. They are to be used when dealing with any of the "attacks" and "holds" used in practice and kept until all the action is finished. They make a big difference in Aiki-do practice.

In *shomen-uchi*, *Nage* invites and attracts *Uke* (***izanau***), joins with him/her (***awase***) and keeps them both united (***musubi***) until the end with a holding or a flowing line of action.

Modalities of practice (*waza*)

Except for the *ushiro* variations previously described, Aiki-do actions are usually practiced in one of the modalities described in this section. They can be used in combinations too but it must be noticed that the work is not the same when *Nage* and *Uke* work on their knees (*suwate*) and when *Nage* is on his/her knees and *Uke* is standing up (*hanmi handachi*) or when they are both on their feet (*tachi waza*).

All actions may be practiced with both practitioners sitting on their knees, a variation called ...

SUWARI WAZA

Then as mobilization expands *Uke* can have *Nage* out of his/her reach, so this makes it necessary for *Uke* to stand up in order to get closer again in order to reach *Nage*. This leads them to work in a situation where the latter is still sitting and *Uke* stands up to go on with the work. This is known as...

HANMI HANDACHI

And as their movements continue expanding both need to stand up, providing them with new sets of angles and stances they can cover while they work.

The work done is different in all these three modalities and it is a common mistake to try to use the same mobilizations in each one of them. Every situation gives a certain perspective that requires a different response.

TACHI WAZA

Any of these modalities of practice implies the use of three most important Aiki elements: *izanau*, *ki awase* and *ki musubi*. Each and every single one contains specific and well differentiated aspects and they cannot be considered as mere stance variations.

NAGE - UKE

SUWARI WAZA   **HANMI HANDACHI**   **TACHI WAZA**

One training modality takes participants to the next one due to an expanding effect:

  a) practitioners start from *suwari waza*, and,
  b) as soon as they get farther apart they must stand up in order to get closer quickly.

This transition from one modality to the next one is also used to teach about *kokyu* (expansion).

Teaching methodology [34]

Aiki-do instructors follow a methodology in which several aspects are contemplated. They go from hygiene, an important personal token of consideration towards our own persons and our practice partners, to the analysis, application and correction of what is learned, involving our person and senses as a whole. The fact is that we learn through our bodies though, since all teachings derive from the meaning and transcendence of our physical action.

- **Body-mind hygiene**: the practice place (*dojo*), the practice uniform (*keiko gi*) and the body of each participant must be perfectly clean.

  Kurita Yutaka *Shihan* points out that our body must be a reflection of our heart. So if we are clean on the outside we must be clean on the inside. Many things and people may superficially clean and yet be intimately dirty. Thus personal hygiene includes our spirit and heart (*kokoro*). Part of a clean living style may consist in getting plenty of sleep, not abusing alcohol or eating wisely before practice, but above all it requires a clean, positive and constructive mind, a will to abstain from putting dirt (selfishness, violence) in Aiki practice since it is an activity intended for cleansing or purification, according to the Founder's true *budo*.

- **Mental attitude**: Aiki instructors regard their disciples as mates. Being like siblings, they care for them accordingly, helping them to get rid of their ego and to unveil their self. Students see each other as companions and not as enemies or competitors. Advanced practitioners must guide less skilled ones and they all must have a big smile when they work, not a big frown or a hostile face. They must enjoy technique and not suffer it. Everybody must always be grateful and

---

[34] Adapted from Tamura Nobuyoshi's *Aikido and Etiquette and Transmission* (see our References).

considerate. The mental attitude emerges from the correct activity of the body (respect) since attending a class is to do our best.

- **Demonstration**: every one must be attentive and fully awake with all their five senses on what is about to transpire in class. The instructor's demonstration has to be as clear and precise as possible, and students must be able to capture everything through their senses. When they emphasize the basic fundamentals they must make it easier for students to understand them.

  Students must not talk during practice: it is considered that their minds open as soon as they shut their mouths. They will only bow to one another at the beginning and ending of each movement as well as when switching partners and asking them to interact. Nobody is allowed to act as the instructor, and when somebody has or thinks they have a better understanding, they can always show it by means of their performance. Words distract their attention and centeredness and lead to verbal disputes or even physical fights.

- **Explanation and mind work** must provide for the purpose and method of practice, highlighting the points that require special attention to achieve a perfect imitation by students. According to Kurita *Shihan*, this means they will first use their understanding (*left brain hemisphere*) during the explanation and as they stand up and start practice they must switch to their intuition and personal talent (*right brain hemisphere*). They are just oriented as to how they can unite all the different pieces of the puzzle and each individual is responsible for their own intuitive learning.

- **Analysis** is done by the left side of our brains. When a technique is demonstrated or explained it can be and is always analyzed or thought about by our left brain's logic. Since it contains multiple aspects and elements, it is usually divided into several fundamental parts. In *Kurita Juku Aiki* it is important to emphasize the internal ('hidden')

components of a technique as well as its spiritual and social application and relationships to everyday life.

Superficial technique is irrelevant, but practitioners may tend to worry too much about it and about mastering it. This will make them fail to understand that it is just a means or tool for the expression of something deeper lying under that surface. They must feel and sense what they do before they worry about mere form.

- **Imitation and pro-activeness:** students need to reproduce each technique/action without questioning it and preferably using their right brain. No questions are allowed unless the instructor accepts them during a verbal explanation. [35] The best way to ask a question is by showing the instructor through our performance. The best way to help a partner to do well too is by working correctly and doing one's best. Movements must be sensed, felt and enjoyed, not just analyzed. Kurita *Shihan* advises to use the right brain hemisphere here so that intuition is put to work, giving a new impulse to the left brain, and taking comprehension to a higher level, even when there won't be any words and thoughts to explain things.

Nobody needs to boast after an excellent performance, and everyone must be happy. Competition is not allowed in any form since it takes students nowhere when they try to show their partners that they are unable to do things. Besides, those who perform well are in control, they can show by example and as the action is going on. No body should blame anybody else before analyzing their own performance first and trying to find what works and what doesn't work in one's self, in one's intentions, will and spirit.

- **Non-mechanical repetition**: it allows for the assimilation of all constituent elements of a "technique" and it must be done more intuitively than intellectually, not just mechanically or, even worse, consciously (*left brain work*). Practice follows immediately after a demonstration by the instructor. It is necessary because we learn from our body movements, but we are always advised against mechanical repetition since it hinders our growth and understanding. Each action must be a new one, like a brand new day. It is to be felt and tasted.

Speed, power, and precision are progressively accomplished so no mistakes will be overlooked. Kurita *Shihan* worries about errors early on in practice and due to bad instructorship or lazy students, since this only leaves them with less and less understanding and quality development for the future. He stops the class right after any mistake, then he pinpoints what is wrong and students have no other choice but to study after class, always reviewing between classes. This also shows their interest to learn, study, and do their best.

---

[35] There are people who say *"When I was O-Sensei's student I asked him such and such a question"*, but as Kurita *Shihan* reports the Founder never answered anybody's questions (emerged from the left brain), since he simply demonstrated instead (he used his right brain, whose work cannot be put in words).

- **Correction**: it is not enough to correct the appearance of our techniques. It is necessary to try and understand them by cutting off all the roots of incomprehension and error. Care must be given to the use of good breathing (*kokyu*, not what we do with our lungs), as is explained in the next Chapter. The work of our feet, the use of our hands, the level changes of our hips as we move and the indispensable use of *ki*, all add to the holistic action of our body and heart abiding by principles such as *izanau, awase, musubi, aiki no michi* and many others in complete absence of *selfishness*.

As we have previously stated, the Aiki *senses* (sight, smell, touch, hear and taste), as well as the use of "breath", are absolutely different from our five biological senses; they are related to our body but also to our practice partners. (Kurita Yutaka *Shihan*) [36]

- **Peer observation**: it is important to carefully observe everybody else's "techniques" which includes the instructor as well as advanced and beginning students. Everybody can visually and sensitively compare their own actions with those from others. One must always observe, meditate and do in order to improve, and double the effort every time so that understanding is eventually grasped.

Chapter 6 includes a discussion on how this also leads to a system based on responsibility and not on authority, thus offering new possibilities in fields ranging from business and administration to our personal lives. It is important to insist that competition must be completely absent during this observation and imitation process.

---

[36] Such senses are basic constituents of *ki*, the "magic force" practitioners look for during practice. If we use *ki* we use our "biology," our whole being. Once more, it is noticeable that Kurita *Shihan* teaches that technique is supposed to breathe (a concept explained in Chapter 5). By the same trend, when he says technique has a taste and a smell, he is obviously not talking about our biological senses. This has to be explored as a new set of five senses. Kurita *Shihan* insists Aiki implies "*seeing what nobody sees, smelling what nobody smells, listening to what nobody listens to, and making technique breathe and have a taste.*" Technique should be alive, not dead or stagnant. Obviously this can only be understood by direct demonstration, since words are always insufficient, inaccurate and/or misleading.

- **Gratitude**: this is an element that must always be present. Appreciation is shown to both instructor and classmates. At the end of class everybody will say: "*Domo arigato gozai mashita*" (thanks a lot for what you've done) because everyone has collaborated for the benefit and development of the whole class. [37]

The methodology described resembles a process followed by ancient *Samurai* as depicted in old woodblock paintings. It consists of: *observation* (watching carefully what happens), *meditation* (thinking about it) and *action* (proceeding to hands-on practice and experience, which is in fact learning through our bodies and senses).

An Aiki wrap up

The Aiki session concludes with a movement designed for stretching our back and vertebrae. It leaves them in place and provides an additional way to care for the body with a final massage. Since there are no slaves in *Aikido*, this last action is also done as everything else in Aiki: in a special and careful way.

HAISHIN UNDO (back stretching)

Observe carefully and you will notice that *Uke* is grabbing *Nage* in such a way that he can let go whenever he wants to do so. In a different paradigm *Nage* would be grabbing and controlling *Uke*, and deciding for both of them. In a usual reaction, when a person takes somebody from the wrists or lapel, it is to lift them up in order to exercise control. This is not so in Aiki, where the last action taken consists of one

---

[37] O-Sensei taught gratitude is fundamental: we must thank the Universe, because it allows us to be in this world; thank our parents, for giving us life; thank Nature because it provides us with all we need to live, and thank everybody else since they give us the social support we need. Please refer to: *Aikido – The Way of Harmony*, by John Stevens, under the direction of Rinjiro Shirata, Shambala Publishers, Boston and London, 1984, p. 61.

person holding their partner by the wrists, so that they can help stretch each other's backs, letting them free to let go whenever they want. Thus, a conclusion is that in Aiki practice *Uke* will never be tortured or punished by any means: practitioners are always free to do as they wish and in accordance to their own selves. *"There are no slaves, nor bosses, in Aikido"*. (Kurita Yutaka *Shihan*)

Chinkon kishin – returning to the source

The Founder used to wrap up the Aiki session with a final bow (*rei*) as a farewell to his God. In current practice everyone says *Domo arigato gozai mashita* meaning "Thanks for what you have done," for your effort teaching (students) and for your effort to learn (instructor). The Founder thought Aiki was possible by means of the grand Divinity of union, confluence and harmony: the "*Aiki O-Kami*".

Immediately after bowing towards the *kamiza* (the place of honor usually occupied by a picture of the Founder) and thanking the instructor, students turn to each other and then their words mean "Thanks for everything you did".

In contemporary practice it is basically a token of appreciation towards O-Sensei.

THE END (closing the cycle)

A word on hierarchy

The idea of an older age and position is natural to the Japanese and it is customary to expect that older sons become a substitute father-like figure for their younger brothers. They are trained for this responsibility, which also gives them an authority position over their brothers and sisters. When they address each other they use special words denoting such a difference and respect. In Aiki practice the oldest person of a *dojo* or the highest in rank may take charge when a *Sensei* is not present.

Together with parents-children relationships, another Japanese kind of human vertical relationship is that between *sempai-kohai*. Senior practitioners are called *sempai* (they are older or superior in ability. The term is used in contemporary Japan to refer to those who graduated earlier from the same school). *Kohai* is the opposite of *sempai*, and it refers to those who are junior or who entered the same school after others.

Aikido follows this tradition with a definite variation: highest ranks are responsible for the lowest ranks during practice and not the mere beneficiaries of honors and distinctions, since O-Sensei himself never pursued them.

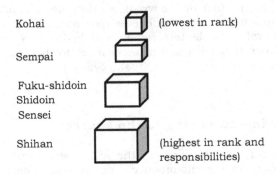

Kohai   (lowest in rank)

Sempai

Fuku-shidoin
Shidoin

Sensei

Shihan   (highest in rank and
                          responsibilities)

Traditional ranking system

A traditionally hierarchical system has traditionally implied the stronger people help or take care of the weaker ones. But in the new Aiki paradigm the lowest in rank, the newcomer, assumed as the "weakest" member, is never to accept any weakness since they can also help the strong ones. Tradition is used for the sake of the mutual respect involved among practitioners. As they grow up and learn they are expected to act maturely and with no selfishness as part of an Aiki-do community, where elders (in rank or age) lead responsibly, and the younger ones (both in rank or age) follow the set example and take it as their own.

Belonging to a group or an organization naturally teaches about respect and consideration towards other people, particularly elders or authorities since we recognize experienced people as important members of our society. We usually learn about rules and cooperation when we play group games, or when we engage in a football match guided by people with more experience who designate the tasks involved in the game. The Founder did the same so Aiki practice teaches us how to share with our partners in order to walk the same path. It sets the rules that teach us how we can protect from any misdoings by non sincere partners or classmates. Aiki practice sets clear gentleman's rules and always reminds us that abuse of strength of any kind is not appreciated. This is part of correct practice since it starts and ends by showing respect, literally meaning *"Do as you must, with a positive spirit, a sincere will and a constructive intention."* Aiki practice offers a chance to have a high quality group play, of the same kind usually abandoned as people grow up. It offers a splendid life experience.

"Aiki is not an ideal or an invisible phenomenon, it's a culture" (Kurita *Shihan*). Collaborating as a group, people use Aiki (union, confluence and harmony) and they put the creating forces of the Universe (*ki*) to work. As we have previously mentioned human history is full of examples that led to the creation of different civilizations, although force, brutality and slavery have been used instead of confluence to join forces in order to destroy our enemies. We need to perform without elaborating on everything but by imagining them instead through the use of our right brain and by following our intuition.

A big goal in few words and concrete actions

- Aiki is meant to be done in union, harmony and confluence with a practice partner. It is not an individualistic but a collectivistic path to be walked along with others. Master Ueshiba's posthumous message *"Takemusu Aiki"* means *"Make Aiki victorious"* (Kurita *Shihan*).

  Takemusu Aiki is another aspect of Aiki-do and in fact it has been an additional training modality in *Kurita Juku Aiki*. There are no *Nage-Uke* parts in *Takemusu Aiki*, since *Nage* can also play the role of *Uke* at the very same time during the same line of action. This is completely different from regular *Aikido* practice.

- The effort put forth by participants must be given 100% and not just 50% of each practicing partner. Then it must be multiplied until they achieve 1, 000 %.

- Aiki-do is a means for evolution and to make us get rid of old paradigms. This tends towards the elimination of the old fighting objectives of training and the dependence on strength, clashing and conflict. Its objective is to take advantage of our energy and to use it in the most efficient way, in accordance to the principles of the Universe and taking them as a source for knowledge and as a life style.

- These precepts are not a mere ideal: practice consists of left hand movements which allow for the right brain work to do its job and use intuition in order to help the left brain construct a new understanding of things that may transform life.

- Aiki rescues intuition, a forgotten or despised element, as well as the impulse to grow and improve; intuition is the driving force that has driven our development as human beings and is also a force related to the concept of *ki*. Transformation is the main goal of Aiki.

People can now have a good glimpse at their own being through Aiki practice.
(Y. Kurita *Shihan* with T.S. Okuyama *Sensei*, c.a. 1995)

Aiki looks for harmony reflected both in our performance in the *Dojo* and in our relationship with others

[*AI* : Aikido's concept of "matching"]

Aiki is the same perfect harmony, order and alignment found between Moon, Earth and Sun

Chapter 5

The Aiki practice session: transformation

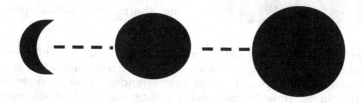

LEARNING FROM THE UNIVERSE

Aiki straightens out whatever is crooked in our minds, hearts and spirits

Aiki practice can correct and improve our posture. By so doing it also helps correct our spirit, heart and mind. It promotes an adjoining work, both individual and collective, that creates a close relationship among practice partners. It helps us to develop the use of our two brain hemispheres, giving us the sensitivity to understand ourselves and others as different and complementary individuals. This is Aiki's way to carry out a fine work of personal cleansing and perfection which eventually translates into personal betterment. The effort made in training serves as the cleansing agent; techniques are the ground for personal improvement. It is just what happens when people wash their clothes and they rub and rub until they are clean. The same happens in the starting warm-up, rowing-like Aiki exercise called *Tori fune undo* shown below.

"Enlightenment" in Aiki means a clear understanding (vision) of things, not their scientific or technical explanation. It is acquired in each and every Aiki movement, starting from this warm-up exercise, which is intended to help us awake our intuition.

As we have already mentioned, an Aiki warm-up helps us to advance our personality. It is like a train going uphill or like people in a boat rowing towards one shared destination. (Kurita Yutaka *Shihan*)

Western philosophers and methodologists make a difference between explanation and understanding. An *explanation* is the reasoning used in the study of Natural sciences; *comprehension* is an understanding gained in what they call sciences of the Spirit. Broadly speaking, enlightenment in Aiki-do embraces both categories: it studies the nature of things and its impact into our beings. *Tori fune undo* must be done not just with stamina and vigor but also with our heart (*kokoro*). It is useless when it is done without the right attitude. When done as a concentration exercise, movements with the left side advance 1,000 miles, trying to reach the Sun and beyond, whereas those made with the right side bring towards us that far away energy sitting at the farthest corner of the Universe (Kurita *Shihan*).

It is also very important to understand and always bear in mind the difference between *activity* and *work*. *Shomen-uchi ikkyo* is the activity and its work involves using all the Aiki ingredients necessary to make it complete and give it a different state. What makes it beautiful and extraordinary comes from more than what is superficially observed. Aiki deals with beauty, perfection and care that lead to a different kind of human expression. It is for all these reasons that a *dojo* is a place for enlightenment or realization, completely apart from the mystical or religious connotations this concept has in our culture. Aiki-do movements make us see what nobody sees, smell what nobody smells, as well as to hear, touch and taste what nobody hears, touches and tastes. The fewer ingredients we use in practice, the more tasteless our techniques are and the less number of chemical reactions will be produced in both *Nage* and *Uke*.

This posture and its exercise helps correct our posture and tune our mind in addition to the "cutting" (*kiru*) action.

Techniques are applied to us and not against an enemy!

Since the beginning of his mission, Kurita Yutaka *Shihan* has taught that learning how to twist a person's arm is not of interest in Aiki-do. However, a wrong message may have been sent out throughout the years by expressions such as: *"If you learn Aikido you can effortlessly defeat an enemy,"* or *"You can redirect the attack if you...,"* etc. Kurita *Shihan* has always made a clear difference between Aiki-do and self-defense because one single technique is good enough to defend against any attack and vice-versa. As in any other system, an attack can be countered with any of the many different techniques available in its repertoire. They can be devastating, and they can send us to jail too, but this is not its goal.

Against the self-defense view, no effort is good enough when it comes to take care of *Uke*, so as to never inflict any harm or even the tiniest pain. Harm of any kind maims both our integrity and that of our partner. As Kurita *Shihan* teaches, *ikkyo* or any other technique is in fact applied to ourselves, given we are the ones who choose between being nasty or considerate, careful or neglectful with the corresponding results of our actions. Caring for our practice partners or neglecting them has a direct impact on our own personalities and true well-being.

To understand this we must bear in mind that when we practice we are literally borrowing our partner's body, which is like both a reference book and our mirror. Doing anything destructive against him is just not OK. It goes against the positive part of our nature, and hinders the chances to manifest non-violence, the most distinct quality Aiki requires from us. Besides, our partner is also urged to have an active participation in order to multiply the work put in training and to take care himself. This was the way discovered and proposed by O-Sensei to be truly victorious. Other thinkers agree with him as can be seen in the case of the contemporary Argentinean writer Jorge Luis Borges who once said:

"Whenever we know of a victory of war, we are facing human failure".

Aiki-do techniques are made of angles, circles, and combinations which are the situations to work with. Technique manipulation *per se* constitutes an inferior level because it does not help us very much in our search for "energy", its addition nor its multiplication either. Only a deeper understanding and growth can be considered a real change, improvement, and a superior practice level.

All Aiki elements and factors are necessary and Kurita *Shihan* makes an analogy to make his point: *"A telephone is incomplete when it has not the buttons or the batteries needed to make a call"*. The same happens if any Aiki-do action is performed without a good and sincere heart, in due ceremony, and containing all its fundamental elements because it is as useless as a telephone with no dialing parts.

Techniques may look like complete Aiki actions but they can be of a totally different nature. Not knowing the difference is like being unable to tell sugar and salt, coffee and coke, or a crystal and a diamond apart. It is only when you have a keen eye that you are able to tell the difference. According to Kaiso Sensei, the application of technique resembles a sports fishing where *Nage* is the fisherman and *Uke* is the fish: the fisherman protects the fish and never kills or despises them. *Nage* and *Uke* can also be compared with the Ocean and the fish:

"The Ocean does not need the fish but it is not arrogant and rejects them; on the other hand, the fish needs the Ocean to live. If Uke is welcomed Nage never torments them". (Kurita Yutaka *Shihan*)

Using an analogy with the sword, Kurita *Shihan* teaches that learning Aiki sharpens ourselves: applying a technique means to learn where the cutting edge is, so we don't waste it. Regarding the actions used, only natural movements are correct. When they are unnatural they are too big or small, uncomfortable, nervous, hesitant, static. When they are rigid they make us feel heavy and inflexible. Correct techniques make us good for real, and not as a mere idea. As we have previously stated it is a big mistake to go backwards in our progress by looking into the older arts Aiki-do has left behind. Fighting arts are "external" since attacks and counterattacks go against the fighters; Aiki-do is "internal" because it affects the nature of the people using its techniques and its work is done for the sake of their own growth.

These ideas are the theory transmitted by an *uchideshi* like Kurita *Shihan* who proudly thinks of himself as the last one who still cares for the Founder's ideals and his fundamental teachings. He instructs about the theory behind Aiki movements such as the different stages found in their application (birth, growth, decline and death), and their similarity to the elements found in Nature, etc.

It is for all these reasons that we have insisted that if techniques lack the Aiki ingredients described up to this point they cannot be considered as complete.

O-Sensei showing his own growth, not how to defeat an enemy.
(Kurita *Shihan*, Uke)

An unusual finish for *ikkyo* (first Chapter): notice *Nage* is not grabbing *Uke*. It is an example of a technique applied and concentrated on ourselves and not on *Uke*. The open fingers are supportive and non-violent. A closed fist is basically aggressive and it does not help to follow the precept that *"True victory is victory over one's self"*.

Three different training levels

If we realize that practicing Aiki techniques is like sharpening ourselves, then we can state that doing so is to refine ourselves as we develop proper *ki* (a right posture bound towards a right action). When a couple of students start practicing they usually lack the adequate skills required and their actions are characterized by the use of strength or tricks. But as they progress and feel the subtleties involved in it their performance becomes much more flexible and mutually complete: they become physically, mentally and spiritually adapted. This can be seen in three common practices and progress levels:

a) ***Strength vs. strength*** – This is the basic and primitive performance found when students are rigid and their muscles are stiff. At this level they usually react in one of two different ways: they will barely move or they will move too much in an apparent disorder. In the first case they seem to be testing techniques, they want to see if Aikido really works. In the second case, they move so much that their practice becomes out of control, totally empty of any content. Competition rises at this level and develops a weird sense of mistrust and a lack of pleasure and confidence between partners due to their scarce *communication* (spiritual and physical contact).

Nage is unable to perform and *Uke* is in fact stealing or wasting the energy of both partners. They just go against each other, in a clashing movement: this is a lose-lose situation, even for the one who is stronger and seems to win.

Nage	*Uke*
(a useless 100 % energy)	(a useless 100 % energy)

b) **Strength vs. flexibility** – This is an intermediate level performance where the old paradigm starts to be changed among students. The more advanced they become, the more they realize there is no need to fake techniques nor to fight or use strength. They move with much more order and they know how to unite and align with their partners since they are able to communicate with them. They are able to catch their mutual "energy" and add to it.

When students are not experienced, they may still make use of unnecessary strength or weak, loose actions, again making them steal their partners' energy. Their practice is then of no use to either one, since those who are more flexible do not receive their partners' share, and those who are working with them are lazy and do not bother to work at all: practice demands and looks for 100% from both and not 50% by the two of them.

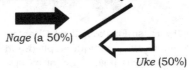

Nage (a 50%)

Uke (50%)

There is no crash here but there is still some separation between them so it is still a win-lose action.

c) **Flexibility plus flexibility** – This level is achieved when practice is carried out in the form of an advanced performance free from mechanical technique. It is reached when both partners actively coordinate their efforts and work during a session. *Uke*'s role is never passive since he/she is not supposed to ever stay still just waiting for *Nage* to work. *Uke* is not indifferent to the sharing and communicating process with *Nage* so he/she must keep aligned and active. When there is union, harmony, confluence, togetherness, collaboration, participation, circulation and contact, Aiki is done at a superior level, leading them to softness and perfection, and allowing for the free and spontaneous creation of living technique.

The 100% added by each partner produces 200% which can still be multiplied as their energy share is augmented and they progress towards growth. Only then there will be no such dualities as loser-winner, weak-strong, fool-smart, common-special, with-without *ki* people, etc. No harm must be present at any time, no hard feelings, and no arrogance from those with more expertise who do not wish to "lower" themselves to practice with novice students. Showing off must not be present since this will make them feel special and beginners will feel below them. It is at this level of progress where we find the basic Aiki formula:

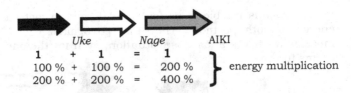

Uke		*Nage*	AIKI
1	+ 1	= 1	
100 %	+ 100 %	= 200 %	} energy multiplication
200 %	+ 200 %	= 400 %	

Both *Nage* and *Uke* join forces and then multiply their mutual energy in a win-win situation. Practice becomes a real pleasure at this level.

Category in practice

Non-alert beginners and advanced students may be using a strength that takes their work in the wrong direction. Claiming their *Aikido* is hard or tough, soft or gentle only shows they are unaware that *Nage* and *Uke* execute highly *positive* (non-fighting), *beautiful* (complete, flexible), and *true* (real) actions (techniques). They must display the same category (*sahō*) of a highly ranked officer and their work should not be stiff, mechanical or repetitive. They must realize their training may be corresponding to one of the following four categories as a result of the kind of performance they show.

HIGHER CATEGORY

4°. Sahō – "elegant and absolutely natural practice". Although this term refers to etiquette in general, it might be applied to natural and complete movements added to "technique"; new features emerge in both performance and applications at this level.

A ← B

Speechless communication between partners is excellent and undiferentiated. There is total communication at an intuitive level by means of the works of the right side of our brain.

3°. Shuden – "strong, intense practice". Practice may be rather severe, but always correct at this level. It is like the forging of a sword so it is like multiple hammering and heating in order to get a beautiful, sharp, and intuitive sword.

A → B

INTERMEDIATE CATEGORY

Verbal communication between partners is low since there is preferably no talking and definitely much more work in sharing actions.

2°. Giho – "explained and reasoned practice". This involves the analysis to understand what makes techniques work and execution variables are taught for this reason.

A ↔ B

Communication between partners at this level also depends on how well they work. They might use a combination of a physical and verbal approach, a combination of both the right and left sides of our brain. This is a fundamental category in the teaching-learning process.

BASIC LOWER CATEGORY

1°. Kihon – "mechanical practice". This term basically refers to teaching about stances and it is usually applied to the mechanization of movements through a repetitive emphasis on its components.

Communication between partners is rather poor and differentiated at this level.

The transformation gained through Aiki practice shows that training will eventually take us from our current material stage (body to body fighting) towards a more spiritual one, where no competition, no sports and no fighting exist. Indeed categories will change their physical state from solid to liquid and then to gas as the following graphic indicates:

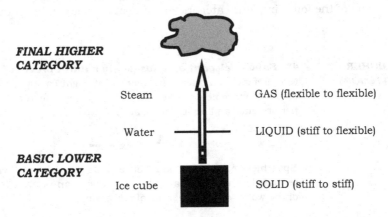

FINAL HIGHER CATEGORY

Steam   GAS (flexible to flexible)

Water   LIQUID (stiff to flexible)

BASIC LOWER CATEGORY

Ice cube   SOLID (stiff to stiff)

All of these training categories used in practice obviously differ: movements are rather square at first, and then they are gradually rounded. Subsequently students may look for a new modality of practice called *henka waza* which refers to technical transformation and change. At this stage participants will be able to show form variables which are rather independent from current technique. They will become new personal expressions. Changing techniques does not mean switching from one technique to another, as it has been explained when *Nage* tries something, and after realizing it doesn't work he/she then tries something else. It means to transform them in such a way as to create new moves and thus work in accordance to the grand Aiki Spirit (*Aiki O-Kami*) which is master Ueshiba's development line.

IKKYO   **IKKYO HENKA**

As we can see in the previous pictures, the relative positions of *Uke* and *Nage* are different but they render the same *ikkyo*. The usual form (A) is transformed in form *B* but although *Nage* is looking to an opposite direction he still ends as in *A*.

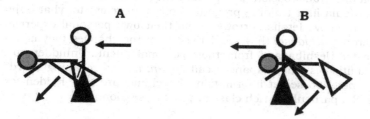

One more difference: the *shiho-nage* grab shown in the picture to the left requires the use of strength, whereas the *shiho-nage henka* one on the right doesn't. The one on the left is aggressive and violent.

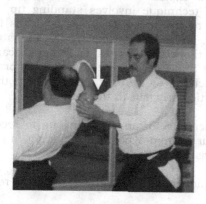 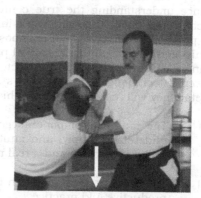

"Changing techniques" has been incorrectly understood as going from one technique to a different one or as a strategy to take our partner by surprise. This is just switching techniques, not changing them. In a different interpretation *henka waza* means transforming, e.g. *ikkyo*, or *shiho-nage*, into a higher class application or performance without losing its essence and leaving room for *Uke* to move flexibly and in constant expansion (breathing). This is the way Kurita *Shihan* teaches about "changing techniques" progressively:

OYŌ HENKA (progressive transformation)

It is from this additional *Oyō-henka* category that free and infinite creation of technique is possible. It is free from technical bindings and other types of longings that only deceive our hearts. Such is the spirit of Aiki, and as such it makes movements pass through different stages and forms, just like the changes seen in car designs year after year. Kurita *Shihan* points out that once O-Sensei Ueshiba discovered the Aiki *do* he was always changing and perfecting his perception and the forms of practice. And everybody has the right and might also be expected to make additional creations with Aiki once they acquire the foundations discovered by Kaiso Sensei and are truly ready to follow his line. [38]

A word on oral transmission is important here since students must be aware of the hidden curricula in a training program. This term refers to what happens in class as instructors show details borrowed from their own personal experience and discoveries. Regarding *uchideshi* they are derived from the chances they had to train directly with master Ueshiba and from their personal talent. Unhidden to absent students, oral tradition is what Japanese call *kuden*, a term meaning "words to be transmitted" and not "top secret information." Teachings are only hidden for those who did not attend a particularly rich class or practice session.

A final note on the main unnoticed elements used in Aiki practice

As we have stated, it is impossible to explain Aiki with drawings or pictures since understanding the true contents of technique involves standing up, taking action and doing the right work in order to feel them. They are a means for the expression of ourselves so it is impossible to perceive and experience them if students only learn the beginning and final parts of the whole process, or if they discard and ignore essential elements and factors that must be present in every performance. Even if techniques are shown in strobe pictures as an attempt to present them in detail they will remain "unseen". This is particularly true in the case of:

a)   The multiple components giving meaning to, and allowing us to recognize, understand, apply, and multiply our *ki* from a posture set aright, a positive will, a right heart and a real non-divisible union.

b)   The different ways in which techniques must be integrated to insure real and productive Aiki practice.

c)   The symbolic significance of all "attacks" which have to be seen as circumstances to be resolved by means of creative and non-aggressive solutions. And the meaning of all "defenses," which must be seen as the orientation and meaning of our own life, as opportunities for growth and for a more subtle and refined communication between *Nage* and *Uke*.

d)   The transcendence of *leading* and *control*, which in fact are a demonstration of respect, in regards to the mutual care given between partners.

e)   The use of distance (*ma-ai* / *mawae*), the invitation or attraction (*Izanau*), the approach and union (*awase*), as well as the unbreakable union and solidarity (*musubi*) required fitting Aiki's requirements which in turn lead to a maximum *efficacy*. All this teaches the value of the non-mechanical repetition of our movements if we see them as responses to circumstances that teach us about the value of adaptation as opposed to the usual confrontation, competition, separation and division.

---

[38] The same has happened, for instance, with Edison's invention of the phonograph: he invented it and others have made important developments and changes with it.

When people ignore these elements they don't have a good Aiki practice and they can't see the nature and color of its path (*do*). Their training sessions lack level and category and the high standards looked for throughout practice. *Mobilizations* won't be related to what happens not only in a *dojo* but in the various aspects of our personal, family or professional lives. This implies that mastering Aiki will never really happen.

When practitioners only know and show its fighting aspects, a self-limitation occurs, even if they argue they are trying to preserve ancient *budo*, understood as a serious martial issue. The same happens if they are naively convinced there are really hard and soft styles without realizing that this is a weak and deceiving argument since according to Kurita *Shihan* a hard style can always be countered by a soft response and vice-versa.

An *Uchideshi*'s glossary of Aiki-do concepts (*Kurita Juku*)

This section gathers many issues Kurita Yutaka *Shihan* has touched as an instructor. His recent additions are now being developed and they will have to be dealt with in another book since they are now being created and changed from day to day; they will have to be digested and correctly practiced before trying to present them in writing or in graphic forms. Besides direct practice, the best way to present them won't be easily chosen, given they belong to a general theory based on the works of the right side of our brain, which is a wordless way to gain deeper insight and is aimed as the future of Aiki practice, Kurita *Shihan*'s legacy.

Much of his special instruction departs from the teachings disseminated up to this date in hope to go beyond the Founder's line. The following is a list of all the terms and concepts he has passed on in more than two decades. Most of them are not usually referred to by other instructors in regular classes or international seminars either. There may be other instructors who teach similar things but they may not be as colorful as Kurita *Shihan* so he deserves the credit here. The next con-

cepts are examples of the original point of view that permeates any other general knowledge we might have, and they have been selected because they illustrate all that must be said about what happens during practice, especially now that he is putting more emphasis on Aiki instruction.

Although it also includes terms used at many *dojo* around the world, it presents those that have been fundamental as part of the first *Kurita Juku* period. But since the Founder barely used many terms by the time Kurita *Shihan* became an *uchideshi*, it also presents samples of a rather unorthodox *Aikido* vocabulary. In his days, he reports, everything was referred just as *kokyu* by O-Sensei, who was seemingly developing *Takemusu aiki* by that time too.

A

- **Action** – The body movement; the activity.

    Aiki-do actions are closely related to techniques and regarded as such, in spite of the *work* they all require. When practitioners follow the way correctly their actions become a *do* (a path and an end to follow) and they go beyond *waza* (mechanical lines of action).

    Yokomen-uchi ikkyo, shomen-uchi nikkyo and *tsuki kotegaeshi* are three different mobilizations and actions but when they are correctly done, the work carried out in all of them is just the same.

    See Work, Technique and Waza

- **Activity** – The external actions; the "attacks" and techniques of *Aikido* practice as seen on their surface.

    A car in motion is said to run, that is its activity, but in order to do so it requires the participation (work) of components such as gas, and means such as the engine, a transmission, an electrical system and the wheels.

    In order to carry out an activity such as *Shomen-uchi ikkyo* we need to put *ki + kokyu* to work. If they are missing Aiki fails, just as when a car runs out of gas and stops running. All the elements included and developed by Kaiso Sensei Ueshiba are the necessary components for a right and complete performance.

    See Work

- **Ai** – The act of adjusting, joining, adding or making two things coincide.

    See Ai in the basic glossary of Aiki terms used by the Founder (Chapter 2)

- **Aiki** – The combination of two personal *ki* ("yours and mine") as an action that connects them with the Universal *ki* .

    For Aiki (combined *ki*) to be good and effective both partners must work equally, they must put the same kind of heart, guts and stamina in what they do. Their actions must be the same size and correspond in every sense. In order to do so they must take into account the following Aiki points:

    Point 1 ("Ichi no aiki") - **gravity**

    Point 2 ("Ni no aiki")   - **calmness**

    Point 3 ("San no aiki") - **initial action**

    Point 4 ("Yon no aiki") - **approach, invitation (*izanau*)**

Point 5 ("Go no aiki") - **sharing, interchange (*ki awase*)**

Point 6 ("Roku no aiki") - **added energy**

Point 7 ("Shichi no aiki") - **indivisible union (*ki musubi*)**

- **Aiki budo** – Two different entities the Founder transformed into one single thing (Aiki (budo) do) based on Aiki.

- **Aikido** – The name by which the philosophy and art of Morihei Ueshiba's work is known to the world.

- **"Aiki-do"** – A way of harmony, unity and confluence as it has been defined here.

    Kurita Yutaka *Shihan* considers *Aikido* as: "*The science of life, a way to enter a new life and strength for the benefit of all humanity*". It is the mold or formula for the creation of a great life. It is the special name used in this book to remind practitioners about the original ideal developed and proposed as a new culture by *Kaiso Sensei* (the correct title to address O-Sensei according to Kurita *Shihan*).

    See Kaiso Sensei

- **Aikido Ki** – "The driving force, the impulse and spirit" of the Aiki way.

    Everybody asks questions about the superficial or technical aspects of the art but its *ki* is its heart, the honorable care and will we put in our practice.

    See Kokoro

- **Aikido ceremony** – The steps taken to make practice special.

    A special class is used to pinpoint the details added in the right Aiki work. And it is by following and taking care of all single details that it becomes a ceremony and goes to a different level.

    As in a banquet many things are put on the table and each one of them has a specific purpose in order to enhance the celebration. People must learn how to use each one of them with refinement and no confusion.

- **Aikido practice** – A chance to grow and join the Universe.

- **Aiki senses** – This term refers to a parallel set of "senses" envisioned by the Founder that are not to be confused with our biological senses; they relate to the concept of "senses" defined as "the quality of being aware". With this in mind we can compare both Aiki and our biological senses as follows:

Biological senses	Aiki senses
Sight	To see what nobody else sees; to see beyond
Hear	To hear what nobody else hears; to hear "silence" (which is "the voice of God" according to Kurita *Shihan*)
Smell	To smell what nobody else smells; to find the scent of Aiki
Taste	To taste what nobody else tastes; to find the special flavor of Aiki; to taste *pleasure*.
Touch	To touch what nobody else touches; to feel the difference and enter a new realm or dimension through the work of our body (our whole *being* and *biology*, unified body, mind and spirit)

When Kurita Yutaka *Shihan* teaches *tai-no-henko*, for example, he points out that most people usually fail to use their sight correctly, something they do in many other actions. He explains that the five Aiki senses refer to the necessary use of our biology (being) from a unified posture and a flowing movement. The training process implies: (a) to see correctly; to give our action a direction with our sight; (b) to listen to what we are doing; no sound is always better; (c) to perceive the texture of our action; to feel it; and (d) to taste it, to perceive its flavor, its scent; to realize everything is manifest through the body as a reflection of the Universe.

When there are signs of difficulty during an activity (technique), and hence the use of strength or any slight manifestation of violence of any kind, it has no *flavor* and we lose direction. On the other hand, when there is relaxation, the nature of all the Aiki senses emerge and manifest. When students achieve this they can say they are sensitive to Aiki and they are being positively affected and transformed by it. This is why *ki* cannot be simply translated as energy. If any of these senses fails to work properly there can be no Aiki.

See Ki-shin-tai in the glossary of Aiki terms used by the Founder (Chapter 2)

- **Aiki sphere**:

The center is right between *Nage* and *Uke*

Nage represents the vertical axis (**Y**)

Uke *represents* the horizontal axis (X)

Nage moves up and down whereas *Uke* moves to the left as well as to the right

It is only by covering all these angles that we can talk of a sphere since it can only be made by the works and union of both partners. (Kurita Yutaka *Shihan*)

In a sphere, all angles are covered

- **Art** – The use of the imagination to create something, such as a musical composition or a poem or a practical skill learned by experience.

   Japanese art has traditionally been a teaching-with-no-words process learnt through direct experience, and it is how it has to be done in Aiki. The characteristics most often associated with traditional arts are:

   a)   **keishikika** (the formalization produced by the establishment of a pattern or form –a *kata*, absent in Aiki–),

   b)   **kata** (mastering the pattern or form, as well as the classification of ability en route to mastery, which results in the granting of licensing and grades such as *kyu* and *dan*),

   c)   **kanzen shugi** (the beauty of complete perfection gained after constant repetition of the pattern –still used in Aiki instruction–),

   d)   **seishin shugyo** (the mental discipline required)

   e)   **tōitsu** (the integration with the skill in order to transcend the pattern).

   The components of a work of art can never be divided or fragmented, so it is only from this perspective that we can say Aiki-do is an art, and in regards to the activities carried out. It can be said Aiki-do is an art just because its dynamic elements –the triangle, the circle and the square– may be combined:

   This is the language syntax used to express different ideas throughout the combination of its elements. Schools emphasize the starting points but neglect the process and the resulting order. And to be able to learn this it is necessary to have a big heart and an open mind. There is a deeper level that has to be unveiled in Aiki-do since Aiki goes beyond mechanical execution. There is no problem in combining these elements at will, but they cannot be mixed with those from other arts since that produces weird results and leads to confusion. Students must always keep in mind the meaning of all these indivisible elements:

Beginning   Duration/process   Result /order

❖	❖	❖
Alignment	Mobilization	Completion
AI	**KI**	**DO**

All works of art have a certain value. A Van Gogh and a Picasso are unique, and although many others might be able to paint they will never be like those who came before them. This is also true with the Founder's way, it is only one and it cannot be changed. Styles obviously belong to someone else whose work came later but will never be as the original one.

When new painters have emerged and used their own talent, they have also succeeded by proposing their own work and a change from previous artists. So those who are now developing different things with Aiki-do will eventually produce a product of their own and they may have to choose a proper name.

See Martial art

- **Atemi** – A real or fake hit to the face, unnecessary in Aiki.

- **Attack/defense** – These terms are not really part of Aiki as well as terms such as escape, separation, projection, throw, break, blocking and many other that reflect and carry negative concepts of the same sort. It is important not only to avoid these words but also their corresponding actions.

  Aikido practitioners know that an "attack" is also a "defense" and vice-versa since there is a lot of relativity in this new paradigm. But the enunciation of its attacks and defenses is relative too. It is not the same to ask students to practice *Shomen-uchi ikkyo* (as is the usual practice) than to work on *Ikkyo shomen-uchi* (a *Takemusu* training version) or to study *Shomen-uchi - katate dori - ikkyo* (*Kurita Juku Aiki*'s new version).

  The first enunciation is the regular way techniques are practiced all around the world. The second one is a transformed way which changes the relative roles of both *Nage* and *Uke*. It is a *Takemusu Aiki* application where *Nage* starts and finishes the whole technique and plays both the *Nage* and the *Uke* roles at the same time, a big difference from the usual *Aikido* practice. In any case all situations must be resolved with *ki*, not with muscle or mind, with something between both partners which helps them avoid aggression and violence.

  If Aiki-do is a path to be entered by two, and there are no enemies but partners in practice, there can be no fights, just as it happens with any couple or team relationship. Attacks represent uncomfortable situations and practitioners must look for positive ways to overcome them and learn from that.

- **Attention** – Consideration, notice, a very important part of Aiki work.

- **Attraction** – The first stage of Aiki work is the act and power to attract like a magnet; to attract is to draw or pull to oneself.

See Magnetism and Izanau

- **Awase** – The second phase of Aiki action is to reach out, to discover, and to unite, according to our description in Chapter 4.

  It is the basis of techniques, their *kihon-gi*. It is one of the two main principles to be studied in Aiki when practicing both static and dynamic actions ("pins" and "throws") and the work they imply. It means overlapping, crossing, and finding out. It is the way *Nage* and *Uke* get together and it is used with *kokyu* (an extension).

  Kurita Yutaka *Shihan* explains this concept by showing how the lapels of his shirt (*gi*) are crossed in front of when he puts it on. It is part of the contact phase of all activities. *Awase* must be present in our actions to help combine the centripetal and centrifugal forces present in them.

  See Izanau, Musubi, Phases, and Brain.

B

- **Balance** – Equilibrium.

  This concept has at least two interpretations by Kurita *Shihan*:

  A) The pyramid △ is said to be the most balanced geometrical form. It can be unstable if it is put upside down ▽ but if it spins it doesn't fall; it is just like a spinning top!

  That is the way the Universe works and it explains why circular movements are used in Aiki-do. Although this could explain balance, there is still a bigger question to be asked: Where is the "ground" that supports our planet Earth and the Universe itself?

  B) An important way to look at balance is by referring to the interaction produced during practice.

  Besides being attained by means of a good posture, with the body perfectly aligned and never bending the head downwards (our sight never goes to the ground), balance also relates to *adaptation* and *compensation*:

Uke = comes and follows

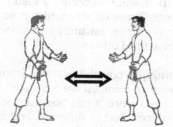

Nage = goes, gets close, and directs

This fact produces a balance formula which basically states that *Nage* always has to compensate for any variations in *Uke*'s force, impulse or intention. For example:

a) when *Uke* comes fully committed, full of strength, speed and a dynamic force of 10, *Nage* doesn't need to do anything but to take advantage of this and act immediately (0 + 10 = 10).

b) when *Uke* comes with a force of only 8, *Nage* needs to use 2 in order to make for that dynamic force of 10 (2 + 8 = 10).

c) and if *Uke* doesn't move at all *Nage* will still have to compensate by using all his dynamic force himself (10 + 0 = 10).

The fact that there is always a result of 10 means activity is not only *receptive* but *pro-active*. It is a big mistake to think of Aiki-do techniques only as a defensive system: *Nage*'s actions can also be "offensive", so to speak, if seen from a fighting perspective. However, Aiki is not aggressive although taking the initiative is the basis of *Takemusu* practice as compared with all the general *Aikido* styles.

Balanced actions work with these values:

NAGE		UKE	
0	---	10	In self-defense terms, 10 is a committed attack by ***Uke***
1	---	9	
3	---	7	
5	---	5	
7	---	3	
10		0	In self-defense terms, 10 could be an attack by ***Nage***

In traditional martial terms under the premise that an attack is 100% a physical encounter, it may be easier to defend from an assassin (who commits 100% attack) than from a thief (who may not be committed 100% and may still surprise the victim with a sudden and violent attack or with some other hidden or dirty trick).

- **Beauty** – A quality that makes someone or something pleasing to look at or listen to.

Aiki makes us feel pleasure. We must have in mind that beauty is found in a moving body and thus Aiki's refinement and softness is similar to the highest class ballet dancing forms. Its flowing movements also touch the public and their emotions as if it were a dance. Practitioners make it seem simple and easy, but their practice and execution is carried on until perfection is reached, not only for one's own sake but for the benefit of others.

Aiki is one of the multiple possibilities the human body has to express itself to create a certain frame of mind: if we practice tough and violent actions our mind will be molded as such since it will become the basis of our approach to resolve our everyday life conflicts. Aiki is different and cannot be compared with martial (fighting) arts and sports.

- **Belt** – The belt used in Aiki-do is more than a band or strap worn around the waist to hold up a uniform: it holds our energy and shows our disposition to work. A black belt means students have started the path, and when a *sensei* grants one he is passing both his and the art's energies as well.

  Kurita Yutaka *Shihan* uses his belt to demonstrate the two most important Aiki elements all actions or techniques must contain:

  a) *awase* (encounter, overlapping: when we put one of the belt extremes over the other on our hips and in front of us), and

  b) *musubi* (union, securing: when we tie the belt in a knot).

- **Body *(tai)*** – The physical structure of a person.

  Kurita *Shihan* sees it as the sheath of our spirit, which is also our "sword" and our "treasure". The corresponding *kanji* for this word indicates "the root of a person", bones and flesh. In addition, our body is equipped with five senses that allow us to perceive and reach the world around us.

  But in regards to our senses it is necessary to be aware that Aiki has its own parallel set of senses. Sight, for example, is crucial in performing Aiki actions since looking to the ground makes us lose our balance, and looking to our partners makes us concentrate on them instead of ourselves and the Universe. And it is only by means of correct practice that we can really taste Aiki techniques which are only complete with the correct *work* done.

  It is essential to learn how to apply techniques with the whole body than just with the hands: the use of our hips and legs is essential at all times. Using the hips helps us gain in heaviness (gravity) which augments our category from the mere effect of our use of our natural gravitational force or centrum (*seika tanden*). Besides, using our chest and back is crucial too.

  See Category, Gravity, Intention, and Senses

- **Brain** – The large mass of gray nerve tissue inside our skull responsible for our thinking, perception intuition and imagination.

  Our brain is an organ formed by two different hemispheres; it has a left side in charge of reasoning and sensibility, and a right side in charge of our intuition and sensitivity. The left perceives a doing and the right helps it to carry it out. Aiki practice involves the use of both: one deals with the practical use of techniques and their logical analysis, and the other deals with its sensitive perception. In Western philosophical terms one is scientific (*apolineal*), and the other is artistic and intuitive (*dionisiacal*).

  The left side thinks in terms of words, whereas the right side thinks in terms of images and they are mutually complementary. Being our most valuable asset in Aiki, the brain helps us do things by perceiving and reaching things out in the world and the Universe with the help of its two complementing sides.

It might be said that *Kurita Juku Aiki* currently focuses on teaching people how to use the right side of the brain and to help them to be more intuitive and imaginative so they can creatively cope with their lives and times.

See Beauty

- **Breakfall** – An action alien to Aiki.

A roll is *"a momentary change of position,"* as defined by Kurita *Shihan.* Falling or slamming actions are violent events existing in Judo or wrestling but unnecessary in Aiki.

Uke must be carefully "put in place" by *Nage*, who has to move them both from one place to another. This should be done with the maximum care and consideration, as when somebody puts fine glass cups on a table. The human body is like such glass cups: if they sit at the edge they will fall and break. So in order to avoid this it is necessary to sit those glasses safely right in the middle of the table, where they will be completely safe and sound. The same is to be done with our practice partners (*Uke*) and at all times in Aiki.

See Rolling

- **Breathe** – The action by which we take in and force out air from our lungs.

This is the usual meaning of one of our most important biological actions. But there are many confused practitioners who –miming arts like *Karate*– inhale and exhale deeply with their lungs when they are executing an *Aikido* movement, something which is completely far from what constitutes Aiki breathing.

When Kurita *Shihan* judges how somebody performs as *Nage* he bases his observations on the kind of life they show. When he says their technique is alive he literally means that it contains all necessary elements and breaths from all angles, including up and down directions. Otherwise he says their technique is dead

The following illustration clarifies this:

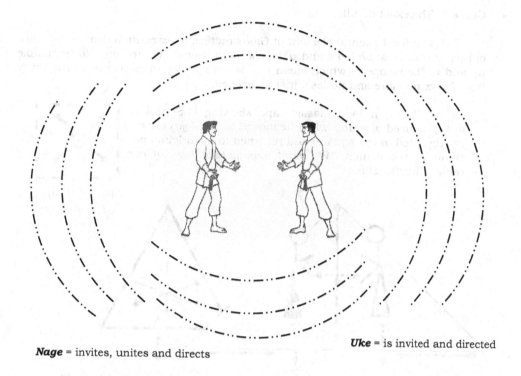

Nage = invites, unites and directs

Uke = is invited and directed

**Getting close and away makes action breathe (when *Nage* receives
Uke he is inhaling, and when he finishes he is exhaling)**

Aikido techniques must breathe, and this is possible through the movements of both partners. By coming and going practice resembles the expanding and contracting action of the Universe. And because of this, there is no time for attacks. Both partners get close (using *awase*), connect and remain connected (using *musubi*) and so they act in unison. Breathing is not an action made by our lungs in Aiki: *Nage* inhales when *Uke* is coming and exhales when *Uke* goes forwards, and vice-versa, with the interaction of both centripetal and centrifugal forces.

This also implies practice must be dynamic and not passive: starting after our partner has already taken our wrist or has finished his *shomen* is too late and passive, and it does not contribute to having the best practice.

See Inhaling / exhaling

C

- **Category** – Refinement, elegance, ceremony.

  See Exercise / practice

- **Center** – The exact middle.

    It is a fundamental element of *Giho* practice, an execution dealing with two old basic concepts: *shikake* and *uketachi* (both seemingly meaning "to be unable to" and to "be trapped") which mean *Uke* is not allowed to escape or to run away from *Nage*: no more and no less, just as needed.

As can be seen in a classic tape showing O-Sensei at work, he used a center when he moved to the *dojo* corners (represented in the square) and returned to his original position at the center. *"We must always take care of our center"* (Kurita *Shihan*).

The Aiki center in *Renzoku waza*

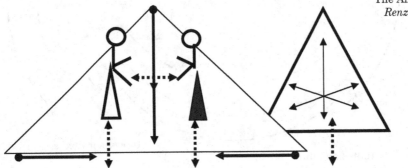

AIKI CENTER: What center are we talking about, a center in Aiki and in our life?

- **Centrifugal force** – A force that makes something go away from a center.

    It is a force we direct towards the farthest corner of the Universe in Aiki training. *"Going away about 10,000 miles from the place we are standing"* is an expression constantly used by Kurita Yutaka *Shihan*. This is not to be confused with anything related to a term such as rejection because that is not the way Aiki uses the forces of the Universe. This concept is applied in *Tori fune undo*.

- **Centripetal force** – A force that makes something come to a center.

    In Aiki practice it is a force we aim from the farthest Universe corner towards us. *"Coming from about 10,000 miles away towards the place we are standing at"* is another expression used by Kurita *Shihan* to explain our contact with the forces of the Universe. This can be considered an attraction, a way in which Aiki uses such forces and it is also applied in *Tori fune undo.*

- **Ceremony** – A series of acts performed on a special occasion.

    A ceremony consists of carefully designed steps; if they go wrong, it will be spoiled. Aiki practice is mostly done as a ceremony so if negative elements prevail the positive elements won't be present to make it a ceremony. Neutrality is thus necessary in our training in order to make it positive and constructive.

    Ceremonies require a careful look at details and the same can be said of Aiki practice. It is highly elaborated because the event celebrated is taken as important or unusual and not as an ordinary one, so the effort is made to make it memorable. It shows progress, a main human goal. Aiki can be practiced as a ceremony, and thus be taken to a special category.

- **Circles** - Curves that are closed.

    Aiki uses circular action. However many *Aikido* styles have adopted straight movements instead, particularly in their *shomen-uchi* style.

In *shomen-uchi ikkyo*, *Uke* cuts downwards to the center, *Nage* attracts upwards to his center.

Then he reverses the motion in a circular way and continues to his center again.

Although the hands must go up and down, they always do so in circles that come along with the vertical movements. Circles are described as a fundamental part of every action with the support of our legs.

Aiki uses circles when attracting or leading *Uke*, when entering or pivoting, when lifting or lowering our arms and that of *Uke*'s, etc. Circles have no angles, no corners; they are simply perfect shapes. Circles are found also in mobilization trajectories and they are always started from our center (*seika tanden*).

- **Circulation** – A movement from person to person in constant flow.

Nage = "negative" energy; *Uke* = "positive" energy

As in a car's battery

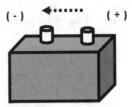

Circulation helps to avoid the characteristic violence of martial (fighting) arts. (Kurita *Shihan*)

When *Nage* proactively responds, not just reacts, they do it in a positive way; that is, in a way that makes them encounter *Uke* without hurting them. Roles are then constantly reversed, interchanged and shared in order to experience and learn from both.

- **Competition** – A contest (struggle or fight) alien to the Aiki-do.

Competition arises when we allow *Uke* to go away and detach and when we make any mistake in our performance or execution since this gives way to fighting (or any other reactions or countering).

If *Uke* can get up, run away, or counter our action, our technique is rather useless. And it doesn't function either when we want to win, when we have a winning-over-the-other frame of mind. A push, an attempt to hurt, a block and a throw are all considered violent in Aiki since they force the resolution of conflict.

- **Consideration** – Concern.

No consideration for our practice partners also means that we have no consideration for ourselves either, so we must consider ourselves.

- **Consistency** – Coherence.

Kurita Juku Aiki's goal is to find consistency between philosophy and actions (techniques) since they are regarded as vehicles and means for growth and development. If we speak of harmony we must demonstrate and keep it up at all times. Aiki practice must be efficient, harmless and non violent, void of any hard feelings, something to be enjoyed at all times during practice.

It must be used to help each other and ourselves to grow and get stronger in union, harmony and confluence, something that may also help improve our culture and civilization.

"Theory and practice, philosophy and technique must be united and consistent; this gets us closer to God." (Morihei Ueshiba)

- **Copy** – Imitation, resemblance.

There is no need for copying because imitations are always parallel images and not originals. If we move mechanically we will be moving like a machine and machines always do the same without going anywhere. No matter how precise and accurate, if we use mechanical actions we are leaving no chance for variation and recreation. Thus we won't be able to develop and transform ourselves and what we do.

"We are not machines... even a monkey can imitate or mimic what humans do, but they are not humans" (Kurita Yutaka *Shihan*).

As Kurita *Shihan* remarks, monkeys are able to reproduce or duplicate what humans teach them too but all they do is just a movement, without any contents or transcendence. The same happens with dogs and many other animals when they obey our orders and we play with them.

- **Courtesy** – Polite or thoughtful behavior.

See Consideration

- **Cutting** – A division made with a sharp instrument (*kiru* is the Japanese word).

    Left and right hands work in a different way as well as do the legs. By working in a different way we use the sphere found in Aikido movements and then we have a complete technique.

    There are four different kinds of actions:

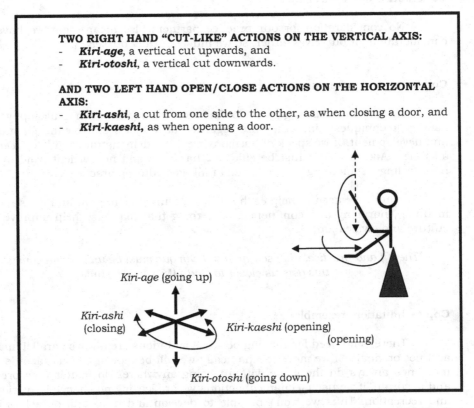

TWO RIGHT HAND "CUT-LIKE" ACTIONS ON THE VERTICAL AXIS:
-   ***Kiri-age***, a vertical cut upwards, and
-   ***Kiri-otoshi***, a vertical cut downwards.

AND TWO LEFT HAND OPEN/CLOSE ACTIONS ON THE HORIZONTAL AXIS:
-   ***Kiri-ashi***, a cut from one side to the other, as when closing a door, and
-   ***Kiri-kaeshi,*** as when opening a door.

Kiri-age (going up)

Kiri-ashi
(closing)

Kiri-kaeshi (opening)

(opening)

Kiri-otoshi (going down)

    In regards to practice with "weapons", the right side is exercised with the wooden sword (*bokken*) in order to study vertical (top-down or bottom-up) action. The left side is trained with the wooden staff (*jo*) to learn from its opening and closing horizontal movements. In addition, Kurita Shihan has used the *jo* to teach about *ichi-no-aiki, ni-no aiki, san-no-aiki*, etc, and is recently using the *bokken* to teach *ichi-no-tachi, ni-no-tachi, san-no-tachi*, etc., fundamental Aiki features from which all actions stem from.

    According to Kurita *Shihan*, cutting (*kiru*) is a pause, a limit, and an extreme. Cuts stop at certain times between alternating upwards and downwards action and when referred to the action of our hands and arms, to be executed from the hips that carry them, they refer to the former four different forms used in Aiki motion:

a) **Kiri-ashi** is an opening motion.

It uses an outwards pivot of the hips and it may be used in combination with *kiri-age* action.

b) **Kiri-kaeshi** is a closing motion.

It uses an inwards pivot of the hips and it may be used with *kiri-otoshi* movements.

(JO ⇨ Left hand)

c) **Kiri-age** is an elevating motion.

It is an upwards standing movement going against gravity so Kurita Yutaka *Shihan* considers it as a "working" action.

d) **Kiri-otoshi** is a falling motion (*otoshi* means "to fall").

This downwards movement uses gravity so its application leads to relaxation and rest, not to a final, devastating or killing action.

(BOKKEN ⇨ Right hand)

"Left and right hands never move the same way on the same axis. When cutting with a bokken, the left hand is firm and the right one is flexible, which makes a complete technique. Doing the same with both hands has been considered the same but that is absolutely wrong". (Kurita Yutaka Shihan)

D

- **Deshi** – A disciple, not simply a student.

    A disciple is someone like those live-in students (*uchideshi*) who believe and spread the teachings (*Aiki*) of their leader (*O-Sensei*).

- **Development** – Growth.

    Each individual is responsible for their own development. If a disciple may surpass the master, as one popular saying goes, it is important to find a way to know the Founder, follow his line of development and then do better. Not to follow him means never reaching the kind of growth and insight (right brain) he was able to achieve since it stays at a superficial or technical level (left brain).

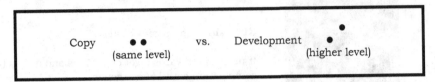

To develop and progress doesn't mean to reach whatever an international technical level may be. It is necessary to go beyond it. Experimentation and study is what really teaches us, not just looking or comparing styles, or just asking someone to teach us and to have fun during practice.

Two relevant terms are: (a) *o-henka*, which is a change, a variety, as when an engine is used in different vehicles, and (b) *oyo-henka*, an application leading to a variation as it occurs when a T-Ford car model is completely transformed into a Mustang or as when the bullet's action to hit its target in a straight direction is transformed in a missile with the ability to follow its target.

Buying or using old technique is like buying or using an old car, and looking at old pictures has to be more than looking at history, at the past, as in a museum: we can always learn from it. (Kurita Yutaka *Shihan*)

See Exercise / practice

- **Dojo** – A place for enlightenment and understanding, and not a mere practice hall.

- **Dosa** – Exercises literally done as mere repetitions.

See Undo and Waza

- **Doubt** – Uncertainty.

There are many doubts in the Aikido world, but Kurita Yutaka *Shihan* always states:

> *"Aiki-do as a proposal is very clear. O-Sensei considered this world is dirty with crimes, war, abuse, etc., so he thought it is necessary to clean it up. But in order to do so we must clean up ourselves first. When practice is correct, Aiki-do is a way to achieve this. We must learn the right fundamentals and practice at a higher level for that, with category (Sahō)."*

See Exercise/Practice

- **Dori (Tori)** – These are not only a grab but a defense against somebody holding a knife.

Dori is a means to connect with *Uke*. It is the door to open communication and it helps to combine the work of two partners. Kurita *Shihan* recalls the Founder and his fondness to make *Mochi*, a kind of bread in which he mixed the dough with his own hands. He referred to it when he talked about *aiki tori*: mixing the bread was originally an action where one person flipped the dough whereas another one hit or kneaded it. O-Sensei took this work in his *katate dori* where Uke grabs *Nage* and he works to combine both *ki*.

Aikido style

Kurita Juku Aiki style

Kurita *Shihan* teaches the right order in which the fingers are to be closed when grabbing our partner's wrist: start with the little finger and finish with the middle finger together with the thumb (as a lock), leaving the index finger opened. Besides, the step taken in order to make a grab with the left hand is different from the one used when grabbing with the right hand.

E

- **Echo** – The reflection of sound waves was used by O-Sensei to explain the mutual synchronized and corresponding actions of both participants (*Nage/Uke*)

When a man sends his voice...

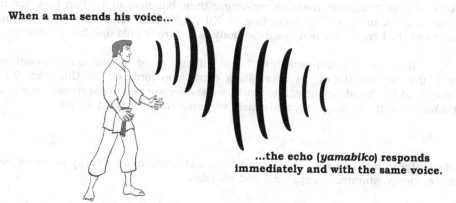

...the echo (yamabiko) responds immediately and with the same voice.

The same must happen between the mutual actions of *Nage*, who never waits, and *Uke*, who is never passive. This shows how relative things are in Aiki: *Nage* can also start the attack and finish it, both at the same time, which in fact is the most distinctive feature of *Takemusu Aiki* variations.

In addition, this allows them to work with exactly the same intention and purpose with a mutually active and real work. Thus they have the same stature and the same technique size (*ki*).

Nage never waits...   ... neither does ***Uke***

Immediate corresponding actions

- **Education** – Training and knowledge given by instructors when they teach.

    It is not necessary to have a new education as long as we have a good (correct) one. Tradition is its support and basis. Education means respect in Aiki, which simply means taking care of our duties and doing as instructed. Regarding education, Kurita *Shihan* pinpoints to the concept of *iku*.

    See Iku and Study

- **Energy** – The ability or will to work.

    It exists in many different kinds, e.g., solar or dynamic energy, etc. "Falling" occurs when *Uke* have no control of their balance, when *Nage* uses the force of gravity against them by nullifying their balance, and when they are not able to work or function. According to Kurita Yutaka *Shihan*, energy basically refers to the heat in our body –a dead body is naturally cold and has no energy.

    It is also a multi-meaningful and difficult word in *Aikido* often confused with the essence (*ki*) of the everlasting expansion force of the Universe. When compared to "the ability or will to work" we see a clear relationship with our heart (*kokoro*) and the courage or enthusiasm we must have for what we do.

    See Ki

    Multiplying our energy – By the end of an execution of an activity we must have more energy, stamina, happiness, and pleasure.

    If each partner works with 100% the result is 200%. If they work with 200% they will get 400%. But this must be done by learning to relax; when we are tired we rest, and it is by resting that we re-charge our energy.

    See Shugyō

- **Etsunen kai** - "Next year's practice"; instruction planned by yearly goals.

Practice has to be planned. An instructor may need to go from mechanical to spontaneous performance one year, for example, and wait to analyze differences in practice levels on the next one. Or he might like to analyze the implicit changes of *kihon gi, henka gi* and *oyo henka gi* this year, and then to move from no category (or non ceremonial) practice to one of a high category (or ceremonial), and leave all special practice for the next year, etc.

Etsunen kai helps to make continuous changes in our Aiki life to be reflected in our lines of action and style. The following is only one example of the way Kurita Yutaka *Shihan* emphasized in 1996 specific technique phases to be practiced according to the rank of his students:

a) That year the *contact* phase (union, *mawae* and *kokyu*) was going to be the main topic for 5th and 4th *kyu* students.

b) The *nagare* phase (major and wider circles) was assigned to be the topic for 3rd. and 2nd *kyu* students.

c) The *free mobility* phase (360° circles instead of the usual 180°) was intended for 1st *kyu* students, and

d) The *ceremonial* (*Sahō*) practice was going to be the goal for instructors.

This ensured each student got what they needed in order to reach their next level: instruction progressed towards superior performance. But Kurita *Shihan* stopped following the usual Aikido contents made popular by some big organizations when he decided they are usually a list of techniques and they are only referred to for testing and promotion purposes without really highlighting important Aiki fundamental aspects.

- **Example/explanation** – Something singled out to show what other things are and reasons to do as demonstrated.

Aikido has different kinds of examples or explanations used to show and illustrate actions that depend on the use of our left or right brains. Two kinds of explanations related to the *left brain* are:

a) the *technical* or *scientific* explanation, as when it is said that, "*Katate dori* is a grab as well as a protection against an attack," "*Irimi* is an entrance of the body," or "*Tenkan* is a pivot", etc., which is often referred to sword actions and the fighting origins of *Aikido*, and

b) the *philosophical and spiritual* explanations like these: "*Katate dori* is an approach intended to promote closeness and communication"; "*Irimi* is an entrance to another dimension"; "*Tenkan* is a change of objective and perspective", etc.).

But Aiki has an additional way to show and illustrate these same actions. It is very important and is related to the function of the *right brain*:

c)   the *imaginative* and *sensitive* explanation: imagining and feeling the order of the Universe reflected in our "techniques", and applied to our own lives since they are the means to discover it.

No words are ever used in this kind of explanation, only sensations, perceptions and feeling. When the union of our *kokoro* and our *energy* (heat) is felt it finally results in the actual manifestation of our *ki*. It is here where we must find the secrets of the Universe, as well as its order and arrangement, its Aiki. Such an explanation allows for congruence and consistency between the first two left-brain kinds.

The two former left-brain kinds of examples and explanations show the evident action executed by *Aikido* practitioners. They might be leaving out all reference to the work done during each action, hiding it to the untrained eye and body. On the other hand the last one –(c)– launches a deeper right-brain vision. It can be used to approach the inner subtleties of the work required to make a difference in Aiki performance.

The right brain explanation is constantly pinpointed and aimed at in *Kurita Juku Aiki* and it is one Kurita *Shihan* is constantly studying and recalling in order to gaining new insight on the ideals inherited by Kaiso Sensei. It leads Aiki-do practice into practical applications in our everyday lives and it is required in order to take *Aikido* one step further.

See Study

• **Exercise/practice** – The work done to train body and mind.

The body can be trained separately, independently from the mind, so to speak, or, to be more specific, without having to use of our left side of the brain, which controls our logical and technical thinking.

Generally speaking **Aikido** has two different ways to learn how to execute a movement and to practice it in response to the student's needs to start and be introduced to the art:

a)   *Kihon* – The first preparation exercise (mechanization of action). It may refer to a basic superficial execution, and it is basically a contact phase.

b)   *Shuren* (shuden) or *Tanden* – It refers to firm and strong practice, done to the limit of our abilities and with great stamina. This term is expressed by two Japanese words: *shure* (with strength) and *tanden* (firm holding) so this practice consists of severe, non-stopping and hurting practice. It leaves the students with a sore body and ego.

Aiki-do has two extra ways to train the mind in order to make it reflect the students' progress as they get rid and independent from empty techniques:

c)   *Giho* – Complete practice. It covers all details that make technique perfect at each level (beginners, intermediate and advanced students). Among some other things *Uke* is always at *Nage*'s center and in front of him in this practice. It is the work made by the distance between them as well as the size and quality of the action, which is executed in a continuous, undivided, non hesitant and united way from start to finish. It makes the difference between mere activity and the application of work.

d) *Sahō* - elevated, superior and refined practice. It shows true development since it expresses movements that have been polished. It also shows the heart and essence of Aiki-do as a ceremony.

It consists of a *Sahō,* water-fire work in terms of a ceremony where all elements are put in place and to their right use. This is what each and every practitioner feels in their technique. It can be shown, seen and felt: it is the spiritual work done rather than the activity performed. Correct practice insures *ki* is part of the job done. Unfortunately, students in many *dojo* are some sort of technique slaves. (Kurita *Shihan*)

- **Exhaling** – The action by which our lungs force air out.

    To exhale in Aiki is to give away, to let go of, to redirect an action: it does not actually refer to the lungs at all or to those well-known breathing exercises practiced in *karate*. In some kinds of performance though, students have to try longer and longer exhalations which are intended to practice a longer and more continuous flow of action.

    See Breathing, Inhaling

- **Extension (*kokyu*)** – A term related to breathing, it is the act of extending or reaching, getting to the farthest corner of the Universe or bringing it to us.

    From a martial perspective it protects us as a shield when *Uke* wants to enter our space because it helps us to encounter their intention. And from an Aiki point of view it helps our technique to be alive, opened and breathing. It is through breathing that we seek for an exit and seek to emerge (this is what the corresponding Japanese *kanji* represents).

F

- **Fighting** – A struggle against, a quarrel or arguing.

    To fight is to treat somebody as an opponent or enemy so it is forbidden in Aiki.

G

- **Gi** – Movement, action.

    A term Kurita Yutaka *Shihan* has used to describe three different kinds of movements:

a) *Kihon gi.-* Basis, foundation, posture.

It refers to the first mechanical actions students learn when they start training and improve as they make progress and develop coordination.

b) *Henka–gi.-* Variation and change.

It refers to an unusual performance or application, almost as if it was a different one, e.g. *Ikkyo* finished with a different stance or posture. It is not to be confused with the moment when students switch, e.g. from *ikkyo* to *nikyo* or *kote-gaeshi,* because technique doesn't work and they choose another one.

c) *Oyo-henka–gi.-* Application, adaptation, mobilization with a change resulting in transformation. It also refers to the practical utilization of a technique. These movements have sometimes been confused with actions against weapons. It is also pronounced *O-henka*: advanced technique with an application. It is transformed into something else on the same basis though.

O-henka and *oyo-henka* refer to change and transformation, which are in a certain way no more and no less than development and improvement from a previous state or condition.

O-henka (variation and change) and *oyo-henka* (transforming change) refer to the evolution of basic techniques. Everything can be transformed, improved, and thus changed. It relates to evolution (*oyo* means "progress").

See Student's levels

H

- **Hanmi handachi** – A situation where *Nage* works from a sitting position while *Uke* is standing up, which means the former has a medium mobilization and cannot have proactive or "attacking" action as compared to *tachi waza.*

  It differs from both *suwari waza* and *tai sabaki,* and it is a mistake to think techniques are done in the same way in spite of their different situation.

  See Suwari waza and Tachi waza

- **Haishin undo** – A wrap up activity where one partner takes another one on his/her back and then stretches him/her so that every single bone from their backs are re-aligned. This must be done slowly and flexibly.

- **Henka waza** – "A *responding line of action; region and vicinity*" (Kurita *Shihan*).

- **Henko** – An alteration, a change in direction or sense (from left to right, or from North to South, etc).

- **Hierarchy** – A system of organization in which people have higher and lower ranks. It usually refers to the most powerful members of an organization.

  It exists in the Aikikai institution but it is not part of Aiki since all practitioners are equal and the Founder wanted no divisions, differences or privileges. The higher the rank, the higher the responsibility and the human values expected from the person holding them.

  See Category

I

- **Iku** – Formation and development, the act of becoming.

  As a result of constant training, a series of *iku* constitute what is called *kio-iku* (education or formation of the individual). Kurita Yutaka *Shihan* talks of the following three:

  a) *Ki-iku* – formation and development of one's essence, will, flexibility and intuition (aiki energy).

  b) *Tai-iku* – formation and development of one's body.

  c) *Toku-iku* – formation and development of one's divine nature and being.

  See Kokoro and Ki

- **Ikkyo, nikyo, sankyo, yonkyo, and gonkyo** – The five common *Aikido* "pinning" activities that are common core of an *Aikido* training program.

  See Study

- **Inhaling** – An action used to receive, take, and absorb *Uke*'s action. Breathing in Aiki does not refer to the work of our lungs.

Inhaling   **Exhaling**

- **Instructor** – Someone who teaches a particular sport, skill, etc.

  Instructors are not to keep things to themselves, but only to manifest and do what has to be done. And even when each one may have their own proprietary style, the way of Aiki is not to be changed at all. The Founder's style and ideal must be imitated and mastered before attempting it.

"Instructors educate, they don't teach techniques". (Kurita *Shihan*)

- **Instruction** – A systematic way to teach Aiki at different *kyu* and *dan* levels gives them a distinct level based on work which takes students from a dissipated to a concentrated use of their nature:

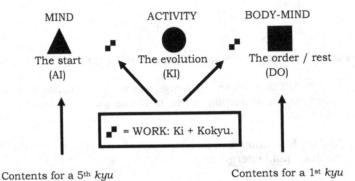

MIND   ACTIVITY   BODY-MIND

The start   The evolution   The order / rest
(AI)   (KI)   (DO)

= WORK: Ki + Kokyu.

Contents for a 5th *kyu*   Contents for a 1st *kyu*

This ensures practitioners go from a lower to a higher rank. It is more or less what happens in general education. So when compared to a regular school system, Aiki-do can be said to progress through the following grades:

Aikido	KIHON is a kindergarten level where the system is presented as a catalogue of techniques. It is like showing the parts of a sword.
	SHUREN is a secondary school level where the system is a set of techniques practiced in a tough way (forging the sword).
	GIHO is a high school level where the subtleties of techniques are practiced (exploring the secrets of the sword).
Aiki	SAHŌ is a College level. Technique is used to make a refined and civilized culture (earning the sword and the rank).

The whole process puts a common soldier of the lowest rank on the way to become an officer of the highest rank.

- **Intention** – Something intended; a plan or purpose.

Intention goes before the body when an *action* (technique) is performed. *Ki* works first and protects us, not the body, which only blocks.

See Kokyu in the basic glossary of Aiki terms used by the Founder (Chapter 2)

- **Interchange (*Aiki*)** – Combination, sharing.

    Students must share their will and energy through correct action. They are not enemies and they must not stick to a mechanical and superficial style. Interchange (Aiki) means "to combine and unite", and practitioners must benefit from each other's work. We must understand and find out the best theory, the best ideology and even if there are any mistakes, the worst ones.

    There must always be honesty, search, and a hunger to develop and improve ourselves and our world. This is obviously Aiki according to Kurita Yutaka *Shihan*.

    See Aiki

- **Internal/external *Ki*** – The Founder never made this difference because *ki* was simply *ki* for him. The essence is partially similar to body posture, flexibility, dynamics, being, attitude, will, and many others.

    "Energy is not outside, but inside" (Kurita *Shihan*). It is Inside Aiki, inside unity, confluence and harmony.

- **Irimi-nage/ kokyu-nage/ kote-gaeshi / shiho-nage/ tenchi-nage** – The most common Aikido "throwing" or dynamic activities described in many books. They are part of most general training programs.

- **Izanau** – Attraction.

    This is the first element used in Aiki action, as mentioned in Chapter 4. In a movement such as *tsuki - kote-gaeshi*, Kurita *Shihan* always goes directly to *Uke* and pivots at the very last second in order to avoid *Uke*'s intention to be completed. By doing this he creates a magnetic attraction which makes *Uke* feel "sucked up" as by a tornado while he places himself in a safer place out of the line followed by *Uke*.

    The effect of *izanau* is like a magnet. It attracts *Uke* and it leads to *Awase* (overlapping) which in turn allows *Nage* to lead *Uke* and control their mutual action. *Uke* cannot escape but is always protected so the initial intention is never broken or stopped, but deviated and free from any possible crash.

    See Awase, Musubi

J

- **Jiyū waza** – Free technique ("doing as one likes it").

    This includes the use of kicks, bites, pinches, and whatever *Nage* wants since it does not focus on the Founder's Aiki.

- **Jutsu** – A means; a technique.

  The original *kanji* for this word is a reference to the means or techniques to be followed or adhered to in order to achieve one's goal.

  This term has a different meaning than *waza* because it suggests a mechanical repetition and refers to the superficial aspects of the work done in the line of action, like twisting an arm or a wrist, slamming an opponent through different actions, stopping him/her in any way or form, etc.

K

- **Kaeshi waza** – Reversing or "countering".

  This situation demonstrates there is the possibility of avoiding any winner-loser situations in Aiki-do, since all actions can be stopped or countered at will by either *Nage* or *Uke*. Instructors and students look like champions when they demonstrate technique, and the public associates *Nage* with "the one who wins" and *Uke* with "the one who loses", which is a wrong message.

  Kaeshi waza is a reminder to get away from selfishness and egocentrism. It is a reminder that cooperation and correct work is essentially a turn-taking chance: sometimes we are up and sometimes we are down.

- **Kaiso Sensei (Ueshiba Morihei)** – This is the right way to refer to O-Sensei according to Kurita *Shihan*.

  The concept is formed by two *kanji*: *kai* (opening) and *so* (beginning); it connotes the fact that master Ueshiba was the first to uncover, envision and unveil the way of Aiki. Although he was its discoverer or inventor, his discovery can still be improved, just as has happened with other inventions like the phonograph, the telephone and the first airplane, to name a few.

  The term is similar to both founder (one who establishes something) and grand master (one who excels other instructors).

- **Kamae vs. hanmi** – *Kamae* refers to the postures used in martial arts whereas the initial position assumed when starting any movement is called *hanmi*. This is the name for all the oblique stances used in Aiki intended to allow for the pivoting actions used to expand the circular and centrifugal/centripetal effects of *ki*.

- **Kamiza** – Literally "the seat for God".

  Kurita *Shihan* has taught traditional classes where all movements are practiced only and exclusively away from the *kamiza*, or either to its sides or to its front, but never towards it. This has to be done as a token of respect but it is no longer taught by many instructors.

The *kamiza* is also the place where important guests sit. So it is also the place where we find O-Sensei's picture in every *dojo*.

- **Kansetsu waza** – The use of articulations.

- **Karate** – This word literally refers to an empty (*kara*) hand (*te*).

    In contrast, hands in Aiki are never empty but full.

- **Ki** – "*A question to be answered, not 'energy'*." (Kurita Yutaka *Shihan*)

    This term has multiple meanings and interpretations. It is part of our being, but it is different from our muscles and minds. It is something between *Nage/Uke* which is neither physical nor mental. It is our intention and will to do things correctly, relaxation and much more. It stems from the body "set aright" and so it is the combination or addition of our heart (*kokoro*) plus the courage or enthusiasm as well as positive will and attitude put on work and action:

    "Kokoro + courage = Ki" (Kurita *Shihan*)

    Ki is the combination of both *kokoro* (heart, will) and courage put in practice plus the right body work done from a correct posture for a specific goal which may in turn mean "life growth".

    There is no such thing as "positive" or "negative" *ki*, because *ki* is only *ki* from O-Sensei's perspective. (Kurita *Shihan*)

    See Ki in the basic glossary of Aiki terms used by the Founder (Chapter 2)

- **Kiai** – As usually taught in *Karate*, *kiai* is commonly thought of as a yell but in fact it means "*God comes to us*" (Kurita *Shihan*).

    As a reversed term *Aiki* is then understood as "*Going to God*". According to the Founder the *do* in Aiki-do is the vehicle by means of which we can literally go to him. By the way, O-Sensei's *kotodama* (chanting practice) was his *kiai*; that is, "*His way to get closer to God.*" (Kurita *Shihan*).

- **Kohai** – A junior student, an obviously none-existing term in Kaiso Sensei's Aiki.

    See Sempai, Sensei

- **Kokoro** – The heart, mind and will put into practice.

    It is a right attitude free from any form of selfishness and winning / defeating feelings.

- **Kokyu** – A factor designed to develop *ki* it is part of all techniques.

  See Extension

- **Kokyu-ho** – The work of chest and legs.

  It is an inevitable work element for all Aiki techniques. It is an integral part of all *Aikido* actions such as *shiho-nage*, *kote-gaeshi*, etc.

- **Kokyu-nage** – Managing inwards and outwards in order to create a breathing and vibrant performance. It is an exercise designed to develop *ki* and train with it. But it is much more than a movement intended to make *Uke* to take a roll because it can be used to work with space.

- **Kokyu-ryoku** – An explosive effect created by the power taken by Aiki movements as they speed up during an action.

- **Kuden** – Oral tradition, instruction given to a student in public or in private.

  Kurita Yutaka *Shihan* states this word must be understood as teachings to be made public and not to be translated as hidden or secret instruction.

- **Kurita Juku Aiki** – Yutaka Kurita *Shihan's* school.

JUKU - traditional school

  The term *Juku* (private school) refers to an old institution where one single teacher had to be in charge of all aspects of students' education. This differs from modern schools since now there is a teacher for each different subject matter. Kurita *Shihan* runs a *Juku* in order to teach in person all aspects related to Aiki. Next to Kurita *Shihan's* name it denotes a renewal of Aiki practice as a legacy freely transmitted by the Founder.

  Since he was sent to Mexico City as a representative of the Aikido Central Headquarters in Japan (*Hombu Dojo*), Kurita *Shihan* taught what he was ordered to. More than 20 years later, Ueshiba Kisshomaru *Doshu* passed away and he spent three additional mourning years before he felt he was able to get apart from the Aikikai style. His goal is seemingly to pass on a series of reviewed original contents and details he learned from Kaiso Sensei in order to present a more refined, comprehensive and integrated kind of practice.

- **Kyu** – class, level, grade or rank; a distinction given to practitioners when they start progressing.

  Right after several *kyu* are granted to them students can start getting *dan* (step, stair) ranks which are traditionally given to high-level practitioners in martial arts. Kurita *Shihan* proposes they should be given to the most sincere students who show the best Aiki progress.

Students who have obtained *kyu* ranks wear white belts, whereas *dan* students wear black ones. Getting a black belt indicates the way has been started. It is a starting point and not an ending one. Unfortunately, many people think of a black belt as a conclusion or final stage in their development.

Both black and white stand for purity, so those are the only colors used. Kidding about it Kurita *Shihan* makes a difference between belts that have become black because they are not washed and the black belts that represent the starting point of a higher enterprise. Practitioners who work with the left side of their brains are always like beginners, whereas those who work through the right heart and their right brain are more advanced.

L

- **Level** – Same height or position.

  According to their progress, the way of Aiki makes a difference between three levels of students' practice: (a) basic, strength vs. strength; (b) intermediate, strength vs. flexible; and (c) advanced, flexible vs. flexible. But there are some other things that constitute a level as, e.g., the size of the line of action which is in turn the size of *ki*, the working level of the arms, the right *kokoro*, etc.

  See Student's levels, Kokoro

- **Left / right** – The sides in reference to a person's hands.

  The corresponding *kanji* for these words contain strokes respectively meaning:

  a) *Migi*, or right side: strength and support;

  b) *Hidari*, or left side: auxiliary strength and support, so it also means to assist.

  It is from these concepts that Kurita *Shihan* finds another direct evidence of the functions performed by our left and right brain hemispheres since although the right hand (left brain) seems to be in charge of conscious actions, the left hand (right brain) is always supporting and complementing it in unconscious or intuitive manner.

  This explains why Nage starts working on the left side in traditional practice in order to use the right side of their brains first. However we have stated that Aiki movements are different when executed with the right or the left hands and legs since they are designed to make them support one another as well as to practice with both brains.

M

- **Magnetism** – The ability to attract.

    Magnetism is an important part in Aiki practice. It is the first step to be taken. *Ki* produces a very special kind of magnetism in Aiki.

    See Izanau

- **Man** – A human being, a person, the human race.

    A man is like a cup over a small plate. The plate is the Universe that supports and sustains him. Without the dish, the cup may fall and the table cloth can get dirty. Aiki allows practitioners to play both roles (cup and plate) in order to awaken their senses and intuition. It deals with the acceptance or rejection of different but complementing roles.

    See Sensei

- **Martial art** – An art related to or aimed for combat (Mars was the ancient Greek god of war).

    The Aiki paradigm puts an end to the negative actions produced from encounters, fights, or any other similar things coming from opponents and helps to overcome their power. Aiki makes us help each other, whereas other arts have a winner over one or multiple losers; no other art leaves any room for people to help each other as Aiki does:

    > *"When learning a 'martial art' (Budo) it is very important not to learn a self-defense form, but to change our perspectives".* (Kurita *Shihan*)

- **Memory** – The ability to remember.

    There are three kinds of memories: two are carried out by our brain hemispheres (one is logic and the other is intuitive) plus the one carried out by our body through the Aiki senses. The latter is the long-lasting memory humanity needs since it is the clearest one, according to the practice system followed by Kurita *Shihan* who states it with a simple formula:

    > *"Feeling, tasting and mastering before we are able to share it with others".*

    See Teaching

- **Michi** – A line, way or direction.

Noteworthy, the *kanji* for this word is the same for *do* (please note that Japanese *kanji* have different pronunciations: one when they stand by themselves and another one in compound terms).

See Aiki no michi

- **Mirror** – Something that reflects a picture of something else.

    We always reflect ourselves in other people: when somebody do something to us we immediately think we are innocent and tend to blame them for their doing. But what we see on them may be a clear reflection of our own doings and we may be unconsciously responsible for what they do to us.

    This is the "Aiki mirror" by means of which we become aware of our responsibilities and we learn about the effect of our actions. So when *Uke* suffers because of our abusive pin or throw we get a good reflection of the kind of heart and intentions we have put in our line of actions. Even worse is the fact that all that pressure will eventually act directly against our own being and upon our own lives without noticing it.

    Many practitioners see the effect of their actions when they hurt a partner, but they may fail to recognize themselves reflected on what they just did. This usually happens when they resist and provoke a fight during practice too, but this should not be tolerated.

- **Misogi** – Cleansing.

    Each practice is a cleansing chance, an opportunity for change. When talking about this, Kurita *Shihan* points out that a waterfall is beautiful because of the rocks, the trees and the sky surrounding it, and hence people like it and may even feel like getting under it. In contrast: no body loves getting caught by plain rain if this just means getting soaked.

- **Misunderstanding** – A failure to understand or agree.

    There are plenty of misunderstandings in *Aikido*, such as presenting it as a fighting art full of non-Aiki terms such as *Nage-Uke*, *randori*, *breakfall*s, etc. Many have arisen from what may be a superficial interpretation of important terms that seem to have been loosely used for the past 40 years.

- **Mobility** – The ability to move or to be moved from place to place.

    The higher the level of (Aiki) performance, the more it is silent in nature. When techniques are correctly performed they are not disturbing or bothering, because they are natural, flexible and silent, something absent in violent applications or performance, as when people slam on the ground.

- **Mobilization** – Comprises entering and circular movements used at will.

Circles are part of techniques, which in fact are variables of the circle made by the direction they follow as practitioners execute them. *Irimi* and *tenkan* are mobilizations whereas *omote*, *ura* and *nage* are techniques (*waza*) or complementing lines of action.

See Waza

- **Movement** – The act of moving (changing the position of something).

  Each Aiki action has an underlying theory which stands as its foundation and helps instructors to explain the Founder's philosophy. In this sense a movement is both the act of moving and the actions taken by practitioners to reach a particular goal.

- **Musubi** – Uniting, tying.

  This is the third element used in all Aiki actions.

  See Izanau, Awase

N

- **Nagare** – From the verb *nagareru* (to flow).

  Kaiso Sensei saw *nagare* (a flow) in the continuous expansion of the Universe made possible by *ki* (see *Ki no nagare,* "the flow of *ki*", in Chapter 2).

- **Nage** – From the verb *nageru* (to throw, to give up); a term not to be confused with *nagare*.

- **Nage/Uke** – Two terms borrowed from *Judo*, or even much more precisely, added by students who studied it (O-Sensei used *shi* and *tori*).

  Nage denotes "the one who throws" and *Uke* "the one who falls", but O-Sensei connotes an absolutely different concept and he did not teach his students to fall in any technical or philosophical sense or in real life.

  The term suggests some kind of passiveness on the side of *Uke,* the one who receives a technique. But Aiki necessarily demands an active work on the *Uke* side too, which is often put aside or neglected for the sake of a training which has traditionally been focused on the role of *Nage.*

  Kaiso Sensei used the term *uketachi* (one that acts as a trapper, as a net; it is one who seems to "invite" but in fact 'reacts') instead of *Nage.* Besides, the combined movement of both participants (referred in this book as *Nage* and *Uke* for the sake of the usual reference) represents the eternal water-fire duality:

a) Besides approaching *Nage*, *Uke* moves upwards and downwards on the vertical axis.

b) Besides approaching *Uke*, *Nage* enters or pivots on the horizontal axis.

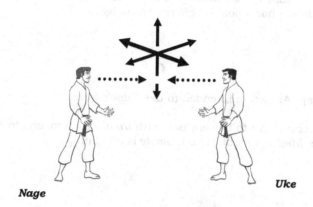

Nage   **Uke**

Together both partners use width and length dimensions. And their mutual approaching and separating movements become complete in its third dimension (depth). Since Aiki has no divisions, terms like *Nage* and *Uke* are not necessary. They may be used to state the different turn taking when activities are practiced. Using dimension and space changes the quality of practice.

See Agatsu, Masakatsu, Katsuhayabi (page 64).

- **Nature** – All living things and events in the world.

  Nature in Aiki is more than a mere reference to the woods, rivers and mountains of our planet. We must see it as Life itself, the life manifested in their beings, states, and composition (*ki* = being/state/composition).

- **Never steal your partner's energy** – By paying attention to practice it can be clearly noticed that:

  ✓ When beginner students practice there is little or no movement, they are static, loose or stiff. They still have to recognize their potential energy and to find their new role.

  ✓ When intermediate students practice only one of them moves correctly and the dynamics changes. They are on their way to apply their energy and potential.

  ✓ When advanced students practice they move in flexible, harmless and effortless actions. They are on their way to become creative and change their practice so each one of them may have a chance not only to give their 100% but to multiply their energy too.

When we do not cooperate, move correctly, or engage in what is being done, we are only wasting ours and our partners' energy and potential. This is what Kurita Yutaka *Shihan* calls *"stealing your partner's energy"* since there is neither circulation nor a positive energy exchange.

O

- **Omote (waza)** - An action intended to use *Nage*'s front.

    This term is not to be confused with *irimi*, which means to enter, by taking a step inside. *Irimi* is a mobilization, *omote* is a technique.

    See Waza

- **One new technique at a time**

    Practice is not made out of mechanical repetitions; the idea is not to repeat movements in a robot-like way. They must be fresh and renewed like a brand new day each time they are performed.

    The different stages of an action are like the three different parts of a day. We can make an analogy with the Sun rising, being at its zenith, and setting, which gives way to the quiet and peaceful night, a time when we can contemplate the Universe. (Kurita Yutaka *Shihan*)

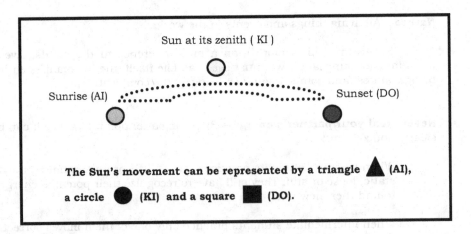

Technique must be fresh and new in every single application, so that renewing ourselves becomes the most important aspect in Aiki training. That is what it was designed for.

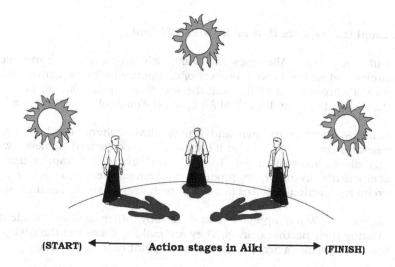

(START) ← ——— **Action stages in Aiki** ——— → (FINISH)

- **Open/close** – Aiki action is made through openings and puts an end to attacks. It is made exactly as when two people are about to shake hands: it opens our hands and hearts. *Kokyu*, e.g., requires us to open our chest and hips.

    The work done helps practitioners to open their mutual postures. It helps them to grow and get rid of violence, making them blossom. In opposition, a closed action makes us go in the opposite direction. But when it is done right as soon as *Uke* is coming *Nage* is already going out of the line of "attack" by using a mobilization designed to avoid crashing and running over each other. This opens *Uke*'s body and puts an end to their initial action. The initial intention fades the attempt away from its start.

    By means of an opening (pivoting action), *Nage* use a different approach towards an "attack": instead of blocking it they open *Uke*'s stance and change their balance. The physical opening also takes place in their minds, and resolves the situation with a completely different approach.

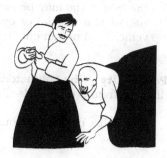

Closed fists and bodies vs. open fingers and bodies

P

- **Philosophical aspects that make Aiki different**

  a) *Path, way (do)* – Aiki uses the Universe's way made of harmonious orbits, circles and waves as well as a set of distinctive order elements. *Do* is the path created through experience and the way that can be used to be in touch with the divine, the Grand Spirit of Aiki (*Aiki O-Kami*), of union and confluence.

  b) *Flavor* – Aiki has its own and unique flavor when tasted, although it may resemble some other arts on its surface. A good taste is achieved when all the ingredients are well mixed. The Aiki work-action set implies using all of its components in order to produce a chemical reaction that results in its exclusive, particular flavor (a taste nobody tastes, smells, and sees).

  c) *Objective* – When applying *ikkyo*, or any other actions, students are not twisting their partners' arms. They are making them feel their *ikkyo*, and they use their partner's arms as an entrance point to that first stage.

  d) *Depth* – Aiki has a profound level and a ceremonial aspect attached to it which makes it different from religion, although Kaiso Sensei used to express his findings in a religious way:

     > *"Aiki-do is an art for the manifestation of the God in us (the divine part in each and all of us)".*

     We must take out the divine within us and make it flourish. That's why practice is done in a *dojo* and not in a gym or hall. Our personality must be refined through training and by so doing everyone can get closer to this particular element. Understood as responsibility, respect is fundamental.

     A *dojo* where the "Aiki O-Kami" *kanji* is not displayed is just a gym or a practice hall and lacks the true Aiki spirit.

  e) *Union* – The result of the Aiki formula is $1 + 1 = 0$ (no attacks, no differences, union, blending and perfection). *"When everybody will do Aiki there will be no more need for it."* (Kurita *Shihan*)

  f) *Freedom* – Aiki has no slaves. Those concerned about learning or performing the best *Ikkyo* may be acting as slaves of technique, and those worried about *Aikido* as a martial or combat art may be the slaves of fear. Technique is a vehicle and not an end in Aiki-do. (Kurita Yutaka *Shihan*)

- **Personality** – The characteristics of behavior and feelings that make one person different from everyone else.

     Aiki helps us improve our personality in a positive, constructive, and refined way.

- **Pleasure** – A pleasant, happy feeling.

Technique must be satisfying, joyful. It is not to be suffered or experienced as something painful. Working Aiki gives a lot of pleasure during practice, a pleasure that can be extended to our lives so it goes beyond fun.

"Smile when you work, it's not a fight!" (Kurita Shihan)

See Smile

- **Polite** – Showing good manners, courtesy.

Politeness is an important element in Aiki. The way we come into the *dojo* and jump into the *tatami* (mats) area affects our relationship with our practice partners. So does the way we behave and show respect to the Founder, to his heart, his way and ideal, as well as to our Sensei and classmates. But most important, it affects our relationship with ourselves. This is known as *Sahō*, the highest level of practice in Aiki, the most refined one.

- **Posture** – The way a person holds the body.

A correct posture must be kept at all times. Practitioners can never use an arm behind their backs or even look at the ground bending their heads down since these postures weaken them. Firm hips are necessary to practice correctly and this has to be maintained throughout all actions.

In a good, balanced and centered posture our weight is distributed like this:

In *hidari hanmi*, for example, the left hand and arm aligns with the right leg. The right hand / arm is aligned with the left leg and all this helps the body to be centered and balanced at all times.

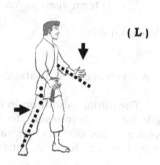

(L)

(R)

Hidari hanmi

- **Practice** – The act of doing something over and over in order to learn it well.

Aiki practice has to evoke the Founder's ideal and everyday, real life at all times. It must reflect positive values, which implies a change of mind and a transformation of our current paradigms; claiming practice is good and effective for combat only means that O-Sensei's line has been lost.

According to Kurita *Shihan*, Kaiso Sensei thought practice must be like a celebration where people get together to relax and enjoy. He used the term *Sho-chiku-bai* (see the glossary in Chapter 2) in reference to the endurance and strength displayed by the pine, the bamboo and the plum. We must have in mind that our effort in practice is the key to open our eyes. It lets us taste the works involved in our action; only effort can lead towards knowledge and understanding (illumination): "*Our ki works when this happens*" (Kurita Yutaka *Shihan*).

See Exercise

- **Pressure** – The force of one person or thing that creates a physical or mental burden.

    Many styles are tough or violent, and many techniques use a lot of pressure against *Uke*. Kurita *Shihan* points out that if we apply pressure on our actions we are also putting that same pressure upon us. This can be felt in practice anytime somebody tries to win or inflict pain on their partners under the impression that they must hurt them to prove they work effectively.

    The less violent or pressing techniques are, the less pressure we will have in our own lives.

    See Pleasure

R

- **Randori** – Multiple attacks.

    A *Judo* term alien to Aiki-do.

    See Renzoku waza

- **Rei** – A reverence or salutation.

    The initial salutation in class to the Founder's portrait on the wall is a way to ask for his permission to borrow his formula. Kaiso Sensei used it as a reverence to his God and he saw as Divine. Practitioners show their respect (*rei*) to each other and to life in general when they bow to each other.

    Rei is what each one can give others, and thus it is like a salutation to the Grand Spirit of Aiki (*Aiki O-Kami*) and not only a reverence. (Kurita *Shihan*)

    See Chinkon-Kishin in the Founder's glossary (Chapter 2)

- **Reigi** – A greeting.

In Aiki, *reigi* is an action meaning that we have category, that our partners respect us, and vice-versa. It is an action similar to that of hosts who receive important guests with all due considerations.

- **Renzoku waza** – Continued, multi-directional, non-stopping application in all directions.

This is a more precise Aiki term than *randori*, which means "multiple attacks" and comes from a word denoting war, riot, and rebellion (*ran*, in Japanese). Similar to the basic practice of *suwate kokyu-ho* (which is used to handle our partner's energy), *renzoku waza* teaches us about connectivity. It consists of following from one technique to the next, keeping *kokyu* (extension) at all times, and moving towards different directions. We can start to the front, then go to the left and then to the right, or we can follow a clock-wise mobilization, or a counter clock-wise one, etc.

The idea in practicing *renzoku waza* is to link one action after another in a flowing and continuous chain. Any techniques may be applied but they must always keep partners attached without any separation between *Uke* and *Nage*.

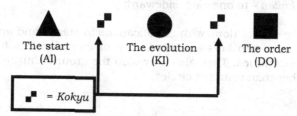

If *kokyu* (contact and extension, represented by ▪◾) is not added and is present between each phase our performance is empty. Any combination of techniques can be chosen and used but our actions must always be united by it. It is not only technique but *kokyu* that matters. The whole formula consists of *ki + work + kokyu* to be complete. (Kurita *Shihan*)

Any combination or chain of actions must be equal in each and every movement; the action must be smooth and orderly, and have a certain rhythm too. *Renzoku waza* teaches us "organization that leads to unity":

Aiki-do is a way to "make" one's self through the works of:

ki *awase* +   ki *musubi*   through   *kokyu* = Aiki
(*ki* overlap)   (*ki* union)   (extended *ki*)

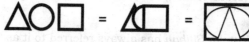

Without these elements we just have mere technique. We must realize that *"the Founder put them all together."* (Kurita *Shihan*)

- **Respect** – Admiration, regard and responsibility.

Respect means to carry out our duties, which in turn means: *"Do as the Founder taught and follow the Grand Spirit of Aiki."* (Kurita *Shihan*)

- **Rhythm** – A regular repetition of a movement, action, or sound.

  Aiki has its own rhythm, speed and vitality.

- **Roll** – A movement made by turning over and over again.

  It is a change in position and it is used as a quick way out from the application of dynamic actions applied by *Nage*. Rolls must always be well concentrated and done with no noise; the body must show the union of mind and body. There are three different kinds:

  ✓ *Kempo kaiten* – to the front (frontward)

  ✓ *Koho kaiten* – to the back (backwards)

  ✓ *Gyaku kaiten* – to one side (sideward)

  They can also be done with modifications in stance and angle. Some styles use rolls combined with falls and need open or extended legs to soften them in order to prevent injuries. They also may slap the ground, but all this may result in squared rather than rounded circles.

  See Circles

- **Ryoku** – The strength or force contained in every action.

  There is a *ryoku* of *irimi*, of *ikkyo*, of *kokyu-ho*, etc. This term is not to be confused with muscular strength: actions gain power as they gain momentum.

S

- **Sahō**

  See Exercise / practice

- **Seika tanden** (*seika no itten*) – A point under the belly button, where the *hakama* is knotted.

  Kurita Yutaka *Shihan* has always referred to it as "point 1" (the "one point" mentioned in many publications), in reference to a central line too. *Seika tanden* must always go up and ahead of us when we move or intend to move. It is used as a reference point for our direction and center. It implies the use of space and gravity but it is usually disregarded as an element that must be present in every line of action. "Attacks" used in practice must always start from this point.

- **Seiza** – A sitting posture.

    Its purpose is to make more energy (it is closer to the ground). It is a *return-to-one's-self* activity that helps us to relax and tune in before practice.

    The work in *Seiza* has both "masculine" and "feminine" counterparts. The masculine is represented by the legs, which work hard in this position (that's why they hurt). And the feminine part is constituted by the chest and arms. They are complementary and create balance.

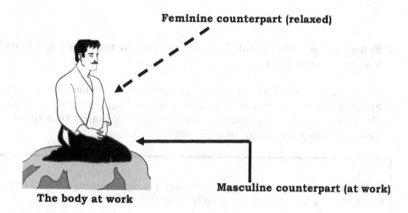

Feminine counterpart (relaxed)

The body at work   **Masculine counterpart (at work)**

    This sitting posture teaches about the difference between doing and not doing, between understanding and not understanding, and between achieving and not achieving. Kurita *Shihan* considers it as the *shugyo* of Aiki-do.

See Shugyo

- **Self-defense** – The act of preventing from the attack of an enemy.

    Aiki-do can be used as a self-defense system but its goals are absolutely different. Thus its application and results are completely different from any fighting forms. As a *budo* form Aiki-do is the way to seriously unite and fit with others as well as with the order of the Universe.

    Kurita Yutaka *Shihan* teaches that "*Soldiers and policemen need self-defense, not us*". Unfortunately, and mostly driven by fear, many people still look for martial arts classes in order to protect themselves on the streets.

- **Seminar** – From the Latin word for "seed", it is a special class or session where a seed is analyzed and planted.

    Since a seminar is not a regular class, the effort applied must be greater. No one can be weak or lazy when attending a seminar since they are intended to gain sensitivity and insight about one's own technique and not just to copy a style. Seminars are intended to go deeper in our knowledge of the art in order to reach a profound insight beyond its technical surface.

- **Sempai** – A senior student, an alien term in Kaiso Sensei's Aiki.

        Since Kaiso Sensei didn't propose any kind of divisions such as *Nage-Uke*, winner-loser, etc., Aiki-do stands indeed as a different paradigm even for Japanese people since it also seems to break the seniority rules represented in their culture by the vertical and hierarchical *sempai-kohai* traditional relationships.

- **Sensei** – "One who came first or is ahead in time", a term loosely translated as teacher or instructor.

        A *sensei* is never above students but "below" them, in a position that enables them to support and take care of them so they can make progress. As shown in the following picture, this can be compared to a plate (representing the *sensei*) supporting a cup of coffee (the students).

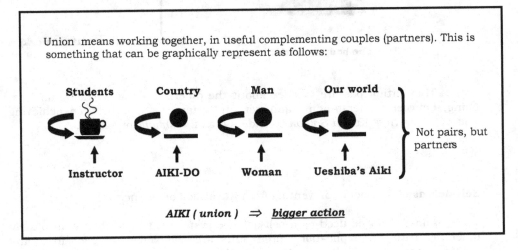

Union means working together, in useful complementing couples (partners). This is something that can be graphically represent as follows:

Students   Country   Man   Our world

Instructor   AIKI-DO   Woman   Ueshiba's Aiki

Not pairs, but partners

AIKI (union) ⇒ ***bigger action***

        Aiki-do *Sensei* never consider themselves as the most important person in the *dojo*. Arrogance is not part of Aiki.

- **Senses** – Any of the powers, such as sight, hearing, smell, touch, and taste, through which a living thing can be or become aware of its environment; also, a quality of being aware, through or as if through a sense (e.g., a sense of fear).

See Aiki senses

- **Shidoin** – This term refers to an advanced practitioner who helps new ones understand and follow instruction correctly. It refers to a monitor who helps out during a practice session.

- **Shihan** – A model *sensei*.

- **Shikake** – A trap. One who 'invites' without 'inviting'.

  Nage must always keep *Uke* united to them, without any pushing, pulling or fighting, only attached. They must take them to the ground without throwing or slamming them.

- **Shikko** – Walking on the knees.

  Shikko must be centered, as when holding a *bokken*. Care must be taken to avoid swinging the head from one side to the other. It helps us to work on our balance and strengthens our legs. This action was used by ancient *Samurai* to move inside castles in order to reduce mobility from any possible attacker.

- **Shisō**– An ideology in the sense of "feelings" in one's brain (*shi*) in addition to careful "examination" in one's heart (*sō*). This means: "to observe carefully, to cogitate (meditate), as in philosophy".

  There should be an ideal, a set of ideas to lead our way and goals that may give sense to our practice. Aiki does not prepare anybody for a big fight so the Founder's ideal was to straighten our crooked world. This is why he ordered his students to "give birth to Aiki", to make it live (*Takemusu Aiki*) !

  See Takemusu (Chapter 2)

- **Shugyo** – Apprenticeship, transcendence, birth, new life or dimension.

  In order to explain this concept Kurita *Shihan* uses the analogy of a chicken: it hatches through to make its way out of the egg in order to enter a new life and dimension. It is a process, a work to be done in order to reach a new level, and to transcend. It may be a hard work, but it is necessary to attain this goal, to grow and to develop.

  If practice doesn't lead to development it only serves to get tired and worn out by the end of a session. Paradoxically, the term also implies: "learning to relax", which explains why Kurita *Shihan* considers *seiza* as the *shugyo* of Aikido.
  See Seiza, Zanshin

- **Shuren (Shuden)**

  See Exercise

- **Smile** – A powerful Aiki resource.

Kurita Yutaka *Shihan* has always advised to "*enjoy technique*". This simple advice helps students to make the difference between violent, aggressive, ill-intentioned practice and a non-violent, non-aggressive and well-intentioned one.

When you smile the right side of your brain is at work. It makes Aiki flourish. Compared to a grin, a smile creates harmony and union.

**Kaiso Sensei always smiled, unless he was absorbed
and lost in the intuitive and sensitive world of
his own, putting imagination to work.**

Aiki was designed by master Ueshiba to become a tradition, so it is never to be changed. In this sense we were advised by him not to modify the way of Aiki but to hear the voice of the Grand Spirit of Unity, Harmony and Confluence (*Aiki O-Kami*) instead.

- **Student**

  See Deshi

- **Student's level** – A practitioner's particular height or position.

There are three general levels: beginner, intermediate and advanced. Advanced students always learn the basics: how to stand and start moving, how to approach and use *ki*, etc. If they don't learn this they cannot say they are advanced. How can they say they are *Shodan* (first class) or *Nidan* (second class) practitioners? What is the difference between them and beginner students?

Ranks are usually granted to people who learn a given curricula (contents), a series of techniques, with or without weapons, applied against one single or multiple "attacks" but never to people who understand the path, the *do* of Aiki. Some instructors confuse their students by making them abide by certain rules and technically fixed aspects that do not necessarily correspond to what the Founder proposed.

See Etsunen kai

- **Study** – A careful examination of something.

     Rather than looking for the best technical trick to make Aiki-do work, we must ask ourselves why the attack is directed to the shoulder and not to the elbow (or vice-versa), why we do grab the wrist and not the neck, what the philosophical and social meaning of *irimi, ushiro, hanmi handachi, katate dori, yokomen-uchi* is, etc.

     According to Kurita Yutaka *Shihan* the answers to these questions help understand Aiki-do, but this is something which is only possible through experience. If students don't feel their action or if they do not perform according to the right principles, they are only wasting their own time. Imagination and creativity are necessary to develop.

- **Support** – Holding in position, preventing from falling.

     The way of Aiki is to support people, as well as Sensei support their students.

- **Suwari waza** – An action from a *suwate* (sitting) position.

     Since it refers to practice on the knees, there is no or little mobilization in this sitting (lowered) situation. Regarding "attacks", the work applied in this situation is quite different from that in *tachi waza* and *hanmi handachi*.

     In this position we have not the same mobility as when we are standing up on our feet. It implies taking different things into consideration.

See Hanmi handachi, Tachi waza

- **Suwate vs. Idori** – Both terms refer to sitting postures but there is one main difference between them: there is no movement in *idori* practice, whereas *suwate* involves action that is made possible through the use of *shikko*.

  Idori can be used with Omote and Ura whereas *suwate* can additionally be used with *irimi* and *tenkan*. Both differ in many ways from practice standing up.

T

- **Tachi waza** – A standing up situation involving a larger mobilization.

  Contrary to both *suwari waza* and *hanmi handachi*, it offers much more freedom of movement, which is its main resource.

  See Hanmi Handachi, Suwari waza

- **Tanto waza** – A stabbing mobilization.

- **Teaching** – Giving lessons, helping someone to learn something.

  Instructors must teach in such a way that there is always relaxation (a *ki* element). Certain feelings are to be relaxed, such as anxiety or anger, and even all wish to win and fear to lose. Instruction should focus on *ki awase, ki musubi* and multi-directional *ki*. The latter happens when actions go up and down or when they switch to the right-left, to the front-back, and when they are heading to the ground in order to end *Uke*'s intention, etc.

  This is what instructors should be teaching and bearing in mind every single session or class. The brain learns only when the body learns: "*The body never forgets*" says Kurita *Shihan* so his teaching-learning formula consists of:

  "Feeling, tasting and mastering"

  This is the condition before teaching others. Instructors cannot teach what they have just learned in a class. Mastering one technique at a time should be the rule before proceeding with another. And a rank should be given only after mastering each important element within the whole Aiki set of components and factors and not to the best mechanical performance.

  See Practice

- **Technical aspects that make Aiki different** – From a technical point of view *Aikido* shows the following differences with other arts:

  1) *mobilization* – It uses an entering (*irimi*) and opening (*tenkan*) movements. *Irimi* is a proprietary action of Ueshiba's Aiki not found in other arts.

  2) *posture* – It is made in triangles (*sankaku*) and alignment (*hito-e*)

3) *defense* – Its movements flow to avoid blocking and countering.

4) *circles* – Straight movements from other (martial) arts are alien to Aiki.

5) *advantages* – It is efficient, and can be applied with minimum effort.

- **Technique** – A special way of doing something.

   Mechanical technique is not as important in Aiki-do as it is in *Karate* or other arts. And they are irrelevant when compared to the work needed to learn Aiki based on the elements proposed by the Founder.

   We must always bear in mind that an *activity* is not the same as *work*, and that all actions in Aiki-do are *vehicles* and chances to express Aiki. The right attitude and work are much more fundamental than technique (*see* kokoro).

   Technique's stages

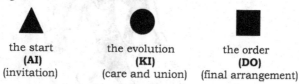

the start	the evolution	the order
(AI)	**(KI)**	**(DO)**
(invitation)	(care and union)	(final arrangement)

The first stage deals with encounter and approaching, it is an invitation; the second one relates to care, attention and union; the third one is a final relaxation and arrangement at one final point, with both partners staying there unattached.

Kurita Yutaka *Shihan* uses an analogy here: think of an eagle trapping a fish and taking it alive to its chicks. Basically, it never eats rotten food nor gives it to its chicks. This means instructors must give their students a live technique and not a dead one. *"What can you learn from dead techniques?"* (Kurita *Shihan*).

Uke are our "fish" in Aiki, so we must not kill or lose them. Technique must have a big size and a strong essence, a quick interaction and a rhythm, a smooth performance and an even arrangement. Techniques are to be characterized by body-mind flexibility which is the source for unification. They must always compensate: if they start soft they must end hard, and vice-versa.

   Schools and instructors may confuse big with height, and strong with muscle, as well as speed with fast, without ever thinking of the rhythm and harmony created by circular movements in order to avoid the emergence of a violent and aggressive style full of blocking and stiff action, with pulling and pushing squared movements.

See Activity, Action, Izanau, Awase, Musubi and Work

- **Technology** – Knowledge put into practice.

   Technology has been used for centuries to change human life, to control Nature. Aiki-do is a new technology created by Kaiso Sensei, its greatest engineer.

Just as computers are used and needed today, Aiki is necessary in our times, according to Kaiso Sensei's ideals.

- **Te-gatana** – The hand used as a sword.

    By opening all of our fingers we avoid violence. An open hand is necessarily used to greet whereas a closed fist is mostly intended to punch. By standing with our fingers opened we make our hand act just as an antenna ready to catch the broadcast signals sent by our practice partners (*Uke*) and this prevents them from hurting *Nage*'s wrists.

- **Throwing / slamming** – Two forbidden actions in *Kurita Juku Aiki*.

    Throwing vs. falling – Aiki students never throw themselves or others, they use *Nage*'s balance to make them go to the ground. *Uke* never falls and they are taken good care of since *Nage* protects them from slamming or breaking down.

    Falling is eliminated in Aiki practice: *"Nobody wants to fall, just as no one wants to see an airplane falling down."* (Kurita Yutaka *Shihan*)

- **Tori** – A term replacing *Uke* in recent books and publications; a term used now and then by Kurita Yutaka *Shihan* since 1996.

    Tori's role is not simply grabbing a wrist but apprehending *Nage*.

    See Uketachi

- **Tori fune undo** – A rowing-like exercise intended to advance our personalities by learning how to extend and attract the Universe's energy to and from its farthest corner.

- **Tsuki** – A punch or thrust.

Tsuki is made by *"going to one point over a certain line and then returning backwards, right on the same line."* (Kurita Yutaka *Shihan*)

U

- **Uchi** – Literally meaning "inside" it is a term commonly used in actions such as *shomen-uchi* (a hit to the front) and *yokomen uchi* (a hit to the side of the head).

    It refers to the most common Aikido attack to the head/nose, an activity described in many books and schools to be a part of *Aikido*'s most common programs.

See Study

- **Uchideshi** – A live-in disciple (*deshi*), one who initially lived at Kaiso Sensei's house (*uchi*).

    Uchideshi were those fortunate and privileged who were able to be accepted to study directly with O-Sensei and lived and helped him out at his house. Kurita Yutaka *Shihan* says it was not easy to become part of this group since keeping it implied many sacrifices. Being an *uchideshi* himself he wonders why not all former disciples follow Kaiso Sensei's line since some seem to have put aside important and fundamental concepts they don't teach.

    Kurita *Shihan* has pointed out that lessons based on *ki awase* and *ki musubi* have been neglected, as well as on some other things master Ueshiba talked about. And since he is still trying to do his best to keep the Founder's line alive and going on, he considers himself to be his last *uchideshi*. But he hopes there will be new enthusiasts willing to follow the original line in the future and who will be as interested in this as he is now.

- **Uchitachi** – One who comes to the trap, so to speak. It is a synonym of *Uke* and an old Aiki term.

- **Uke** - From the verb *ukeru*, it means to catch, to receive, to be affected; it is a term opposed to *Nage*.

- **Uketachi** – One who acts as a trap (*shikake*). It is a synonym of *Nage* and an old term used by the Founder. One who reacts and responds.

  See Tori, Uchitachi

- **Undo** – Exercise, as sports define it.

  See Dosa and Waza

- **Ura (waza)** - An action intended to use *Nage*'s back direction by leading *Uke* with a backward step.

    This technique is not to be confused with *tenkan*, which is a pivoting and opening mobilization.

  See Waza

W

- **Water–fire** – A duality technically referring to the intention of an attack as well as to the horizontal and vertical axes used.

    1. On the horizontal axis, and in reference to one's knees or legs, the right one is fire and the left one is water. So when *Uke* comes with a fire intention of 8 with the right foot, *Nage* uses a water intention of 2 and the opposite (left) foot as he gets out of the line of the attack.

    2. On the vertical axis, and in reference to the arms, they are fire when they go up and water as they come down. Countering *Uke*'s actions with their arms is possible when *Nage* uses *izanau*.

    The water-fire principle - This principle teaches to reach right balance. It shows people how to adapt. When somebody comes yelling at you (an intention of 8), you can always speak in a lower voice (an intention of 2). When they grin with anger (10) you can always smile (0), and when they fight you just don't. This fundamental Aiki principle can be used in real life. We may say it summarizes O-Sensei's ideal of adaptation and confluence.

    Omote-ura, irimi-tenkan, and thus attack-defense are all different but complementary since one is fire and the other is water just as left-right, man-woman, teacher-student, or boss-employee are complementing dualities too.

    See Balance

- **Waza** – Literally craft and skill; lines of action.

    The *kanji* for this word implies an intricate task. This is something to be remembered whenever it is translated as "technique", because this concept accurately refers to both a line of action and a vehicle, a means. Aiki has different *waza* (lines of action) and the effect is different when students use one or the other. And it is important to always have in mind that they are:

✓ First, and above all, chances for communication.
✓ A chance to learn to integrate ourselves.
✓ A chance to relate to others and to integrate with them.
✓ A chance to learn how to get together and unite, how to discover and understand, and how to develop our intuition to take a useful lesson for our lives. When they are done in a different or non-conventional way then they become varied forms (o-*henka waza*) that can still be applied and transformed (*oyo-henka waza*).

Kurita *Shihan* has transformed the dynamics of all these *waza* in order to change the usual way of practice at one point in space (the mutual center of *Nage* and *Uke*) in order to move in a broader and dynamic *katsuhayabi* practice (*katsu means* "besides", "in addition"; *hayabi means* "speedy").

Three different kinds of waza:

a) **Nage waza** (from the verb *nageru*, "to throw").

Nage waza is an action going outwards in what has been commonly taken as a big circle or a lead towards a throw. However its real intention and purpose is to make *Uke* follow through from one side to the other. *Uke* might use a quick solution (a roll) in order to get up and go on to engage the next movement.

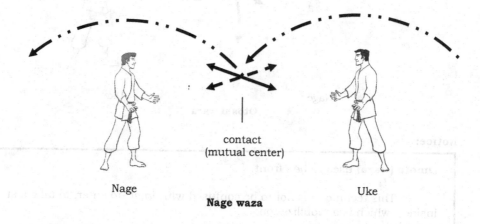

contact
(mutual center)

Nage   Uke

Nage waza

b) **Osae waza** (from the verb *osaeru*, "to suppress", "to control"). It has been translated as pinning.

It is an action in which *Nage* acts as a baseball catcher, doing his/her best to stop *Uke* and not allowing them to go away or pass through as in the previous action (*nage waza*). The idea is to keep *Uke* where he/she is in order to "*square things up*".

Nage   Uke

Osae waza

c) **Otoshi waza** (from the verb *otosu,* "to drop").

The action here goes to a lower position since it is intended to literally trap *Uke* in order to put him/her down. *Nage* move towards his/her own center with a definitive effect. It is a strong move and the idea is to apply through it the whole force of gravity by sinking the body and making it heavy, as heavy as that force might be.

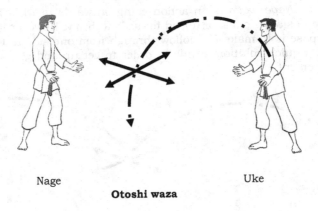

Nage   Uke

Otoshi waza

Notice:

Omote (waza) uses *Nage*'s front.

This technique is not to be confused with *irimi* –to enter, to take a step inside–, which is a mobilization.

Ura (waza) uses *Nage*'s back direction by taking a step backwards.

This technique is not to be confused with *tenkan* –to pivot and thus to open–, which is another mobilization.

Waza are the actions used in different circumstances or situations.

Waza found in many standard Aikido programs

✓ *Suwari waza* – a sitting, Japanese style action on the knees. This situation has room for small or no mobilization for both *Nage* and *Uke*.

✓ *Hanmi handachi* – a situation where *Nage* is sitting down and *Uke* is standing up (medium mobilization).

✓ *Tachi waza* – a situation where both *Nage* and *Uke* are on their feet and with the possibility of large and varied mobilizations.

✓ *Atemi waza* – an exposing action that helps to distract *Uke* with a fake or a real slap or hit to the face.

✓ *Jiyu waza* – a free action where even biting and kicking might be expected to be used. This is certainly not part of Aiki-do.

✓ *Tanto waza* – a stabbing action practiced with a wooden knife and the basis to explain and correct most activities, as well as to show where they have been derived.

✓ *Kansetsu waza* – an action made through the use of *Uke*'s articulations.

✓ *Kaeshi waza* – a reversing action that shows both *Nage* and *Uke* there are no winners or losers in Aiki-do since they both borrow their mutual effort in order to learn and grow.

Additional waza found in Kurita Juku Aiki

✓ *O-henka waza* – an action responding *"in a certain region and vicinity"*.

✓ *Oyo-henka waza* – an action meant for *"a big transformation or improvement"*.

✓ *Renzoku waza* – a continued, non stopping and organizing action covering all directions.

See Dosa, Undo, Jutsu, and Work

- **Weapons** – Anything used to overcome and defeat somebody.

    No weapons are in fact needed in Aiki training, except for the fact that many correct postures and actions can be clearly referred to and illustrated by relating them to its martial origins. The practice of *Iaido*, for example, is usually a means to understand Aiki-do's roots or simply to manifest beauty through the use of the body. Instead a *bokken* and a *jo* are used; they are not considered as weapons but as extensions of our body and means to connect and avoid the use of muscles or muscular strength. The *jo* (staff) and the *bokken* (wooden sword) teach all we need to know. As a personal conclusion, these "instruments" must be the most suitable vehicles the Founder could ever think in order to realize and use *ki* since they are extensions providing a connection between *Nage* and *Uke* to develop a good sense of *ki*.

This posture attracts the energy from above

From our definition of *ki*, these instruments are that "something" needed between practitioners which is neither the mind nor the body, so they constitute an "indirect" way and means to put both partners in touch by avoiding the use of any mind (thinking) or body (muscle). In this sense weapons may be the vehicles for *ki*, hence they help materiallize it when used as such and not as ordinary wea-pons.

See Ki

- **Weight** – The force of gravity pulling on an object.

    Expensive things have a much better quality and tend to be heavier. Compare a VW with a Cadillac, or a Rolex with any other less expensive watch. Size (height, width, length of something) relates to quality and the same happens with Aiki actions: they need a certain size and a weight in order to be expensive.

    Weight can be noticed in O-Sensei's calligraphy from his last late period too (go to page 221). Kurita Yutaka *Shihan* refers to heaviness as Aiki's strength, but it is not to be confused with muscular strength since it relates to the force of gravity.

- **Work** – Causing to function; the effort made to do something.

    It refers to the practice contents needed for adequate, correct practice. It is different from activity which is what we see on the mere surface.

    See Activity

- **Zanshin** – Creativity, originality.

    According to Kurita *Shihan*, zanshin is an old term used in martial arts but it does not belong to in Aiki, so it is not used in *Kurita Juku Aiki*.

Kaiso Sensei instructing Kurita Yutaka *Shihan*

Kurita Yutaka *Shihan* and his role as an *Uchideshi*

Strong beliefs and a stubborn attitude seem to define Kurita Yutaka *Shihan*. Aiki-do's goal is human improvement so it is sad to see high-ranked practitioners who prefer to practice only among themselves and refuse to work with visitors or novice people because they usually consider them as bad, weak, or stupid merely because they show a poor technical skill. Even when they might have technically improved, their hearts have obviously lost their human value making them slaves of their ego and their useless technique. It all results in confusion for them, and their improvement is simply an illusion due to their own selfishness. It is also ridiculous when they try to show off before a class starts, trying to impress new participants. People in *Kurita Juku Aiki* are always reminded that their *hakama* and skills do not necessarily represent Aiki.

We must not forget that the way of Aiki is not only the way of the union of our spirit-mind-body, but a way of union, confluence and harmony with ourselves and others. If we stop the progress of our spirits and hearts (*kokoro*), everything will stop and stagnate. A spirit rejecting other people, ignoring how to accept them, or just concerned with an individual progress, reduces itself to selfishness and cannot be in union with the Universe, since everyone is part of it. We are the children of our galaxy and we are also brothers/sisters of all members of our own species. If there is a time for Aiki to be useful it should be now since our globe has been put in danger by many human mistakes and selfish interests of all kinds.

Kurita Yutaka *Shihan* states that our practice partners (*Uke*) are there for us and that when we play the role of *Nage* we are responsible for their safety and must creatively resolve the interactions created. Without a partner, it would simply not be possible to discover a new world and this is why we thank them at the beginning and end of class. It is from their presence and willingness to be there with and for us that they make our progress and evolution possible.

This is represented as:
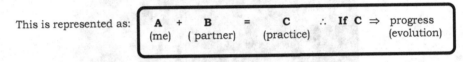

$$A + B = C \quad \therefore \; \text{If } C \Rightarrow \text{progress}$$
$$\text{(me)} \quad \text{(partner)} \quad \text{(practice)} \qquad \qquad \text{(evolution)}$$

It is with the presence, participation and work of a partner that we can improve and also share the joy of practice. Thus in order to do so it is imperative that we have a grateful heart: to help less advanced people implies a lot of patience and care, and that results in a great personal benefit. To understand the causes and obstacles that hinder the performance of a less skilled partner it is necessary to progress in our own search and personal understanding first.

According to Kurita *Shihan*, our traditional paradigm tells us that the strong one must help the weak, just as the smart one must help the stupid. But from an Aiki point of view even the weak and the stupid are not supposed to accept their weakness and stupidity. The new formula proposes to do one's best in order to reject such personal ghosts and enemies so as to eventually get rid of them.

Our task is to find how this may be possible. This is another form of *circulation*: a form of correspondence with which society gains fairness and justice by countering abuse from any sides. There is no worse mistake in the world of *bujutsu* (the art of the warrior) than depending on technique and becoming selfish, and just being proud of mere power and efficiency. The force that can help us overcome our selfishness is much more important in an Aiki culture.

In general terms, we must accept that practice cannot be reduced to the yearning for becoming powerful and having the capacity and knowledge to injure people. If we understand power comes from the application of Aiki (order and arrangement, *Cosmos*), we can see the strength of a person results from abiding by its principles as the only way to become a real winner.

For those *uchideshi* who have dedicated their lives to spread the practice of Aiki, this frame of mind maybe the only way to lead to true victory as proposed by Master Ueshiba (*Kaiso Sensei*). One must defeat evil spirits like anger, laziness, or fear in us since there are no greater enemies than these true monsters. As soon as the idea appears that our technique is good our progress stops. We must always bear in mind that the constant flow of the Universe never stops. Stopping even for a moment implies falling behind and dying since living things are always growing and changing. This is how things in Aiki become a matter of life or death.

An integral education makes men and women more humane. It needs to include subjects which can make people become more civilized instead of just filling them with information. The physical aspect, so disdained by Western intellectuals can be the vehicle through which sensitivity to others can be trained in aspects like respect, conscience and tolerance so much needed in our contemporary world. Aiki can give us a self-control no empirical science has ever been able to provide. It can be our supply of wisdom, especially when dealing with our own beings. This is the "*Victory over one's self*" that other great men in history also knew about:

"There is no conflict as severe as the one faced by someone who fights to defeat himself". (**T. A. Kempis**)

"Nothing provides a greater advantage over others, than keeping calm and immutable under any circumstance". (**T. Jefferson**)

AIKI O-KAMI
(The grand union, confluence and harmony spirit)

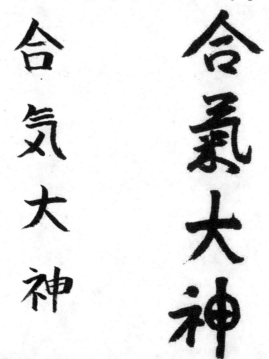

COMMON WRITING vs. **KAISO SENSEI'S WRITING**
(LIGHT AND SQUARE)   (HEAVY & ROUND)[39]

---

[39] Taken from: *A Guide to Remembering Japanese Characters*, by Kenneth G. Henshall, Tuttle Publishing Co., 1998 and *The Essence of Aikido* by John Stevens, Kodansha International, 1993.

**Aiki teaches us to help others succeed
and by so doing we win over ourselves and become
stronger**

[*AIKI-DO:* **A path to help ourselves and others
in unity, confluence and harmony**]

*"Civilization has been created so we must learn how to
live in it" (Kaiso Sensei, Ueshiba Morihei)*

Chapter 6

Beyond the *Dojo*

IKKYO
– FIRST CHAPTER –

Aiki and other self-improvement systems

Going from theory to practice summarizes the purpose of *Kurita Juku Aiki*, a school that covers many important aspects of our lives. Since it is through correct work and activity that we can reach our goals, we know it is only through hard work that we can make the changes we may be yearning for. Aiki action prepares for a new rational action, giving students a characteristic advantage successful people have and makes them different from the rest: their skill to force themselves to take physical action. It opposes all the rational improvement models which may just remain as mere rhetoric, good intentions, and raw, unfulfilled plans.

Will (our human *energy*) is the basic element used in Aiki to do whatever a given action requires. Aiki is *self-knowledge* and its practice helps us to see how we feel towards the acts we subject our personal matters to and the context of our work in personal, family and business fields.

A *positive attitude* towards life, us, the world, and our profession is a prerequisite of Aiki self-knowledge. It demands a correct and harmonious mental attitude. The body is responsible for molding our minds through practice and it explains why union, confluence and harmony define Aiki. This three-fold term constitutes a new set of *beliefs* directed towards respect, attention and tolerance to others. Respect equals harmony in Aiki. These factors help us deconstruct or re-engineer the old attitudes carried from childhood: we have suggested that Aiki helps us to straighten out whatever is crooked in our minds, bodies and spirits already.

From an Aiki perspective we learn our partners and fellowmen are in fact the mirrors where we can see that what they do is an exact reflection of our own doing. This is true for individuals as well as for entire communities. It is from mirrors that we can realize how people look at us and how we really act (Kurita *Shihan* has called this the *mirror principle*). Practice allows us to align (Aiki) our attitudes with those from others so that our non-verbal and verbal behaviors can stimulate them too and help them to become *positive* and *receptive* towards our own beings.

Aiki is *adaptation*, and with the *adaptability* it affords we can modify our behavior and function effectively in any situation by means of four basic actions: *omote* (acting frontally to the situation), *irimi* (anticipating and entering it with our own perspective), *ura* (reconsidering its origin), and *tenkan* (opening and leading it to a different perspective).

To *grow* is *to adapt and change*, one of the most necessary capabilities in our times. From the Aiki perspective we understand that "more adaptable" means "more aware of ourselves", and a greater capacity to use the growth choices which can help us to collaborate and grow with others in confluence and harmony. If we are in such a position, we can always be in control. Practice helps new leaders to stop giving orders and to start *giving support*, to achieve shared benefits as well as to abandon abuse; it helps people to forget about defeating others and to learn how to look for a consensus instead.

The term *Aiki* means "to be in line with", "to walk in the same direction or on the same path with others" (*confluence*). Experts in personal development affirm that *alignment* takes place when our values and beliefs correspond to a positive and constructive conduct. This avoids the creation of excisions in people, as well as in the vision and mission of the group creating a *collectivistic sense*. The main cause of non-alignment is the subsistence of old paradigms which translates into paradigmatic paralysis. True change implies *transformation of skills and aptitudes*. Aiki props up values and helps defeat weaknesses and fears, so that practice, the *aptitude-creative* physical activity, always has an immediate application that transcends explanations.

Aiki promotes *self-esteem* (the value we give to ourselves) and *well being* (a good mental and physical condition). We use these elements to face challenges in our search for success. While proposing the idea of union, confluence and harmony, Aiki helps us eliminate the need for competition and direct fighting. This avoids the risk of losing and guarantees our chances of doing better at all times. It supports our need to feel *valuable*, *capable*, *accepted* and *welcome* for what we are: a need we must satisfy by ourselves. By rescuing us from our own lethargy, it makes us live the present and prepare for the future. It stops us from putting ourselves in a stagnant position. Kurita *Shihan* states the past is small and the future is large so we might also expect to have a great future for ourselves and for Humanity as a whole.

There is no improvement or development without change. Those who do not change are either dead or on their way to extinction, since they have lost their vitality. *Change* consists of acting and not just of discussing or thinking about the things to be changed or that require transformation. Our will is important and Aiki presupposes a greater *energy*, awareness, well being and capability to do so; it breaks old patterns and destructive or unfavorable habits. Correct practice develops our intuition and gives us an iron will, the energy we need to change.

Finding solutions to our problems, instead of dwelling on them, is one characteristic of the constructive thought proposed by Aiki training. If we think all problems have a solution, and keep our senses alert, we can ensure the *optimization* of the possibilities to find solutions. On the other hand it is often said that changes bring about fear, but this does not happen when the ones who change are the individuals themselves. Contrary to those who remark that *being centered* is a mental state, the Aiki paradigm maintains that centeredness is a physical state which helps to situate the mental one. A quiet mind is like a mirror where we are able to see a neat reflection of ourselves, and the body must be centered in order to get such a mental state.

To experience our beings from our center (body) and not from the periphery (externals) implies the need to do it physically and not mentally, although it happens through the unconscious work of our right brain!

People find Aiki techniques difficult to perform because it is not easy for them to change their habits. The first time they try them they work with their logic and their hands instead of just using the whole body. This new paradigm resembles other disciplines like *Yoga* and *Tai-chi* based on exercises to *control the body* and not the intellect. When we are *centered* we look at the world with objectivity and this is one of the most evident results derived from Aiki practice.

Aiki is learned through the active and dynamic efforts of two people who center and concentrate during motion. This differs from practices like the static *Zen* and *Yoga*. Aiki training consists of the execution of harmonious, soft and rhythmic movements. It is the way in which we control and handle our center (the contact point between two practice partners) in this new paradigm. In turn it provides calmness, serenity and the control we need in our lives and in our personal interaction with others. It makes us receptive to external stimuli. By means of this practice, our thinking becomes as clear as a mirror in a dynamic way.

From the Aiki viewpoint it is considered that activities of a *competitive* nature against others, and eventually against ourselves, only diminish our *performance*. They hinder the *joy* in what is done because someone is always on the losing end with the resulting loss of self-confidence. On the other hand competition basically leaves only one winner who sometimes ends full of a new set of hidden *complexes* or *insecurities*. These are created by the tension to go on winning and derive from their need to maintain themselves in that winning level. This literally traps them in somebody else's triumphs and always makes their own victories ephemeral.

Tony de Melo, a renowned Brazilian priest, gives a good example of the mechanics of competition. He tells the story of a great archer who always hit his targets until the day he is invited to participate in a tournament. The story goes that he loses his dexterity at the moment he faces the expectation of having to defeat a series of opponents. He loses control when he changes his attention towards competition and his competitors and his performance drops. Competition works as follows: no body wants to lose, and even when everybody wants to win, there will only be one winner. This doesn't necessarily mean that all those losers cannot really use their skills in different fields and situations. The same happens when people take any test: they tend to perform in a different way as compared to their usual, painless, and spontaneous everyday performance.

Training in Aiki entails the requisite of an *adequate* (relaxed) *atmosphere* or environment in order to promote learning. It must be *free of any threats and pressure*, affording students a high level of challenge and opportunities to get ahead. Attacks are seen as chances for growth and not aggressions. We can change reality just by changing our point of view. Aiki stimulates *experimentation*, techniques become the context, and learning is derived from direct experience. This stimulates *self-reflection* (meditation) and a deep, intuitive understanding. Practice is founded on a profound respect for life and people, so Aiki-do cannot be considered a martial, war-bound art. This gives practitioners the *importance, consideration, opening* and *confidence* plus the *freedom* and *individuality* for the endowment of their best personal expression, without any fear for reprimands. True and correct Aiki-do practice distances itself from all military climate or spirit: students take care of themselves and of each other.

Aikido teaches us to *accept compromise* and to *strengthen our spirit*. It develops our personal efficiency by helping us to always choose a positive answer. At the same time, practice builds an enormous personal congruence state, a state of harmony. Training (*aiki activity + aiki work*) is the way to access the way (path, code), since it constitutes a *help process* and guidance that leads to personal development. It is a way to reach our own individuality and enlightenment, understood as a *high level of consciousness*. It is used to develop our *intuition*, defined as knowledge coming without conscious efforts, and to manifest it in positive attitudes and relationships in the personal, familial and managerial fields.

It is worth insisting that Aiki-do is a path where we learn to explore and *manifest our energy*. It allows us to *recognize it*, to *apply it*, and then to *multiply it*. Given it is not a fighting or self-defense system, it helps us to discover ourselves. Aiki allows us to change our attention from the external world to our internal being (what we really are). It helps us to *return to ourselves*, as in *Seiza*. Aiki is an excellent *healing method*: its interest in handling the body is to strengthen it and improvement is aimed not only at our physical well being but at recapturing our total human beings. In turn this helps to heal and improve our relationships at all personal and professional levels, as individuals and as whole societies. The same goal is being currently intended by Western models of *integral education*. Not only does Aiki give us the personal power needed in our personal life, but also in our work life, a power we can call *entrepreneurial energy*.

When our life heals we leave behind fear, anger and the things that hurt us in the past. This is what *Budo* was all about for the Founder since it has an application in the most diverse aspects of everyday life. Aiki has:

    a)   a potential for an integral education,

    b)   a role in dealing with interpersonal and personal conflicts,

    c)   an application in contemporary business,

    d)   a role in leadership, and

    e)   an opposition to any falling, breaking, destroying or defeating ideas or practices.

Aiki as an integral education system

As part of our outline of the way of Aiki in and out the *Dojo*, we can compare its system with a contemporary integrative Western education model in order to understand its benefits.

Integral Development Model (IDM)[40]	The *Aiki* System
1. Its goal is to form an integrated person, capable of living a complete life. Anthropologically oriented, it is nourished by the development of existential values, achieved through the integrative development of five aspects developed in the following order: ① **Mind** ② **Body** ③ **Emotions**, ④ **Identity** and ⑤ **Society**.	1. Its goal and values are the same as in the IDM, and it is also anthropologically oriented, but all of the same five aspects are developed in a totally different order: ① **Body** ② **Emotions** ③ **Identity** ④ **Society** and ⑤ **Mind**

2. It is a formation process seeking:
   a. to relate dichotomist concepts,
   b. to develop values and beliefs, and
   c. to know the psychological, pedagogical, social and cultural structure of the person, as an autonomous process undergoing a life-long development that takes into account all the five aspects encompassed.
	2. It is a formation process seeking:
	   a. to eliminate dichotomist concepts,
	   b. to strengthen constructive values and beliefs, and
	   c. to know the psychological and socio-cultural structure of the person, as a process undergoing a life-long development through assiduous and conscientious practice of all five aspects in one single physical practice.

3. The learning process is experiential and directed, and special attention is paid to introspection, conscience taking, and self-reflection through concrete guidelines of an educational teaching nature in each one of the five aspects mentioned in (1) and defined as follows:
 	
   a. **Mind**: analysis of reality, and use of rationalization. This aspect analyzes, rationalizes, and values things (the role of our left brain hemisphere).
	3. The learning process is experiential and directed, introspection is realized through sensitivity and reflection by means of partner activity and concrete guidelines of an individual acting nature through techniques of a martial resemblance:
	
	   a. **Body**: expressivity (extroversion), confidence and will power development, health care and self-knowledge fostering (reflection). This aspect is the depository of spiritual and sensory perceptions and/or intuition (the work of our right brain hemisphere).

[40] Taken from: *Modelo educativo: Desarrollo de la identidad personal. Los ámbitos de la persona, el aprendizaje autónomo y la organización cooperativa* by Begoña Salas García and Inmaculada Serrana Hernández , Ediciones Universidad de Barcelona, Spain, 1998.

b. **Body**: expressivity (extroversion), confidence and will power, health, reflection and self-knowledge development (introversion). This aspect is the depository of sensory perceptions.

c. **Emotions**: development of feelings, expression and reception of affection, trust, singularity, sexuality, personal roles, love and self-esteem. The feelings expressed through the body belong to this aspect but physical activity is secondary.

d. **Identity**: integrity, dignity, balance, coherence in the physical, social, affective, cognitive and attitudinal aspects (capacity of feeling and living our total being). This is the wise, not programmed aspect.

e. **Society**: solidarity and tolerance, detachment and devotion, generosity, deliverance, sensitivity, respect, discretion, balance and harmony, as well as responsibility (compromise, sincerity and honesty). It is through the development of this aspect that a person can have an impact on society.

b. **Emotions**: expression and recaption of affection, trust; acknowledgement of singularity, and of personal roles, sexuality, love and self-esteem. Positive feelings are expressed through the body.

c. **Identity**: justice, honor, truth, valor and loyalty (integrity); balance, coordination and coherence with the physical, social, and affective-attitudinal aspects (capacity to act constructively, in union and harmony). It is the wise and programmed aspect of the body shaping the mind.

d. **Society**: union, confluence and harmony in the same values of the IDM (solidarity, tolerance, etc.), plus *respect* embodied as responsibility. The person makes an impact on society through the harmonic contact with people (starting with their practice partners), as well as the trust earned through the execution of techniques.

e. **Mind**: way of acting and perceiving life (operational knowledge). It analyzes reality in order to understand life, and does not center on information interchange; it rationalizes and values things, guided also by what is known as the five parallel Aiki senses.

Education, from the Aiki perspective, consists in learning about the order of the Universe through one's own body and sensory experience, and in particular by means of the use of the right hemisphere of our brains which leads to the development of our intuition.

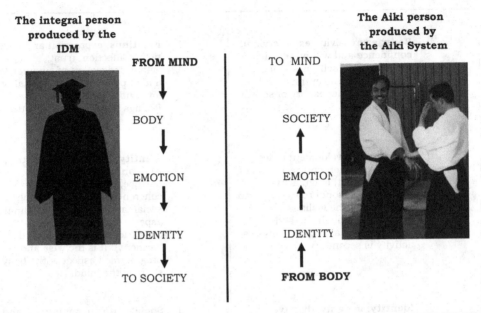

The integral person produced by the IDM		The Aiki person produced by the Aiki System
FROM MIND		TO MIND
↓		↑
BODY		SOCIETY
↓		↑
EMOTION		EMOTION
↓		↑
IDENTITY		IDENTITY
↓		↑
TO SOCIETY		**FROM BODY**

UPSIDE-DOWN LEFT HEMISPHERE WORK   BOTTOM-UP RIGHT HEMISPHERE WORK

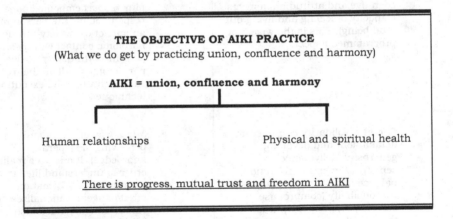

THE OBJECTIVE OF AIKI PRACTICE
(What we do get by practicing union, confluence and harmony)

AIKI = union, confluence and harmony

Human relationships   Physical and spiritual health

There is progress, mutual trust and freedom in AIKI

The main difference between Aikido and all Western educational models is that Aiki favors a physical means to reach the same goal, but it definitely pursues the same objectives as the IDM. It searches for the expression of the universal order through the body and its application to practical, everyday life. It searches for the natural flourishing of the personality, work, education and quality relationships with others as a personal, familial and social path of group confluence union and harmony.

Aiki is an integral model that appeals for the use of the right brain in order to support the left one to creatively transform and take our current perception of things a step further.

We have forgotten about relationship with our bodies, the place where our minds reside. The psychomotor development started in elementary and middle schools should have never ended. Physical education is commonly thought of as a means to develop dexterity, coordination and related benefits in children, but Aiki actions serve to refine and promote this development throughout our lives. Movements are so refined that they may require years of constant practice, the only way to achieve the best execution and the best adequate mentality. PE classes suffer from two main unfortunate circumstances: on one hand they stop too early during childhood or youth; on the other hand they are practiced so much as sports that they end imprinted in our minds making it too difficult to be overcome and affecting Aiki practice. The strength actions and competitive tactics learned in sports and PE classes remain stuck in our subconscious mind as an indestructible paradigm.

The first thing we are taught in our lives is that we can depend on our strength and that we can support ourselves on it, something we cannot easily change. On the other hand, physical exercises have also become shows to be watched as mere events, just increasing the risk of the diseases associated with the modern, sedentary, and urban way of life. We must insist that the intensive activity of Aiki also favors self-understanding of our beings as well as spiritual elevation: there is never a separation between the physical, mental, and social aspects. Aiki-do promotes all of them.

Aiki and interpersonal conflict

Thomas F. Crum (1987) has proposed a practical application of Aiki principles and philosophy to the resolution of interpersonal and family conflict. He takes the basic teachings of *Aikido* to help us analyze conflict and establish an Aiki way to perceive it and deal with it accordingly. In his opinion, conflict tends to scare us, making us to try to avoid it in its many forms without realizing it is a natural part of life since it is always present. He proves that all the different conflicts in life constitute our best opportunities for growth and learning.

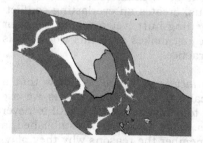

He supports his view by reminding us that conflict is present everywhere in Nature, with a constructive effect which models rocks, mountains and the like. As an example, he reminds us how difficult it is to tie our shoes for the first time by ourselves, how disheartening it is to accept that our balloon may fly away from our hands into the air, or how sad to see our delicious ice-cream cone lying all fresh on the ground. He states that we experience changes throughout our lives: in our personal appearance, in our work place, in our professional lives, etc. All of these changes are usually produced by conflict or even have caused it in turn. Crum makes us realize that from each one of those conflicts we have always obtained some good amount of knowledge, given we have always overcome those crisis.

His ideas summarize the main foundation of Aiki: since conflict is omnipresent, we must adapt and regard it as an opportunity for growth rather than moaning, complaining or self-justifying for what makes us suffer. From an Aiki point of view, our work must be channeled by taking advantage of conflict itself instead of wasting our efforts trying to avoid, deny or fight it. Although it always seems unavoidable, we can always find a way to overcome it.

Although conflict and struggle are always there, he states, we can radically change our relationship with it by transforming our viewpoint and our resulting actions. That is what Aiki training is all about.

Examples of human conflict happen in everyday situations for Crum: when children want to do something parents do not approve, or when a couple has problems in their relationship and cannot communicate. We can also say that this is what happens between countries that seem to have no chances of mutual understanding. In such cases, we must be able to distinguish between a clash of forces (power), and reasoning (a chance to change their situation into one of greater union, communication and adaptation). To do this they should accept the responsibility each part has in a conflict first and then use an Aiki strategy, instead of allowing people to see themselves as opponents before they say something. It is always wiser to stop fighting and start finding creative solutions and adaptation.

Aiki is simply about never clashing, about never being indifferent or apathetic. The best way to do this is to assume the role and viewpoint of the other person, putting ourselves in their place in order to understand problems and negotiate the best possible solution. Sometimes we fail to see we are imposing barriers, assaulting or undermining what is happening to others. And such indifference, tied to our primitive instinct of not letting anybody win over us, creates an everlasting conflict. Anger is a protective response to keep us from getting hurt, yet a raging behavior produces another anger of greater intensity which just makes problems worse. This explains why *Nage-Uke* roles are interchanged in practice.

Aiki-do teaches us to use the *water-fire principle* by which we know that if someone shouts we must lower our voice and calm down. If the persons we are talking to lower their voice, we might increase our tone always being careful to never engage in a shouting match, as it usually happens. Once a balance is established, a middle point is naturally reached. People must remember the reasons why they play, work, live and are together. They must always remember what made them connect their lives, and what has given quality to their relationships in order to strengthen them. That is the only way they will be able to rescue what has kept them together (their *energy*), instead of just seeing the negative factors or adhering to a one-sided reasoning.

Aiki teaches about constructive collaboration, instead of destructive competition; alternatively, we play the roles of a winner and a loser to always be able to experience both sides of the game. When people only win they lose perspective, whereas at the same time the loser develops a bad, self-denigrating inferiority complex. These situations are not desirable, since it makes both become losers in the long term.

There is no place for destructive competition in Aiki. The challenge is to defeat our own selves, our ego, our fantasies, our arrogance and weaknesses, without ever hurting others or stepping over their integrity as individuals.

We know that bad tempered people usually tend to intimidate those around them, seemingly obtaining what they want. Many learn to be strong, to defeat others, to do just what they want, trusting too much on this system which in the end is a reminder of their weakness. They can defeat others but not themselves in order to overcome their fears, indifference, selfishness, apathy, disdain, etc. If this is the case they impose authority and respect, but they never earn them. They may eventually and inevitably lose if they end up all alone and tend to isolate themselves in the process: no body wants to get bitten by a rabid dog.

Aiki makes us firmly believe it is of no use to defeat others if we can not handle our own selves, and we could also maintain that, even when someone attacks us there is no reason for a counterattack. "Know thyself" is still great advice; Socrates promoted knowing about both our conscious and unconscious selves too.

We have learnt to fight back from childhood, and this has made us unable to understand each other. When we argue we seldom listen to what others have to say: we just wait for our turn to counter-argue, without listening to them first. We use our intelligence just to think of a way to defeat and demonstrate they are wrong or unable to understand us. This is not the best strategy for communication: people need to learn to see the different points of view from others, to accept them and to value them accordingly, so they can in turn respect our personalities, ideas, and concerns. Definitely, our acquaintances, friends and people in general are the mirrors which reflect our actions (Yutaka Kurita *Shihan*).

When things do not go as desired we become tense and anguished. However, we must learn to calm down and relax: "If things can be fixed there is no need to worry, and if they cannot be fixed all we can do is to relax" (a Tibetan saying). We can always see things clearly if we are flexible. We can analyze and find an answer whenever we are dealing with conflict. Aiki teaches us to remain in control, facing multiple situations and adapting to them in order to change.

Human violence is an unmistakable demonstration of weakness. Societies and their most violent acts always result from the weakest and poorest fear-driven choices. Violence is generated from within and from the most varied forms of undoing. The same thing happens with fear or with any other negative feelings and thoughts. On the other hand, a positive mentality gives us the necessary strength. An acute concentration gives us clarity of mind, and reflection helps us to see all things well, attaining greater intelligence and leaving our ignorance behind. Aiki teaches us how not to pay attention to our destructive internal enemies.

The challenge is and will always be the same for humanity: to try to find the way of union, confluence and harmony, internally and externally, beginning with themselves and then transcending to things and people around them. This can be attained only through the diligent, earnest practice of Aiki, not by dissertation, theories, promises or good intentions. After all, *"Only practice makes perfect"*, as our popular wisdom teaches.

Aiki and contemporary businesses

Aiki-do is a paradigm change and evolution system which can also modify the way contemporary business organizations and the modern managerial culture is run since it can also be applied to the issues related to the human and commercial relations inside and outside companies. Aiki has the capacity to create a trusting, calm, and cordial environment that can be part of them if they learn to see it as a system used to create *entrepreneurial energy*. This is the energy needed to endure difficult times, once the old paradigms related to the way of doing business seem to have fallen apart and the sense of security has faded away in many businesses.

Based on *Aikido* principles, some authors have written about such possible applications among entrepreneurs. Hiroaki Izumi offers a perspective based on the way Eastern and Western companies are usually organized. Izumi detects an important element that keeps a *dojo* united. It is an aspect that from his point of view marks a big difference when you compare Japanese and American corporations: traditional US companies operate through an *authority system*, while *dojo* do it through a *responsibility system*.

According to his view, people's behavior inside an organization is not only structurally dictated by hierarchy but by the perception people have towards power, politics, work division, and people as workmates. For him, traditional corporations have been established in terms of an arrangement that shows who is and has authority over somebody else, as can be noted by the fact that a board of directors is over the President, who in turn is over the vice-presidents, and these over directors of several subdivisions, etc.

Authority and the power given to an individual, Izumi states, come with position, and it is used over lower levels from top to bottom.

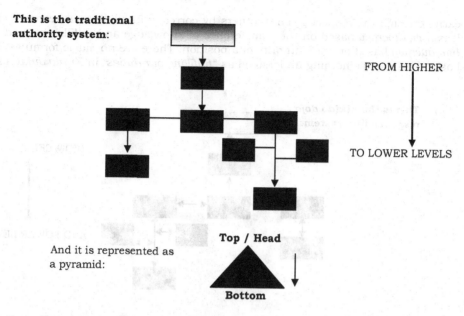

This is the traditional authority system:

FROM HIGHER

TO LOWER LEVELS

And it is represented as a pyramid:

Top / Head

Bottom

According to Kurita *Shihan*, this hierarchical position arrangement is not completely Aiki since it represents the ancient paradigm of a ruler over his people. Although he is supported by the base it is formed by a majority that has no power to help decide what is best for the company. Even worse, the top has no communication with the bottom, in order to coordinate their efforts. They act as a body with a separated head.

In Izumi's opinion it is not usual to talk about responsibilities in Western managerial circles because these follow a descending vertical line and they always fall on lower levels –the responsibilities of the manager towards the Board of Directors, or of the Board towards the shareholders. This demonstrates that very little is said about the responsibilities from higher levels towards subordinates. Attention is centered on power and authority of one over others with a seeming lack of responsibility for their actions, and that's all we hear about, he remarks.

According to Izumi this opposes the responsibility system typical of a *dojo*, where hierarchy is not synonymous with authority but responsibility towards lower levels. A good *Aikido* instructor, he states, has to teach and take care of students who in turn are responsible to learn, practice hard and help higher rank members. In the training hall, the *sensei* ("the one with more experience") provides the *sempai* ("the middle levels") with the technical learning adequate to their level of knowledge. In addition he/she instructs them on how to become good teachers themselves, by allowing them to practice as apprentice instructors under his guidance. Monitors must watch over the learning of all members in the *dojo*, and ensure everyone pays correct attention to their instructor. Everyone takes care of the learning and safeguard of those under them, while taking care of their own study.

Izumi calls this a "cascade of responsibility" which flows downstream, reaching even the newest club member (the *kohai*), whose sole responsibility is to practice correctly and enthusiastically. This creates a system of total incorporation where authority is not provided by rank (hierarchy) but something each individual earns through the respect given to others by correctly fulfilling their responsibilities. It is a *meritocracy* based on the transference of knowledge and fulfillment, and not a *bureaucracy* based on the authority of a position. There are no magic formulas, but a basis of respect (something understood as "*fulfilling our duties*" in *Kurita Juku Aiki*).

This is the *Aikido dojo* responsibility system:

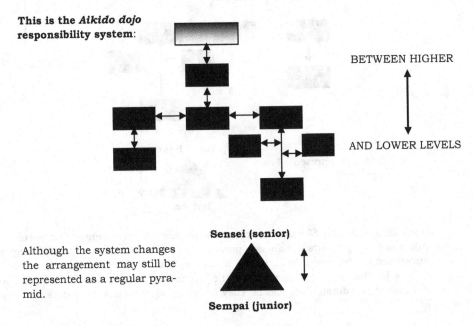

BETWEEN HIGHER

AND LOWER LEVELS

Although the system changes the arrangement may still be represented as a regular pyramid.

Sensei (senior)

Sempai (junior)

According to our exploration of Aiki, the Founder originally proposed unity without any *sensei-sempai* division, since it must promote communication, union, respect, trust and confluence, which in turn brings out harmony. But in a traditional *dojo* model the basis is still integrated by a large minority with a certain power and control over those at the bottom. This becomes particularly obvious when each club or organization imposes what is to be considered correct or when *sensei* become arrogant and self-centered or when they end believing they deserve distinctions they have earned. However one point in favor of this system is that communication and interaction among all members is highly promoted. There are no real ranks in *Kurita Juku Aiki* but if they would exist they could only bring more responsibilities than privileges.

Izumi points out one more fact: experts in *Aikido* might have attained great technical prowess or expertise, but if people in lower ranks feel any lack of authority over them, they simply do not have it, even though they might be able to slam everybody in the *dojo*. The same happens with top executives or experts in many fields whose power is limited to fire people. If a higher rank uses power to make people obey, as he remarks, authority is lost and this only brings about struggle and conflict. No union, no confluence and no real harmony can be seen at all, no sustaining *ki*, and without it power is useless according to Kurita *Shihan*.

For a *dojo* to work well, Izumi adds, everyone must understand and take care of their responsibilities. Everyone must be alert to everything that happens in the *dojo*, help as much as possible, and be careful to always be attentive to everybody else. The club system works, according to him, because people show respect to the

Founder (they know his ideals and take care of the *dojo*). It works because everybody looks after everybody else to keep from being injured, among other things, thus bringing harmony along.

There are many companies where new employees ignore how they are organized, and everybody should be responsible to teach and bring them up to date. Even more important, they should help them fit. Kaiso Sensei didn't talk of authorities, positions or commanders. Kurita *Shihan* recalls that when Master Ueshiba was invited to a reunion he always looked for the regular seats instead of the VIP ones. Going back to the combination (*Aiki*) examples presented throughout this book we can take a step farther and change the paradigm so as to consider an opposite structure where higher levels support and are the basis of lower levels, which need to be helped and oriented. It can be represented like this:

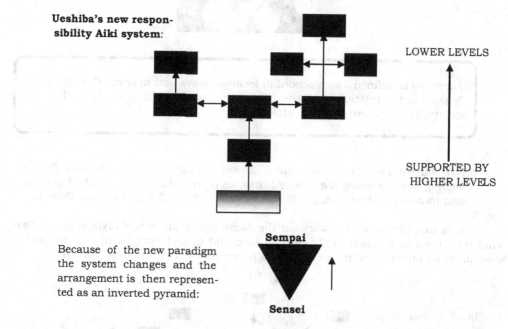

Ueshiba's new respon-sibility Aiki system:

LOWER LEVELS

SUPPORTED BY HIGHER LEVELS

Sempai

Sensei

Because of the new paradigm the system changes and the arrangement is then represen-ted as an inverted pyramid:

This new arrangement might seem illogical and "unstable". But, we must remember that the top, with all of its power, control, decision, knowledge, and expertise, which are never lost or renounced, can support those "under" him/her by placing them over. This is a much more comfortable and protective position for them. It is like a parent protecting their children, like a growing tree, as the plate that holds a cup of coffee in place. (Kurita *Shihan*)

The support system changes and we are not looking at a triangle but a square.

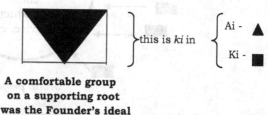

}this is *ki* in

Ai - ▲

Ki - ■

A comfortable group on a supporting root was the Founder's ideal

▲ Ai = an initial element;   ■ Ki = its complementing work, order and arrangement

This might still
seem unstable...

... until we realize the Earth is in fact sustained by all the
Aiki forces of the Universe (Kurita *Shihan*'s theory).

Harmony is defined as an accord of feelings, ways and actions. It is an orderly state in the relation of all the different parts of an entity (individual, family,
society, business corporation, etc).

*"We must always remember that Ki is not a magic, invisible element, force or
energy, but something we choose to use, as a part of a pre-established process,
and that Aiki is the science of life and a new culture"* (Yutaka Kurita *Shihan*).

It is just like when we work on the same single project, everyone, no matter
what their rank or position might be, can help and in fact does build it (it would be
wise not to let hierarchies hinder their own personal success and development).

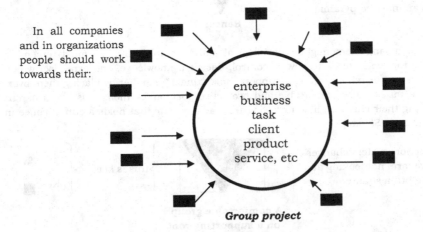

In all companies
and in organizations
people should work
towards their:

enterprise
business
task
client
product
service, etc

Group project

Collaborating as a group means working on the same direction, thus leading to
Aiki (union, confluence and harmony) with the loving and embracing force of the
Universe's *Ki* at work.

Aiki and leadership

John O'Neil (1977) explores another concrete non-martial angle of *Aikido*. He addresses executives and entrepreneurs in order to make them see that the old business practices of dominance and control, based on what he considers an "act-first-and-think-later-and-at-any-expense" paradigm, have fallen behind. Borrowing *Aikido* principles, he proposes a new style of leadership, whose foundation is not to defeat others, nor to abuse them. This is a good example of the overall effect Aiki can produce in our contemporary life.

Following the principles of *Aikido* practice, O'Neil affirms that:

a)   new leaders are modifying the entrepreneurs' perception about the way they are doing things;

b)   they must start by knowing and controlling their own selves if they want to count on values to make their decisions on a foundation different from mere stock market fluctuations; and

c)   they can always find support in the *Aikido* ideal: the true and only worthy victory is the one we can have over ourselves and not upon others.

And, from what we have already explored in this book, we can see two different managerial paradigms:

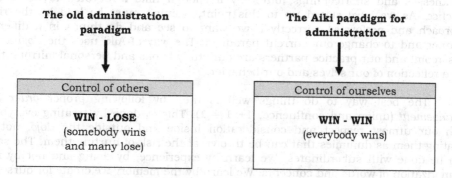

The Founder's expression "*Agatsu* (all is well with me), *masakatsu* (my action is at all correct), *katsuhayabi* (and I use space)", can be interpreted as: "We have a good combination if my partner and I are well and I use space". By being 'OK', we really work at 100% and we are transformed. That is Aiki (Kurita Yutaka *Shihan*).

O'Neil sees a world of possibilities for Corporations with the *creative resolution* of the multiple conflicts now existing within them. By means of several traditional martial art analogies, he points out three important things:

a.   *Aikido* is a {combat} art whose most profound purpose is to avoid conflict or bring it to a harmonious resolution. In fact, Aikido holds that winning is not possible if anyone in the contest, even the aggressor, is harmed (...) an idea with profound implications for the peaceful resolution of conflict in all arenas, including business competition, our families, our communities and ourselves.

b. *Aikido* is founded on the principles and skills of balance, movement, and dynamic flow. Aikidoists prevail by moving toward and turning away, rolling out of danger, deflecting the opponent's attack, and redirecting its energy to their own benefit but without hurting anyone. They look from the opponent's point of view without losing their own. These skills, O'Neil states, can be used in dealing with fast-changing playing fields and players from different countries, something necessary in our contemporary global world of businesses.

c. *Aikido* deals with the same raw materials that compose the day-to-day fabric of the working world: our aggressive instincts, our desires for achievement, and all our human fears.

In this respect, Kurita *Shihan* holds that Aiki can help us overcome our weaknesses and shortcomings, but only if enough time is devoted to its correct practice. As we have stated up to this point, training must be lead by the right approach and performed correctly if we want to see and do things in a different manner and to change our current paradigm. The way of Aiki uses the *dojo* as its classroom, and our practice partners are our study books and personal mirrors: they are a reflection of our selves and our behavior.

The best way to do do things well is then by following proper *order* and *arrangement* (union and confluence, 1+ 1 = **1**). This is done by treating everybody with our utmost respect and consideration inside and outside the *dojo*, not by treating them as dummies that can be thrown at the risk of hurting them. The same can be done with subordinates. We learn by experience, by doing and not by rote memorization of words and concepts. We learn by the memory we create for ourselves by performing concrete, positive and correct actions. Using a contemporary and fashionable expression we can say this is the *do* of Aiki. It is based on the work and actions practiced which are the grounds for learning and understanding (illumination), and is a means to transcend ourselves.

DO = Actions ⟶ AIKI
(the way is paved by techniques that lead to Aiki)

"One has to enter Aiki, to go to it, because it doesn't come to us." (Kurita Yutaka *Shihan*)

O'Neil wants entrepreneurs to see the need for a greater tolerance, since acceptance and earnest understanding are an important part of leadership in the new millennium. As such, he states, it must be based upon something else than just defeating or winning over our adversaries, abusing them, and a host of many other old concepts that no longer have place in our times. In his opinion leaders don't succeed due to several internal enemies such as their failure:

a) to grow emotionally;
b) to make creative connections;
c) to empathize;
d) to manage ego, and
e) to overcome alienation and boredom.

Kurita *Shihan* points out that a lack of connection brings about division and Aiki helps because it promotes no divisions. An example of a division contrary to Aiki is found in the contrast between *communication* and *information* within a corporation. Information is by definition a one-way process where somebody lets somebody else know and be aware of a fact about a particular event or subject. Communication is a two-way process where one gets a message across and then gets some feedback in relation to such an event or subject. This is what usually happens in many companies and business places, at an internal (among personnel) and external levels (between companies and clients or suppliers):

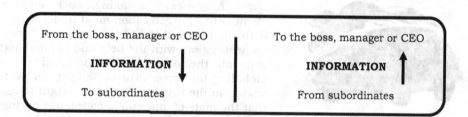

A lack of communication, and circulation, between subjects or viewpoints from either participant characterizes the usual process, where the flow of facts occurs from top to bottom (from a CEO down to the workers). A flow in the opposite direction is usually neglected simply because workers do not let CEOs know how things are going, how they are doing, and what they need in order to do a better job, or because they are simply been ignored.

Is such a division of the component parts of the same issue, process, and affair good or necessary? From an Aiki point of view if entrepreneurs want the participation of ever single member in their companies towards one common mission and vision, information must flow bottom-up, too. This action and its corresponding work is exactly the same found in Aiki training where both *Nage* and *Uke* have a 100% active participation and take turns to act each role.

CEOs and subordinates are two roles found in the natural make-up of a corporation but there must be no separation between their work and benefits and between the results and impact of their actions –they need all the elements that create *ki*: attraction (*izanau*), togetherness (*awase*) and union (*musubi*)–.

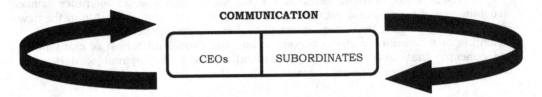

COMMUNICATION

| CEOs | SUBORDINATES |

AIKI circulation is the active participation of both sides

We have already explored the way Aiki eliminates binomial paradigmatic terms such as attacker-attacked, strong-weak, superior-inferior, since in spite of the role we play, or precisely because of it, we can conform to a well integrated whole. We can reach a unitary total vision, a perspective giving us the opportunity to eliminate differences which only seclude. It shows a way to separate and differentiate things, a vision which allows us to use our resources in a better, unifying way, taking advantage of all of our differences.

Just as an instructor who needs students waiting to be instructed, the best boss does not exist when there are no subordinates around. Instead of basing their actions in the position they already have, it would be better if they allow subordinates to use what they know in order to complete a whole personal experience.

A car takes us to our destination. So does Aiki-do

Allegorically speaking, each and every member of an organization must understand that both the rear and front wheels of a car take it to its destination, with the help and in combination with all the other hidden parts of the car, including the driver (Kurita *Shihan*). As we have said from the beginning, it is important to realize that the mate of our cup of coffee, our partner in the *dojo* supporting us and whom we rely upon is our perfect match and complementing element: both become a couple and not independent parts. The Universe is full of many natural combinations (Aiki forms) who were the source of Kaiso Sensei's inspiration: couples, mates, complements, partners (*Nage-Uke*), and many other natural, indivisible units and not even a single divided element.

In short, Aiki offers a new perspective from which it is possible to grow in a positive direction, enabling people to make all types of decisions sprung from its unique point of view. This is why *Aikido* has even been adopted for the first time in a Spanish University as part of their Administration program. [41] Those scholars see the benefits of master Ueshiba's system, which can be compared to the values expected in contemporary business managers:

---

[41] See what Universidad Politécnica de Valencia (Spain) is currently doing. They have formally integrated an *Aikido* program to their educational model. They highlight *concentration, control, balance, virtues, values,* and Aiki principles, as part of the benefits of their curricula. Please refer to: <http::/www.euiti.upv.es/aikido/Paginas/Principal.htm>

Against the manager's skill...	**...Aiki:**
• to operate without the power of his/her hierarchy,	• fosters unity with no divisions (hierarchy takes a new role).
• to learn to compete as to increase cooperation and not to lessen it,	• approaches competition by turning it into an opportunity for mutual growth, making cooperation much more efficient and true.
• to operate according to the highest ethical norms,	• puts ethics into real practice by means of the application of positive work rather than speech or nice intentions.
• to show some humility,	• fights and defeats personal arrogance.
• to develop a process approach...	• controls cause-effect processes and goes beyond them.
• to be multi-faceted and ambidextrous,	• takes the body (the organization itself) as a unit symbol, showing us how to see left, right, up and down angles as emerging and different possibilities, complemented by circular and breathing movements that help embrace a new reality versus lineal mobility.
• to obtain satisfaction from the results,	• identifies, applies and multiplies the positive use of our energy, making us enjoy our growth in communion.
	These are managerial skills Aiki translates into *Entrepreneurial energy*.

The Aiki (union) formulas are $1 + 1 = \mathbf{1}$ or $1 + 1 = \mathbf{0}$ since everyone (represented by a *"Nage"* and an *"Uke"* group) uses their individual talent to multiply their energy to reach a common goal. As seen from the new Aiki paradigm, corporations, businesses, institutions and even governments can look for the total integration of all players when they understand all wheels take them to their destination. They can do so when they take care of all components, like a car's tune up. They can use the new paradigm that keeps the different roles, functions and responsibilities performed in people's lives in their right position.

From an Aiki perspective we can understand when O'Neal states business enterprises can win if they are able to eliminate the differences which actually make the work force personnel (at all levels) feel relegated, ignored or scorned, since it seems they would also be interested in the elimination of the differences they have with labor unions, which also happens to be affected by their own traditional labor paradigm reflected in an organization that blocks their sight to see new growth possibilities (and improvements to labor force). From an Aiki point of view labor unions should also be there to work in favor of workers but also of the corporations or institutions and not only against them, since they originated from them. Labor unions owe protection to corporations, and vice versa, and they win nothing when they weaken the conditions and strength of the enterprise they work for.

As a new paradigm Aiki teaches about self-congruence, self-growth and self-control as pre-requisites for guiding others. It develops leadership and proposes unifying ways to help an improvement which can only be achieved by self-improvement and by taking care of one another, by forming constructive and sincere alliances, and by reaching agreements based on trust and harmony. It uses the body as an allegory and a direct example of an entrepreneurial structure, since each and every organization is in fact an integrated body made up of:

- the *head* (the general director, CEO, mana-ger, the Board, or owner);

- the *upper body* (higher level executives, area heads, etc.; this area houses vital organs and connects the head with both arms and legs); and,

- the *limbs* (sub-directors, heads of depart-ment heads, supervisors and plant workers who provide support and extension to both the upper body and the head); plus

- the partners who help us function and grow.

**Interdependent parts
in one single body**

This representation of the body as a family or Company clearly shows that none of its parts can be isolated. All parts must be cared for in a similar way. For example, if we don't take care of our teeth we lose them and our digestion suffers. The participation of practitioners as partners and not as enemies represents an opportunity to move as an integrated total and literally as an amplified circle of influence.

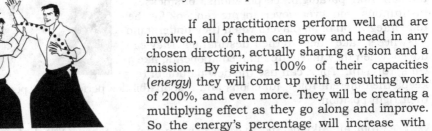

If all practitioners perform well and are involved, all of them can grow and head in any chosen direction, actually sharing a vision and a mission. By giving 100% of their capacities (*energy*) they will come up with a resulting work of 200%, and even more. They will be creating a multiplying effect as they go along and improve. So the energy's percentage will increase with each new try or attempt, and it will perfect itself just as it happens with practice. Such a formula can also be extended to the way we actually coordinate with our employees, clients, providers and even competitors. The way to do so is pretty simple since all we must do is lead by example, everyone can learn from everybody else. They can learn from us if we begin with ourselves and try and do well by uniting with others (*awase*) and connecting (*musubi*) because, in the end, everyone will be able to do just as we do.

Aiki and the falling-rolling opposition

Aikido has no tournaments, since they are unnecessary when individuals pay more attention and interest on their own growth. So, if we accept tournaments are not transcendental, the Aiki perspective shows there is no need to worry about falling and the possibilities of being defeated, so we can always emerge victorious. With respect to falling, literally or figuratively, we can also take it voluntarily and choose to take a roll instead. Knowing a roll is not something to be feared, and that when it happens against our will and induced by an opponent or something out of our control, we can always regard it as a chance to gain a more advantageous position. Aiki teaches that falling does not mean defeat as the old paradigm has made us believe. But we cannot take a roll if our partners block our movement and make us slam on the ground.

Aiki practitioners come down gliding into the mat, just like airplanes do. They always do so out of their own undertaking, and never against the flow, fully aware of the benefits they obtain from it. In sports, and generally in regards to interpersonal relationships, falling down always has a negative connotation. Whether it is on a moral and personal level, falling down is not good mainly when this happens at a business level when a Company is trying to place a product in the market. A fall produced during a tournament or any other sort of competition can be a reason for frustration, vengeance and desperation. But this will make people ignore its true lesson and will hide a creative solution. It has to be applied to the improvement or victory over themselves, which means defeating their own weaknesses.

A downfall, a fear to be defeated, and any crisis are the main sources of conflict in our lives. This is why throughout this book a constant has been to ask in as many possible ways if it is really necessary to fall, to fight, to crash, to run over others, to confront, to hurt and abuse, or if it is better to find a new way to overcome our problems by using Aiki as the right tool. Technology has always made it easier to carry out many tasks, and Kurita Yutaka *Shihan* strongly believes Kaiso Sensei's Aiki is not only the tool but the science needed to enter the way of union, confluence and harmony in our new millennium.

That is the first lesson (*ikkyo*) to be learned, and the Founder used it again and again in order to close the whole cycle of his life development and his final legacy:

TAKEMUSU AIKI !
(Give life to Aiki!)

Kurita Yutaka *Shihan* in his *Dojo*
(Mexico City, 2008)

Supplement:

An Interview with Kurita Yutaka *Shihan* by the Mexican TV conductor Raul Velasco (ca. 1995)

This interview shows how Ueshiba Morihei's Aiki differs from previous martial arts. It took place in a TV show called *Cosmic Vibrations*, hosted by late Mr. Raul Velasco in 1995 and broadcast from Mexico City.

It started by introducing Kurita Yutaka *Shihan* to the audience, and after a brief outline of *Aikido* as a tool enabling us to find harmony and a guide for self-improvement, his first question to Kurita *Shihan* was about Aiki-do's philosophy, its origins and the goals aimed at by its practice. This following is a partial transcription of the interview:

Mr. Velasco - How did it all get started?

Kurita *Shihan* – There are several disciplines akin those of the *Samurai* era. The Founder of Ai-ki studied the situation of the world in regards to combat and the arts of war, and he derived from it his ideal of how to change our world's way of thinking. He focused his reflection on finding a way to unite his discipline with the order of the Universe.

Mr. Velasco – Does "Aikido" mean "the way of harmony"?

Kurita *Shihan* – Yes. I believe that is the easiest way to define it in a language other than Japanese. But it must also be understood as the confluence of Ki used to eliminate negativity, as unification conductive to social development, which is the objective of our practice. As such, when there is any struggle, the question arises as to the way we can advance humanity, irrespective of our social strata or place of origin. The main question is and will always be: how can we improve our planet?

Mr. Velasco – You say *Aikido* helps us to defeat our crises and fears.

Kurita *Shihan* – Absolutely. We must overcome them thru practice, which is never a form of combat. People who engage in combat want to die, that is the meaning and goal when you practice a "martial art".

Mr. Velasco – I was not aware that we can find *Aikido*'s philosophy in some commercial films...

A cut to a commercial segment. O-Sensei's image appears on screen with the following text where viewers read:

> *"Heaven is where ever we are, which is the place where we must practice".*

(Back to program).

Mr. Velasco – I know we can find *Aikido's* philosophy in movies like "Star Wars", for example. Can you help us here?

(A scene is shown here where Obi-Wan Kenobi is telling Luke Skywalker about "the dark side of the Force", also stating the Force penetrates and unites the whole Galaxy.)

Can you elaborate on that idea about the seduction of the dark side of the Force?

Kurita *Shihan* – (Nodding) Yes. The ideal is to never have a war in this cosmic moment, so we must unite humanity with the Cosmos and vice-versa. In this movie we see a cosmic war, which according to the Founder must not ever happen since war stuns and hinders our development.

Mr. Velasco – Can you explain how is it that *Ki* is contained in the past as well as in the future?

Kurita *Shihan* – I cannot translate this word *Ki*, which even in Japanese is difficult to understand. There is always growth, and that is *Ki*, some say it is velocity, but that is not correct either... *Ki* just is.

Mr. Velasco – You say strength is not in our muscles...

Kurita *Shihan* – That's correct (nodding).

Mr. Velasco – Evidently, there are differences in other disciplines like Tae-kwon-do and Kung-fu. A few days ago, while we were both witnessing a demonstration you pointed out something for me. Would you like to share it with our viewers?

Kurita *Shihan* – Sure *(he pauses)*. In *Aikido* we build, we are concerned to find a way to fix what is wrong or destructive, but not doing it as it used to be done in the past, like breaking wooden block or stones. No, not like that, we need something more than destructive methods to show our power and skill. If something is amiss, let us work on it and improve every time.

Mr. Velasco – I understand a basic difference: in *Karate* bricks are broken while in Aikido they are used to build up something.

(Kurita Shihan nods again).

Let us watch Star Wars again to prove we are not just making all this up.

(A new scene from the film is run here: the characters talk about the dark side of the Force, etc.).

Well then. We will present you a demonstration.

(Cameras switch to two students who start working)

Kurita *Shihan* – (Explaining the basics of what they do) The movements, the manifestation is called Ki and, and by joining their *Ki* together they get what is called Aiki. Energy emerges from *Ki*.

Mr. Velasco – Can it be used in the streets?

Kurita *Shihan* – Yes, which would be the only place where it is allowed to use it: if something negative comes to me I have to look for a way to control and lead it, without having to end or destroy anyone's life.

Mr. Velasco – (still watching the demonstration) Is strength needed?

Kurita *Shihan* – No. These young men are using strength because of their age (*he laughs*), that is their level, but on the other hand a woman or an old man can do it in a different way: just by moving their body.

Mr. Velasco – I can see them using some strikes.

Kurita *Shihan* – Oh yes. That's a carry over from the combat forms from which Aikido was derived. Yet, they are used as a "deterrent" or a way to say "stop" the attacker.

Mr. Velasco – You have stated that *Aikido* is a medicine for a world ill by anger.

Kurita *Shihan* – (Nodding). The attack never reaches me and I do not run into it. The attacker wants to strike me but his violence never reaches me if I place myself outside of his line of attack!

Mr. Velasco – In the "The lion King" movie we also found some of the philosophy of *Aikido*, when Raffiti teaches Zimba a lesson, am I right?

(A scene of this film is run. We find Raffiti is teaching Zimba that we can learn from the past).

What is the meaning of Raffiti's thump on Zimba's head? When I visited a temple in Japan I saw something similar the monks call "mercy tap"...

Kurita *Shihan* – (*Smiling and nodding*). The forging process of a *Katana* (sword) requires the use of ice together with repeated hammering of the iron, which is thus transformed into art. By the same token, in the old days students were tapped or thumped when making a mistake, which was a way to "clean" them. But this is no longer necessary when things are done right. For example, a child can be tapped mildly on the hand when doing something wrong; in Japan this is done on their little heads on the idea of doing away with all negative habits.

Forging a sword means getting it free from all impurities, which is the goal we try to achieve through *Aikido* practice. Weapons are nowadays used in practice just as learning tools and not as means of annihilation.

Mr. Velasco – Are students taught pressure points and certain holds to escape an attack and things like that?

Kurita *Shihan* – That is very dangerous in a real attack. Since it can be painful to the attacker and this can turn him more aggressive. All we need is to nullify such an attack and not to increase or provoke any greater countering. This is why we do not use force or violence in *Aikido*.

The show finished with an interview with Steven Seagal by of one of Mr. Velasco's reporters. The actor explained how he has learned that in spite of the obvious "violence" behind martial arts there is a philosophy related to the resolution of conflict and self-improvement, in addition to the self-defense side to it.

They go back to the interview with Kurita *Shihan*.

Mr. Velasco – Any final thoughts?

Kurita Shihan – Well, Mr. Seagal makes action movies, but his words are right though.

Mr. Velasco – I have reached the conclusion that Aikido is a way to defeat one of our worst enemies: our own selves.

The use of force is conductive to war, but today we have been talking about peace.

This concludes our program.

(The End)

COMMENTED AIKI REFERENCES:

Ueshiba, Morihei. ***Budo Renshu.***

This is the first of two books endorsed by the Founder. It appeared in 1933, which means it belongs to his Aiki-Budo period before World war II, and is a part of his initial *jutsu* (technical) teachings. His final *do* or spiritual period was only to be known to just a few of his closest *uchideshi*.

This book was translated into English by Larry E. Bieri, and published in Japan with the word Aikido annotated on the original title by the Founder's son, the late Ueshiba Kisshomaru, and so it is to be found in English as: *Budo Training in Aikido - Morihei Ueshiba, founder of Aikido*, published by Sugawara Martial Arts Institute / Japan Publications, 2001.

_____. ***Budo***

The second of the two books endorsed by the Founder, it was privately circulated in 1938. The Founder was fifty-five years old, an age wrongly considered by many as the age when he was at his physical and mental prime. As we have stated in this book, it should now be clear O-Sensei was constantly changing; these changes occurred in spans of every 10 years, as Kurita *Shihan* points out –as an *uchideshi*, he was able to witness this.

This book was originally an instruction manual full of photographs illustrating techniques and including philosophical verses written in a cryptic style, which let all the work being developed in each action hidden to its readers since pictures only reflect their surface. Such a work is now being unveiled by instructors such as Kurita Yutaka *Shihan*.

It was translated into English by John Stevens, and published in Japan with the subtitle *"Teachings of the Founder of Aikido"* annotated on the original title and with an introduction by the late Ueshiba Kisshomaru, and so it is to be found as: *Budo - Teachings of the Founder of Aikido*, published by Kodansha International, Ltd., 1991.

_____. *The art of peace.*

In this book, translated and edited by John Stevens, you find the didactic "poems of the Way" written by O-Sensei. His quotes were gathered from the corpus of written literature and oral tradition which includes tape recordings of Master Ueshiba speaking, transcripts of his talks and interviews, and sayings as recalled and collected by his many students, supporters and admirers, as the author quotes himself.

The ideas conveyed here by the author as well as the calligraphy included in this book clearly shows changes and consolidation of O-Sensei's *budo*. It was published by Stevens as: *The art of peace – Morihei Ueshiba*, Shambhala Publications, Inc., Boston and London, 2002.

To read this book is a chance to see how Kaiso Sensei relied on the right side of his brain in order to pass on to his students so many imaginative, non-verbal explanations of his findings.

Stevens, John. *The essence of Aikido.*

This book is for those who are interested on a reference to the original *kanji* used by the Founder to record many of his concepts, a must for those who want to check on the original concepts in accordance to the written language used to convey them. It contains his didactic poems, a collection of his calligraphy and a gallery of techniques as he was performing them between 1936 and 1938.

A good look to the past, it is a compilation by John Stevens. It was published in Japan as *The essence of Aikido – Spiritual teachings of Morihei Ueshiba*, Kodansha International, Ltd., 1993.

_____

GENERAL *AIKIDO* REFERENCES:

Crum, Thomas F. *The Magic of Conflict*, Touchtone Books, 1987.

Ferres Serrano, Juan Jose. *Gunkan – Diccionario de Kanjis Japoneses*, Ediciones Hiperión, Madrid, 2001.

Henshall, Keneth G. *A Guide to Remembering Japanese Characters*, Tuttle, Boston and Tokyo, 1998.

Morgan, Forrester E. *Living the Martial Way*, Barricade Books, New Jersey, 1992.

Nakao, Seigo. *Japanese-English / English-Japanese Dictionary*, Random House, New York, 1997.

O'Neil, John. *Leadership Aikido*, Three Rivers Press, New York, 1997.

Saito, Morihiro. *Traditional Aikido*, Sugawara Martial Arts Institute, Inc., Tokyo, Japan, 1973, 5 volumes.

Stevens, John. *Aikido – The Way of Harmony*, under the direction of Rinjiro Shirata, Shambhala Publishers, Boston and London, 1984.

_____. *Secrets of Aikido – the hidden teachings and universal truths of Aikido, as taught by its Founder, Morihei Ueshiba*, Shambhala, Boston, 1997.

Ueshiba, Kisshomaru. *Aikido*, Hodansha Publications, Co., Tokyo, Japan, 1985.

_____. *The Spirit of Aikido*, Kodansha Intl., New York, 1987.

_____. *The art of Aikido – Principles and Essential techniques*, Kodansha International, New York, 2004 (previously published in Japanese as *Aikido Shintei* in 1986).

ELECTRONIC *AIKIDO* SOURCES

Izumi, Hiroaki. *The dojo system vs. the Corporation system* as consulted on c.a. 09/17/96 in the following address: http://www.aikidofaq.com/a_section55.html

Okuyama, T.S. *A look at Japanese Culture* as consulted on 09/17/99 in the following address: http://www.aikidoonline.com/clmn_okuy.html

Tamura, Nobuyoshi. *Aikido and Etiquette and Transmission* as consulted on 06/09/2000 in the following address: http://www.aikidoonline.com./feat_0500_tmra.html